GCSE

Modern World History

TEACH YOURSELF BOOKS

GCSE Modern World History

Nicholas Tate

Hodder & Stoughton

A MEMBER OF THE HODDER HEADLINE GROUP

British Library Cataloguing in Publication Data

Tate, Nicholas
GCSE modern world history —
(Teach yourself books)
1. World. 1900–
I. Title
909.82

ISBN 0 340 51273 3

First published 1989
Impression number 10 9 8 7 6 5 4 3
Year 1998 1997 1996 1995 1994 1993

Photoset by Rowland Phototypesetting Ltd., Bury St Edmunds, Suffolk.
Printed in Great Britain for Hodder & Stoughton Educational, a division of Hodder Headline PLC, Mill Road, Dunton Green, Sevenoaks, Kent TN13 2YA by Cox & Wyman Ltd., Reading, Berkshire.

CONTENTS

1 **GCSE Modern World History** 1
1.1 Why study modern world history? 1.2 How to use this book. 1.3 The objectives of GCSE History courses. 1.4 Examination questions. 1.5 Coursework. 1.6 External candidates/Further reading/Addresses of Examining Groups.

2 **Handling historical evidence** 11
2.1 Why evidence is important. 2.2 Primary and secondary sources. 2.3 Primary sources for the study of modern world history. 2.4 Evidence questions.

3 **The First World War and the Paris peace settlement** 20
3.1 The causes of the First World War. 3.2 Why the Schlieffen Plan failed. 3.3 The Western Front, 1914–17. 3.4 The Eastern Front. 3.5 Other theatres of war. 3.6 Why Germany lost the war. 3.7 The Home Front in Britain. 3.8 The Paris peace settlement. 3.9 Key historical terms. 3.10 Questions.

4 **Russia 1917–39** 35
4.1 Russia before the Revolution. 4.2 The causes of the Russian Revolution. 4.3 The Revolutions of 1917. 4.4 Russia under Bolshevik rule, 1917–24. 4.5 Russia under Stalin. 4.6 Key historical terms. 4.7 Questions.

5 **Mussolini and the rise of Fascism in Italy** 49
5.1 Fascism. 5.2 Mussolini's rise to power. 5.3 The consolidation of Mussolini's power, 1922–29. 5.4 Mussolini's domestic and foreign policies. 5.5 The Second World War and the collapse of Fascism. 5.6 Key historical terms. 5.7 Questions.

6 **Germany 1919–39: the Weimar Republic and the rise of Hitler** 57
6.1 The Weimar Republic, 1919–24. 6.2 Weimar: the years of recovery, 1924–29. 6.3 The collapse of Weimar Germany, 1929–33. 6.4 Hitler and the National Socialist party. 6.5 Why Hitler rose to power, 1929–33. 6.6 Hitler establishes his dictatorship, 1933–34. 6.7 Hitler's domestic policies, 1933–39. 6.8 Key historical terms. 6.9 Questions.

7 **International relations during the 1920s and 1930s** 67
7.1 International relations during the 1920s. 7.2 The causes of the Second World War in Europe. 7.3 Key historical terms. 7.4 Questions.

8 The Second World War in Europe 74
8.1 The war in the East, 1939. 8.2 German conquests in Western Europe. 8.3 The war in North Africa and the Balkans, 1940–41. 8.4 Operation Barbarossa: the German attack on the USSR, 1941. 8.5 Europe under Nazi rule. 8.6 The Home Front in Britain. 8.7 The decline and fall of Nazism. 8.8 Key historical terms. 8.9 Questions.

9 Britain during the twentieth century 84
9.1 Liberal governments, 1905–15. 9.2 The General Strike (1926). 9.3 Developments during the years 1929–39. 9.4 The Labour governments of 1945–51. 9.5 Britain's changing world role since 1945. 9.6 Key historical terms. 9.7 Questions.

10 The rise of Japan and the Second World War in the Far East 93
10.1 Japan in the early twentieth century. 10.2 Why Japan became an expansionist power in the 1930s. 10.3 Japanese expansion during the 1930s. 10.4 War with the USA: Pearl Harbor, 1941. 10.5 Reasons for Japan's defeat. 10.6 Key historical terms. 10.7 Questions.

11 China in the twentieth century 100
11.1 China in the early twentieth century. 11.2 Civil war between the Kuomintang and the communists. 11.3 Mao Zedong and the creation of a communist society, 1949–76. 11.4 China since the death of Mao. 11.5 China's foreign policies, 1949 to the present day. 11.6 Key historical terms. 11.7 Questions.

12 The USA: internal developments since 1919 110
12.1 The Twenties. 12.2 The Wall Street Crash and the Depression. 12.3 Roosevelt and the New Deal. 12.4 US foreign policy, 1919–41. 12.5 Truman, the Fair Deal and McCarthyism. 12.6 Eisenhower (1953–60), Kennedy (1961–63) and Johnson (1963–69). 12.7 Race relations and civil rights since 1945. 12.8 Richard Nixon, 1968–74. 12.9 Key historical terms. 12.10 Questions.

13 The USA, the USSR and the Cold War 122
13.1 The origins of the Cold War. 13.2 The formation of two power blocs. 13.3 The Cold War outside Europe. 13.4 Coexistence and detente. 13.5 Spheres of influence. 13.6 Key historical terms. 13.7 Questions.

14 Colonialism and its aftermath: an introduction 136
14.1 Colonialism. 14.2 Why did decolonisation take place? 14.3 How the transfer of power came about. 14.4 Developments since independence. 14.5 Key historical terms. 14.6 Questions.

15 Colonialism and its aftermath: Asia 141
15.1 British India at the beginning of the twentieth century. 15.2 The growth of Indian nationalism. 15.3 Independence and partition. 15.4 India since independence. 15.5 India's relations with neighbouring states. 15.6 Pakistan and Bangladesh. 15.7 Decolonisation elsewhere in Asia. 15.8 Key historical terms. 15.9 Questions.

16 Colonialism and its aftermath: Africa 150
16.1 Independence in British Africa: (i) Nigeria. 16.2 Independence in British Africa: (ii) Rhodesia/Zimbabwe. 16.3 Independence in French Africa. 16.4 Independence in the Congo. 16.5 Independence in Portuguese Africa. 16.6 South Africa. 16.7 Key historical terms. 16.8 Questions.

17 The Arab–Israeli conflict 163
17.1 The Palestine mandate and the origins of the state of Israel. 17.2 The First Arab–Israeli War, 1948–49. 17.3 The Suez Crisis, 1956. 17.4 The Six Days War, 1967. 17.5 The Yom Kippur War, 1973. 17.6 The resurgence of the Arab world. 17.7 Peace moves. 17.8 Israel and the Lebanon. 17.9 Key historical terms. 17.10 Questions.

18 International cooperation 172
18.1 The League of Nations. 18.2 The United Nations Organisation. 18.3 Regional cooperation. 18.4 Key historical terms. 18.5 Questions.

19 International themes 183
19.1 The population explosion. 19.2 World poverty. 19.3 Communications. 19.4 The environment. 19.5 Key historical terms. 19.6 Questions.

20 Specimen answers 190
20.1 Essay questions. 20.2 Source-based questions. 20.3 Evidence questions.

21 Glossary 195

ACKNOWLEDGEMENTS

The Publishers would like to thank the following for the use of copyright material:

Associated Press Ltd, p. 171; Imperial War Museum, p. 83; Popperfoto, p. 121 (both); Punch Publications Ltd, p. 149; Novosti Press Agency, p. 47.

1.1 Why study modern world history?

Look at the headlines below. They are all taken from recent editions of British newspapers.

Solidarity's leaders arrested as Gdansk shipyard strikes

Israelis relive march to independence

US looks towards a second summit

Waldheim cancels speech at Anschluss ceremony

Can you understand what these headlines are referring to? What is Solidarity? Which anniversary were the Israelis celebrating? What is a 'summit'? What does 'Anschluss' mean?

Unless you can answer questions like these you will find it very difficult to make sense of a lot of the things that happen in the world around you. Every day we are bombarded with information about world events: in the press and on radio and television. Much of this is meaningless unless you understand the historical background to what is happening. If, for example, you know something about the history of Poland since the Second World War you will understand what Solidarity is and why it is important to many Polish people. Likewise, if you have studied the events of the 1930s you will know what 'Anschluss' was and why it is still an issue in Austria today.

This is one of the main reasons why so many people choose to study modern world history at GCSE. By doing so they are able to understand better the world in which they live. There are other reasons, of course, for studying twentieth-century history. It teaches you to think, to weigh evidence, to detect bias, and to write clearly. What appeals most, however, is seeing how we have got to where we are today.

1.2 How to use this book

The purpose of this book is to help you do well in your GCSE course. It aims to do three main things:

1 Explain what GCSE History is all about.
2 Show you how to tackle the different kinds of questions you will be asked, both in the examination and in coursework.
3 Give you the knowledge and understanding you need to make sense of the various historical topics you have chosen to study.

In order to make best use of this book *it is important first of all to be clear which modern world history syllabus you are studying*. World history syllabuses are offered by each of the Examining Groups responsible for GCSE: the London and East Anglian Group (LEAG); the Midland Examining Group (MEG); the Northern Examining Association (NEA); the Southern Examining Group (SEG); and the Welsh Joint Education Committee (WJEC). Topics in modern world history are also a major part of the GCSE History syllabus offered by the Northern Ireland Schools Examinations Council (NISEC). In addition there are a number of Mode 2 and Mode 3 syllabuses concerned with aspects of twentieth-century world history (a Mode 2 syllabus is one devised by a school or group of schools, but with an examination set by the Group; a Mode 3 syllabus is one where both syllabus and examination are produced by the school).

Whatever syllabus you are following, it is important to get hold of both (a) a copy of the actual syllabus and (b) specimen examination papers. You can do this in one of two ways: either by asking your teacher/lecturer or by writing direct to the Examining Group. The addresses of the Examining Groups are given at the end of this chapter.

All world history syllabuses offer candidates a choice of topics (though some syllabuses contain compulsory elements that everyone has to follow). Most offer a very wide choice. If you are following a course at a school or a college,the topics you have to study will already have been chosen for you. If you are not sure which they are, ask your teacher or lecturer. If you are an external candidate (p. 9) you will need to decide which topics you want to study. Either way, once you know which topics you are studying, it should be obvious which chapters in this book you will need to read and which you can afford to miss out. Whatever topics you are studying you should read both this chapter and Chapter 2. These are concerned with the objectives that are common to all GCSE syllabuses, i.e. the kinds of skills that you need to have in order to do well in this examination. You should also look at the specimen answers to questions in Chapter 20.

This book has been planned so that the various chapters fit the topics listed in your GCSE syllabus. In most cases therefore you will be able to tell at a glance which of Chapters 3–19 you need to study. Some syllabuses, however, have sections that are arranged differently. The list below gives the other GCSE topic titles that you may come across and shows which chapters and sections of chapters you will need to study for each of these topics.

The Population Explosion and Global Resources since 1945 (LEAG): 19.1 and 19.2
The Vietnam War and its impact on Indo-China and the USA (LEAG): 13.3, Chapter 14, and 15.7
The Search for International Order between 1919 and 1939 (MEG): 3.8, 7.1 and 18.1
The Collapse of International Order in the 1930s (MEG): 5.5, 7.2 and 10.3
Tension and Cooperation since 1945 (MEG): Chapter 13, 18.2, 18.3, 18.4 and 19.2
Conflict and Conciliation (NEA): Chapters 3, 7, 8, 10, 13 and 17
The Military Events of the Second World War (SEG): Chapters 8 and 10
The Development and Impact of the USA and the USSR as World Superpowers (SEG): 3.6, 3.8, 4.5 12.4, and Chapter 13
Imperialism, Decolonisation and Post-imperial Relationships (SEG): Chapters 14, 15 and 16
The Effects of Technological and Scientific Change (SEG): Chapter 19

There are three stages therefore that you have to go through: (a) get hold of a copy of your particular syllabus; (b) find out which topics in this syllabus you are studying; and (c) list all the sections of this book that relate to those topics. Once you have done this (and once you have read this chapter and Chapter 2) you will be ready to begin.

In working your way through the book, pay close attention to the sections headed *Key historical terms*. These explain clearly and simply some of the most important terms and concepts (or ideas) that you need to understand in order to make sense of the topics you are studying. These terms are explained and discussed in detail at the end of the chapters where they are most relevant. Many terms, however, apply to more than one topic, e.g. *Marxism* (discussed in 4.6) and *parliamentary democracy* (discussed in 6.7) are used again and again throughout the book. Each term is listed wherever it is needed for the understanding of a particular topic, with a page reference indicating where it is discussed in detail. All major terms are also listed in a *Glossary* at the end of the book, again with page references to show where a term is discussed at greater length. It is well worth spending time thinking about these terms or concepts. In GCSE History it is much more important to *understand* than to memorise long lists of facts – though factual knowledge is important as well.

1.3 The objectives of GCSE History courses

All GCSE History courses have the same *assessment objectives*. These tell you what you are expected to be able to do as a result of following a GCSE History course. They are what you are tested on both in the examination and in the coursework. As they are so important, they are given in full below (the numbering is that used in the National Criteria, the regulations that all GCSE History courses have to follow). Don't worry if some of the language is difficult. The rest of this section explains what these assessment objectives actually mean in practice.

All candidates will be expected:

3.1 **to recall, evaluate and select knowledge relevant to the context and to deploy it in a clear and coherent form;**

3.2 **to make use of and understand the concepts of cause and consequence, continuity and change, similarity and difference;**

3.3 **to show an ability to look at events and issues from the perspective of people in the past;**

3.4 **to show the skills necessary to study a wide variety of historical evidence which should include both primary and secondary written sources, statistical and visual material, artefacts, textbooks and orally transmitted information**

3.4.1 **by comprehending and extracting information from it;**

3.4.2 **by interpreting and evaluating it – distinguishing between fact, opinion and judgement; pointing to deficiencies in the material as evidence, such as gaps and inconsistencies; detecting bias;**

3.4.3 **by comparing various types of historical evidence and reaching conclusions based on this comparison.**

It will help you to make sense of these objectives if they are grouped under three general headings:

Knowledge and understanding
Concepts
Skills

Knowledge and understanding

GCSE History syllabuses assess you on what you *know* and *understand* about the topics you have been studying. Although you will need to remember (*recall*) a great deal of information, that is only the beginning. No-one is going to do well in GCSE History if all they have done is memorise long strings of facts. You are also required to show *understanding*. The following question illustrates what this might involve:

Write a paragraph explaining the problems experienced by the Provisional Government in Russia in 1917.

In order to answer this question you certainly need to know some facts about events in Russia in 1917. You won't be able to answer it, however, unless you are also able to show that you *understand* these facts, i.e. by explaining why events occurred, by interpreting the motives of the Provisional Government, and by assessing the effects that its actions had. You also won't be able to answer it unless you can *evaluate and select knowledge relevant to the context*, i.e. choose from all your information about Russia in 1917 those bits that help to answer this question, discarding any other bits that are not relevant. You will also need to *deploy* this knowledge *in a clear and coherent form*, i.e. use all this relevant information in order to write an answer that is well argued and clearly expressed.

In studying your topics, always remember therefore to make sure that you *understand* what you are doing. Keep on asking yourself questions such as the following: what is the *meaning* of this word? *Why* did this happen? What *effects* did it have? Why is it *important*? In particular, make sure that you are familiar with all the *key historical terms* listed for each of your topics.

One aspect of *understanding* is referred to in assessment objective 3.3: 'to show an ability to look at events and issues from the perspective of people in the past'. This is essential in studying history. Unless you appreciate that people in the past had feelings, attitudes and beliefs that were often very different from your own, you will have great difficulty in understanding the topics that you are studying. This skill is sometimes referred to as *empathy*, i.e. the ability to put yourself in the position of others and to look at events and issues from their particular perspective. This is *not* the same as *sympathy*. For example, it is important to try and understand why Hitler acted as he did (i.e. to 'empathise' with him) but that is a very different matter from 'sympathising' with him and his views.

Your GCSE History syllabus will encourage you to develop the skills of empathy through a study of *evidence* (see Chapter 2). In trying to do this, remember the following points:

(i) Never forget that past societies were divided into different groups or classes and that these groups and classes had different views and attitudes. Don't therefore write about 'the British people' wanting this or doing that as if they always thought and felt the same.
(ii) Never forget that, even within a particular group or class, individuals might have very different views, e.g. some middle-class Germans supported Hitler, others bitterly opposed him, and some might have had no strong feelings one way or the other.

You can find an example of an essay question testing empathy on p. 48.

Concepts

The concepts here are those referred to in assessment objective 3.2 (p. 4).

These are cause and consequence, continuity and change, and similarity and difference. All GCSE History syllabuses will test your ability to handle these concepts. It is important therefore to be clear what they mean.

Perhaps the most important thing about these concepts is that they are a reminder that history isn't just a matter of telling stories about the past. Narrative – the telling of a story – is certainly an important part of history. It is also something that you are likely to be asked to do as part of your GCSE History course. There is more to history, however, than telling stories. As well as narrating (telling a story) and describing, you will also be required to *analyse*. This can involve many things, for example, explaining why a war broke out, trying to assess the impact of a political leader, comparing economic developments in different countries. Whenever you are doing any of these things you are likely to be making use of one or more of the concepts listed above. You may not be conscious that this is what you are doing. That doesn't matter – as long as you have got into the habit of doing it. Further guidance about the meaning of these concepts is given below.

Cause and consequence

These involve questions such as 'why did this happen?' and 'what effects did this have?' Causes and consequences may be both short-term and long-term. The outbreak of the Second World War, for example, can be explained partly in terms of the events of August and September 1939. It cannot be explained fully, however, without reference to developments going back over many years. Remember also that some causes (and some consequences) are likely to be more important than others (e.g. the effects of the First World War were probably a more important cause of the Russian Revolution of February 1917 than the personality of the Tsar). Finally, don't forget that causes and consequences may be very complex. In some cases it may be difficult, perhaps impossible, to decide why something happened.

Continuity and change

Like cause and consequence, continuity and change are opposite sides of the same coin. History is obviously about change: how it occurred; why it occurred; what effects it had. Changes can be sudden or gradual. They can also be limited or wide-ranging in their effects. This is where an understanding of continuity is important. This involves identifying those aspects of a society which do *not* change. What is most striking about China since 1949, for example, is the extent to which the country has changed. There is much, however, that has not changed (e.g. many of China's attitudes towards the outside world). When studying all of your topics, keep on trying to identify these elements of change and continuity.

Similarity and difference

These are important as a way of helping you to understand more fully what you are studying. By comparing two events or situations with each other, we learn more about both. For example, it is a useful exercise to try and compare the ways in which Mussolini and Hitler ruled their countries. By identifying similarities and differences, we may highlight features about both countries that we were previously unaware of. Keep on making these comparisons throughout your course. In particular, don't think of the different parts of the syllabus as being wholly separate from each other. The more connections you make between them, the more you will understand.

Skills

The assessment objectives refer to a number of skills. These are things that you have to be able to *do* (as opposed to things that you need to *know*). It is partly this emphasis on skills that makes GCSE History very different from many previous history courses. This is so important that it is dealt with separately in Chapter 2.

GCSE MODERN WORLD HISTORY 1
1.4 Examination questions

GCSE History examinations are designed to test the various objectives that you have already read about. Think of each question as having a *target*, e.g. 'to show understanding of the causes of the Russian Revolution' or 'to identify differences between two accounts of the same event'. In your answer try to hit this target. Only put down what helps to answer the question. Anything that does *not* help to answer the question – however interesting or accurate – should be ignored.

Find out from your own syllabus (and from specimen examination papers) the kinds of questions you are likely to be asked. Make sure you know how long you have for each paper (most syllabuses have two papers), and each section of each paper. Notice the marks allocated to the different sections. This gives you a guide as to how much time you should spend on each of them. Examinations in GCSE World History syllabuses usually include each of the following three main types of questions. All are illustrated in the Questions sections at the end of each of Chapters 3–19. You can find specimen answers to some of these questions in Chapter 20.

1 Essay questions These take various forms. Some are just a one sentence question. Others provide a structure for your answer by breaking up the question into various parts. In some cases you are given a list of points that you might wish to include. Examples of all types are given at the end of the following chapters.

In answering these questions, never lose sight of what you are being asked to do. Exclude all irrelevant material. Write precisely (i.e. illustrate general points with specific examples). Don't make rash general statements that you don't really mean, e.g. that '*all* Germans supported Hitler' or that 'Germany was *totally* to blame for the outbreak of the First World War'. It is important that historians are always cautious about what they write. Organise your answer into different sections – and use paragraphs. And above all, argue a case – show that you can *think*.

2 Source-based questions Again, there are examples of these at the end of the chapters that follow. They consist of a piece of source material – an extract from a document, photograph, cartoon or map – followed by questions that refer to the source. The questions may be of various types (e.g. a word, phrase, sentence, couple of sentences, or paragraph). Some lead on from these shorter questions to an essay question which links in some way to the theme of the source. Usually the questions can only be answered using some background knowledge. In other words, the source is being used as a 'stimulus' or trigger in order to help you remember what the topic is about. This is why they are referred to here as source-*based* questions, as opposed to the *evidence* questions discussed in Chapter 2. Occasionally, however, some questions may require you to interpret and make use of the source in the ways mentioned in the next chapter.

3 Evidence questions These are discussed, along with the skills mentioned above, in the following chapter.

GCSE MODERN WORLD HISTORY 1.5 Coursework

1

GCSE History syllabuses allocate between 20% and 50% of the total marks to coursework. The most common pattern is 30% coursework and 70% examination. Coursework arrangements vary from one Examining Group to another – another reason for getting hold of the syllabus regulations. In studying these regulations and in discussing coursework with your teacher or lecturer, make sure you find out the answers to the following questions:

(a) How many pieces of coursework count for assessment?
(b) What are the word limits for each piece of work?
(c) When do coursework assignments have to be handed in?
(d) How does coursework have to be presented, e.g. in ring binders, etc.?
(e) Do coursework assignments have to be done in class, in your own time, etc.?
(f) How much assistance is the teacher able to give?
(g) What are the objectives that each piece of work is trying to assess?

(h) How will the assignments be marked, e.g. how many marks for each objective, section, etc.?

As in the examination, answers to all coursework assignments must constantly keep in mind the question you are trying to answer. It is also vital to pay careful attention to detail – both in what you write and in how you present it.

GCSE MODERN WORLD HISTORY 1.6 External candidates/Further reading/Addresses 1

External candidates

Examining Groups (e.g. LEAG and SEG) offer world history syllabuses for external candidates. These are candidates who are not in full-time attendance at schools and colleges and who are unable to fulfil the requirements for coursework. External candidates sit the same two examination papers as all other candidates, but instead of submitting coursework sit a third examination paper instead. This third examination paper will assess some of the skills (e.g. evidence skills and/or empathy) that would otherwise be tested in coursework.

Further reading

This book aims to provide you with a summary of the major topics that you will be studying in your GCSE History syllabus. You may need to supplement this summary with a more detailed discussion of some of the topics. This can be found in the present author's twentieth-century world history textbook, written for GCSE: *People and Events in the Modern World* (Hodder and Stoughton, 1989).

Addresses of Examining Groups

In order to obtain copies of syllabuses and specimen papers, contact the following:

London and East Anglian Group: ULSEB, Stewart House, 32 Russell Square, London WC1 5DN (01-636-8000)
Midland Examining Group: Publications Dept., University of Cambridge Local Examinations Syndicate, Syndicate Buildings, 1 Hills Road, Cambridge CB1 2EV (0223-61111)
Northern Examining Association: Joint Matriculation Board, Manchester M15 6EU (061-273-2565) or write to any of the other examining boards that form part of the NEA
Northern Ireland Schools Examinations Council: Publications Dept., Beechill House, 42 Beechill Road, Belfast BT8 4RS (0232-704666)

Southern Examining Group: Publications Dept., Stag Hill House, Guildford GU2 5XJ (0483-503123)
Welsh Joint Education Committee: Publications Dept., 245 Western Avenue, Cardiff CF5 2YX (0222-561231)

HANDLING HISTORICAL EVIDENCE 2

2.1 Why evidence is important

One of the most important features of GCSE History is its stress on handling *evidence*. This chapter looks at the different types of historical evidence that you might use when studying modern world history. It also gives you examples of the kinds of tasks that you will come across when you are handling evidence, both in the examination and in coursework.

This is what the assessment objectives say about evidence:

> All candidates will be expected . . . to show the skills necessary to study a wide variety of historical evidence which should include both primary and secondary written sources, statistical and visual material, artefacts, textbooks and orally transmitted information . . .

Let's be clear first of all what *historical evidence* means. It is best to think of evidence as *everything that has been left behind by the past.* The past of course no longer exists. But it has left behind traces (evidence). These help us to piece together what happened. Without it we would know nothing about the past. This is why evidence is so important to anyone studying history.

Test this out by turning to any part of Chapters 3–19 in this book. On every page you will find statements about historical events, for example, that the Japanese bombed the US naval base of Pearl Harbor in 1941 or that over 10 million Soviet citizens were sent to labour camps at the time of Stalin's purges. When reading these statements, keep on asking yourself: how do we know this happened? How do we know this is true? When you think about it you soon realise that many of these statements are only possible because of the existence of a vast mass of evidence: contemporary photographs; eyewitness accounts; people's memories; newspaper articles; secret government records. Statements such as 'over 10 million Soviet citizens were sent to labour camps at the time of Stalin's purges' are just the tip of the iceberg. Underneath is all the evidence that helps to hold them up.

In this book you won't find every statement backed up by the evidence that supports it. That's because this is a particular kind of book – one that aims to provide you with a *summary* of events. Such a summary is only possible, however, because out there in the archives (collections of documents) or in people's memories is all the evidence on which it is based. Don't forget this. Don't ever assume that everything you read is necessarily true – even in *this* book! Keep on asking yourself 'what is the evidence for this statement?', 'how could I set about checking whether or not it is accurate?'. Many of the evidence questions later in the book will help you to do this.

2.2 Primary and secondary sources

In studying the past you will be using many different *sources* of information. These sources can be divided into two main types: primary and secondary sources. A *primary source* is one that came into being at the time of the events you are studying and that is in some way close to these events. A *secondary source* is usually one that came into being at a later date. It is therefore more remote from the events that you are studying. To take an example, primary sources for the study of Weimar Germany during the 1920s would include all of the following:

> Letters, diaries and government papers written at the time; books and newspapers published at the time; photographs taken at the time; cartoons drawn at the time; buildings erected at the time and still surviving today.

By contrast, secondary sources for the study of Weimar Germany during the 1920s would include:

> a book about the governments of Weimar Germany published in Britain in 1968; a book on Weimar foreign policy written in Germany in 1955; an article on life in Weimar Berlin published in an American magazine in 1988; the sections of this book that deal with the history of Weimar Germany.

What all the primary sources have in common is that they came into being at the time of Weimar Germany. What all the secondary sources have in common is that they came into being much later. The distinction between primary and secondary sources is not always quite so simple. For example, what do you call the spoken memories of someone who lived in Weimar Germany but which were not recorded until many years later? In one sense they are 'primary'; in another sense they are 'secondary'. However, you won't go far wrong if you remember this general rule:

primary source = one that came into being at the time of the events being studied and that is in some way close to these events

secondary source = one that came into being later on

Remember that a primary source does not have to be reliable or unbiased. It can have many defects (e.g. can be very biased and inaccurate) and yet still be a primary source – as long as it is close to the event being studied.

HANDLING HISTORICAL EVIDENCE
2.3 Primary sources for the study of modern world history

2

This section describes the main types of primary sources that you are likely to come across when studying modern world history. It is very important to know what these are. It is also important, when studying each type of source, to ask these questions:

(i) What is the value of this particular type of source to someone studying history?
(ii) What problems are likely to arise when using this type of source?

These are the kinds of questions that you may be asked, both in examinations and in coursework.

1 Written sources

This is perhaps the type of source that you are likely to use most often. Written sources consist of many different kinds. These are some of the most important:

(a) *government records* These include official reports of meetings, reports sent by ambassadors, official letters, and the records of debates in parliament. The value of such sources is that they often reveal the views and attitudes of influential people. If you are studying how government policies are formed, they are a particularly useful source. Documents that were secret at the time when they were written can be especially revealing. These may tell you what people *really* thought, i.e. the kinds of things they may not have said in a public speech or report. Governments are also often in a strong position when it comes to getting hold of information about what is happening in a country. Many government records therefore are likely to be detailed, precise and reasonably accurate. Like most types of source, however, government records can also be misleading and biased. Sometimes they can set out deliberately to mislead, e.g. giving the impression that policies are much more successful than they really are. You will need, as with other sources, to decide whether or not you think the writer is trying to tell the truth and whether or not he or she is sufficiently well-informed to be able to do so.
(b) *private diaries and letters* These are often useful because they tell us what people really thought and felt. This is perhaps especially true of diaries, as long as they were not intended to be read by anyone else. With letters, people sometimes conceal their feelings. For example, a soldier writing home from the Western Front in the First World War might have (i) not wanted to tell his relatives what conditions were like and/or (ii) been prevented by the army authorities from doing so. In deciding how reliable letters are likely to be, it is important therefore to think about why and to whom they were being sent.

(c) *memoirs* These are the written reminiscences or memories of people. They relate to events in which the people themselves were involved. Their advantage is that they are often eyewitness accounts of events. They also tell us, from the inside, how people felt. Their main disadvantage is that they are often written down long after the events they describe. Memory can play tricks with people. Some memoir writers also set out to present themselves in the best possible light – and some may even deliberately distort the truth.
(d) *newspapers* These often contain a wealth of information: about politics, about social and economic developments, and about the attitudes of the journalists who write for them. In deciding how reliable a newspaper account of events is likely to be, it is important to find out who owned the newspaper, who its editor was, whether or not it was controlled by the government in power, and whether it was the kind of newspaper that at least *tried* to present an accurate account of events (rather than one that was mainly concerned with telling sensational stories and increasing sales).
(e) *books* For most topics and periods there is a large number of these, written at the time. Books written at the time can be of many different kinds (e.g. books on politics, housing, fashion, travel, etc.). Don't forget that they also include novels and books of poetry. These can often be very revealing of attitudes, as well as helping to bring the past to life. As with other sources, it is important to ask in each case: (i) who was the author? (ii) what were his/her motives for writing? (iii) how well-informed was the author about the events described? (iv) how free was the author to write what he/she really felt and thought?

2 Visual sources

These are of four main types: photographs; films and television programmes; posters and cartoons (including advertisements); paintings. All can be very useful, but all have to be handled with great care.

Photographs can be carefully taken to present a very false picture of events (e.g. photographs of the Germans invading Czechoslovakia in the spring of 1939 which give the false impression that most Czechoslovak people welcomed the invasion).

Films and *television programmes* can be similarly used for purposes of *propaganda*. They can therefore tell the viewer much more about the attitudes of the film-maker than about the events they claim to depict. This, however, can be very interesting if your main concern is to find out what sort of influence films had on those who viewed them. *Posters* and *cartoons* have similar advantages and disadvantages.

Paintings are often neglected as a primary source. They can give glimpses into the past that you might not get from other sources (e.g. details of everyday customs or an impression of what places looked like). They also tell you about the attitudes of the artists who painted them.

3 Statistical evidence

This might seem to present fewer problems. It has the advantage of usually giving precise information. Its disadvantage, however, is that statistics can often mislead. As with other sources, ask yourself whether or not the compiler of the statistics was in a good position to gather accurate information. As with other sources, make sure also that his/her purpose was to try and tell the truth. For some topics, such as Soviet agriculture in the 1930s (pp. 42–44), different sets of statistics tell a very different story, the Soviet government figures showing a much higher rate of production than many others.

4 Oral evidence

This is spoken evidence, recorded either on tape or transcribed (copied down). It can include recorded or transcribed interviews, radio or television programmes, parliamentary debates, and popular songs. It is often very vivid first-hand evidence. Like other sources it can sometimes be biased or unreliable – though this is not a disadvantage if it is people's attitudes you are investigating. Interviews in which people reminisce about the past can also suffer from the disadvantages mentioned under *memoirs* above.

5 Artefacts

These are physical objects that survive from the periods you are studying. They include buildings, monuments (e.g. war memorials), clothes, household items, postcards, old cars and aeroplanes, weapons, etc. These are particularly useful in helping you to piece together the details of everyday life in the past. In doing so they help you to imagine what it must have been like to have lived at a particular time.

HANDLING HISTORICAL EVIDENCE 2
2.4 Evidence questions

At the end of many of the following chapters you will find examples of the kinds of evidence questions likely to be asked both in the examination and in coursework. The various *types* of evidence questions are listed below, together with at least one example of each type of question. These questions relate to the following set of sources. Study these sources before reading the rest of this section.

Sources for evidence questions in this section

All these sources relate to the *collectivisation* of Soviet agriculture in the early 1930s and to the famine that accompanied these events. *Collectivisation* means the reorganising of agriculture into collective farms, i.e. farms owned by the state or community rather than by individual landowners.

Source A: from an account, published in 1933, by an English journalist.

On a recent visit to the Northern Caucasus and the Ukraine, I saw something of the battle that is going on between the government and the peasants. The battlefield is as desolate as in any war and stretches wider; stretches over a large part of Russia. On the one side, millions of starving peasants, their bodies often swollen from lack of food; on the other, soldier members of the GPU (State Political Police) carrying out the instructions of the (government). They had gone over the country like a swarm of locusts and taken away everything edible; they had shot or exiled thousands of peasants, sometimes whole villages; they had reduced some of the most fertile land in the world to a melancholy desert.

(Malcolm Muggeridge, in an article in the *Fortnightly Review*, May 1933)

Source B: an account by a survivor of the famine, recording its effects in the village of Fediivka in Poltava Province.

The first family to die was the Rafalyks – father, mother and a child. Later on the Fediy family of five also perished of starvation. Then followed the families of Prokhar Lytvyn (four persons), Fedir Hontowy (three persons), Samson Fediy (three persons). The second child of the latter family was beaten to death on somebody's onion patch. Mykola and Larion Fediy died, followed by Andrew Fediy and his wife; Stefan Fediy; Anton Fediy, his wife and three children . . .

(Quoted in S. O. Pidhainy, *The Black Deeds of the Kremlin*, Toronto, Canada, 1953)

Source C: from a letter by the Soviet Foreign Minister Litvinov to a US Congressman who had written expressing his concern about news of the famine.

I am in receipt of your letter of the 14th instant and thank you for drawing my attention to the Ukrainian pamphlet. There is any amount of such pamphlets full of lies circulated by the counter-revolutionary organisations abroad who specialise in work of this kind. There is nothing left for them to do but spread false information and forge documents.

1 *Comprehension questions.* These questions ask you to show that you have understood the source. They often require you to explain *in your own words* what the source is trying to say. An example of such a question relating to these sources might be:

Describe in your own words what Muggeridge (Source A) is saying about the activities of the GPU.

A good answer to this question would summarise those parts of Source A that are relevant to the question. It would therefore concentrate on the last sentence of that source. Remember that the question asks you to answer *in your own words*. An answer that simply quotes the source would therefore receive very little credit. Other comprehension questions might test your understanding of key words or ideas in the sources, for example, you might be asked to give the meaning of *counter-revolutionary* (Source C).

2 *Questions asking you to distinguish between fact and opinion*. These can be quite difficult as the difference between fact and opinion isn't always clear-cut. An *opinion*, *judgement* or *interpretation* is someone's view of an event that not everyone would necessarily accept. It is something about which people are likely to disagree – hence the common phrase 'a difference of opinion'. A *fact* on the other hand is something about which there ought to be no disagreement – either it is true or it isn't. If you were asked to give one example of a fact in the above sources, you might refer to the statement in Source B that 'the first family to die was the Rafalyks'. Either this is true or it isn't. The writer may not be telling the truth, but that wouldn't make it an opinion, just an incorrect fact. If you were asked to give one example of an opinion, you might refer to the statement in Source C that 'counter-revolutionary organisations . . . [have] nothing left . . . to do but spread false information and forge documents'. This is a particular view or opinion about a situation, i.e. that there are various organisations outside the USSR whose sole purpose is deliberately to deceive the world about what is happening inside that country. There may or may not be elements of truth in this statement, but it is quite a big claim and one about which people are likely to disagree. It would also be very difficult to prove or disprove. It is therefore a statement of opinion or interpretation.

3 *Questions asking you to identify the attitudes revealed in a source*. These questions are often similar to those asking you to distinguish between fact and opinion. Sometimes you may be asked specifically to identify an author's *bias*. This simply means his or her view, usually one-sided (hence the word 'bias'), of a situation. When studying historical sources get into the habit of trying to work out what the author's views or attitudes are. Remember that this applies to all types of sources. Attitudes and bias are just as likely to be revealed in posters, cartoons and even photographs as in written sources. A question based on the sources above might be:

> Describe in your own words the attitude towards the Soviet famine of the early 1930s shown by (i) Source A and (ii) Source C.

Another version of such a question might be:

> Compare the attitudes towards the Soviet famine of the early 1930s shown by Sources A and C.

In both cases answers would have to focus simply on *attitudes*, pointing to the way in which Source A blames the authorities for the famine and gives the impression that it is an appalling disaster whereas Source C simply denies that the famine has taken place.

4 *Questions asking about the reliability of particular sources.* In using sources, it is important to think how *reliable* they might be as evidence for the situations to which they refer. To do this you need to look very closely at the sources. Take this question, for example, based on Source B above:

> Do you think Source B is likely to be a reliable account of the events to which it refers?

In order to answer this question you would need first of all to look at where Source B comes from. Always remember to look at when the source was published or written, where it was published, and who its author was. In this case notice that the date of publication is some years after the events to which it refers, that the place of publication is outside the USSR, and that the account is by a survivor of the famine. If it is an eyewitness report, that would seem to suggest that it is more likely to be reliable. Certainly the source itself is very precise and full of facts, suggesting that the author knew what he or she was talking about. On the other hand it may have been written down a long time after the event and may thus be distorted in some ways. There is also the *possibility* of bias, even if this does not seem very likely – notice that the title of the publication is *The Black Deeds of the Kremlin.* This is certainly worth mentioning, even if in general you think that the source seems reliable.

5 *Questions asking you to comment on the value of a source.* These questions either ask about the *value* of a source or about the *advantages* and *disadvantages* of a source for someone studying a particular topic. These are really two ways of asking the same question. You might be asked to comment on the value either of an individual source or of a particular type of source. Questions such as these based on the sources above might include:

> How valuable is Source A to someone studying the Soviet famine of the early 1930s? Explain your answer.
>
> What are the advantages and disadvantages of reports by foreign journalists to someone studying the history of the USSR during the 1930s? Illustrate your answer by reference to Source A.

In answering such questions, think carefully again about who the author was, what reasons he had for writing his account, whether he was well-informed about the events he is describing, and what his attitudes and biases were. In this case you might comment on strengths such as the fact that the writer had recently visited the famine areas and is thus an eyewitness of the events he describes. As far as we know, he also had no reason for not telling the truth, as he saw it, about what he had observed. In these ways the source appears to be valuable or useful. On the other hand you might point to the fact that the writer gives very little precise information about the situation in the USSR. You might also mention that he was an English journalist travelling in a country that he may not have known well and whose language he may not have been able to speak. This may well have led him to misinterpret some of the things that he saw. These are some of the possible disadvantages of this source. An answer to this question might conclude by saying that, before we reach any firm conclusions about the source's value, we would need to find out more about the author.

6 *Questions asking you to test the evidence against a particular statement.* An example of such a question might be:

> 'Collectivisation led to the deaths of millions of peasants.' Do these sources support this statement? Give reasons for your answer.

In trying to answer a question such as this it is necessary to think about what you learn from each of the sources. In order to do this you will have to decide how reliable you think the sources are (see 4 above). In addition you will need to think also about what the sources do *not* tell you. In the case of this question the sources actually tell you little or nothing about collectivisation. You learn from Source A that there was a major famine in the USSR and that the authorities were to some extent responsible for it. You learn from Source B about deaths in one particular village. You learn from Source C that some people outside the USSR also believed that there was a famine, but that the Soviet government denied such reports. Nothing, however, is said about collectivisation. You may know from your own knowledge that the famine was a result of collectivisation but you do not learn this *from the sources.*

In answering questions such as these, always remember to be very cautious about what you write. Don't jump to conclusions about the things that sources can tell you. Often they tell you very little by themselves. Don't be afraid to say this if that is what you think – but give reasons why you think it. *Being cautious* applies to all other types of evidence questions as well. It is one of the historian's most important skills.

You should now be ready to try out some of the evidence questions to be found at the end of the following chapters. Have a look at all of these questions, even those in chapters that you are not studying for your particular syllabus. These will show you the range of questions you might be asked, as well as the different types of sources on which questions might be based.

THE FIRST WORLD WAR AND THE PARIS PEACE SETTLEMENT 3

The changes that have taken place in the twentieth century have probably been greater and more rapid than those of any previous century. These changes have had many different causes. One of the most important of these causes has been the impact of war. The twentieth century has seen wars on a scale previously unknown. New methods of warfare have led to situations of *total war*, conflicts in which everyone is involved, including civilians, and which strain the resources of a country to the utmost. Two of these conflicts have had effects far greater than any others. These are the First World War (1914–18) and the Second World War (1939–45). Both wars have helped to shape the world in which we live today. It is impossible to understand this world unless we know something about these wars and the impact they have had. This chapter examines the First World War, its causes, events and effects. You can read about the Second World War in Chapters 8 and 10.

THE FIRST WORLD WAR AND THE PARIS PEACE SETTLEMENT

3.1 The causes of the First World War

3

On 28 June 1914 the Archduke Franz Ferdinand, heir to the Austro-Hungarian empire, was assassinated on a visit to Sarajevo in the Austrian province of Bosnia. His assassin was a Serbian nationalist who objected to Austrian rule in Bosnia, a province largely inhabited by Serbs. The Austrian government accused the neighbouring state of Serbia of being involved in the assassination. It presented the Serbian government with a set of demands, threatening in effect to go to war if these demands were not met. When one of them was turned down, Austria declared war on Serbia. The conflict soon spread outside the Balkans (south-eastern Europe) when Russia came to the aid of Serbia, Germany to the aid of Austria, France to the aid of Russia and Britain to the aid of France. A local conflict had turned into a general European war. It is very important that you try to understand *why* this happened. These are some possible reasons:

1 Rival sovereign states Europe was divided into different sovereign (i.e. completely independent) states. These states had always competed against each other for power and influence within the continent. When they had been unable to achieve their aims by peaceful means, they had often resorted to war. There had been no major European war, however, for over sixty years. Some of the rivalries which divided the Great Powers at the beginning of the twentieth century included: the French government's desire to avenge its defeat at the hands of the Germans in 1870–71; Austria's conflict with Russia over which of them should have the greatest influence in the Balkans; Germany's challenge to the naval and economic power of Britain; Germany's fear of encirclement (being surrounded on both sides) by hostile powers such as France and Russia. In 1914 rivalries and ambitions such as these turned a local conflict into a major war.

2 Nationalism and the problems of multi-racial empires The nineteenth century had seen an upsurge in nationalism. At the same time many parts of Europe continued to be ruled by large multi-racial empires, i.e. empires inhabited by peoples of many different races. These empires included the Russian empire (which contained more non-Russians than Russians), the Austro-Hungarian empire (including Serbs, Croats, Poles, Czechs and many others) and the Ottoman or Turkish empire (which until the beginning of the twentieth century still ruled considerable areas in the Balkans). Nationalist movements within these empires had caused much conflict during the half-century before 1914. The problems of the Austrian government were particularly acute. As you have seen above, it was Austria's desire to curb the activities of Serbian nationalists within its own lands that led it to try and crush the independent state of Serbia in 1914.

3 Economic and colonial rivalries These were not a direct cause of war, though the growing economic strength of Germany had caused considerable anxiety in Britain. Many people in Britain could see how their country was gradually losing its position as the 'workshop of the world'. Germany's acquisition of a number of overseas colonies in the late nineteenth century also seemed to threaten British interests in various parts of the world. Most colonial conflicts had been settled well before 1914 without resort to war. Their effect, however, had been to create even greater distrust among the Great Powers.

4 The alliance system In order to protect themselves against their rivals, the Great Powers had formed two competing systems of alliances during the years before 1914. On the one hand were Germany, Austria-Hungary and Italy in the *Triple Alliance.* On the other hand were France, Russia and Britain in the *Triple Entente.* In most cases powers allied to each other had committed themselves to helping their allies in the event of a war. This had two important effects. Firstly, it might encourage powers to act rashly in the knowledge that they would receive support; for example, the Austrian government's actions in provoking a war with Serbia in 1914 can be partly explained by the knowledge that Germany was likely to back them up. Secondly, it meant that if war broke out between any two powers all the other powers in the two sets of alliances were likely to be dragged in as well. This is precisely what happened in 1914.

5 Popular nationalism and the power of the popular press The peoples of Europe in general greeted the outbreak of war in 1914 with enormous enthusiasm. This can partly be explained by the way in which governments

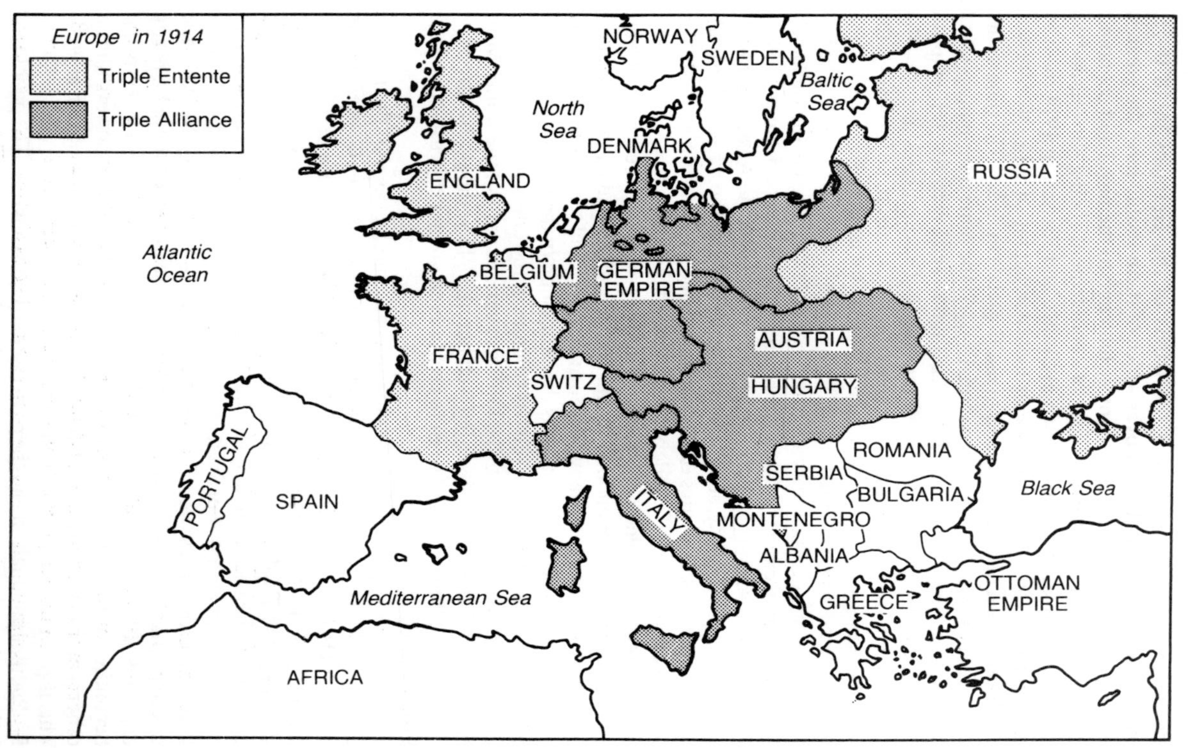
Europe in 1914
Triple Entente
Triple Alliance
NORWAY
SWEDEN
Baltic Sea
North Sea
DENMARK
RUSSIA
ENGLAND
Atlantic Ocean
BELGIUM
GERMAN EMPIRE
AUSTRIA
HUNGARY
FRANCE
SWITZ
ROMANIA
SERBIA
BULGARIA
Black Sea
PORTUGAL
SPAIN
ITALY
MONTENEGRO
ALBANIA
GREECE
OTTOMAN EMPIRE
Mediterranean Sea
AFRICA

had whipped up patriotic feelings among their own people. They had often been aided in this by the popular press which had grown up in many countries at the end of the nineteenth century. As more and more people became literate (able to read and write) and as new technology made possible the production of large numbers of cheap newspapers, so the power of the press grew. It was often used in ways that did not promote the cause of peace.

6 Military plans and the arms race Rivalries between powers had been made worse by the way in which they competed with each other in building up their armaments and increasing the size of their armies. Germany, for example, had been trying for some years to build up its navy in order to rival that of Britain. Countries had also made plans about what they were going to do in the event of war. Germany's *Schlieffen Plan*, for example, envisaged that Germany would at first concentrate almost all its forces on defeating France quickly, only then turning against Russia, whose forces, it assumed, would be very slow to mobilise (get ready for action). The effect of such a plan was to discourage Germany from trying to solve a dispute by peaceful means once mobilisation had taken place. Any delay would mean Germany having to fight what it most feared, a war on two fronts at the same time.

The one country that was not committed by treaty to going to the help of its allies in the event of war was Britain. The British government, however, was determined that Germany should not be allowed to dominate the continent of Europe. In order to prevent this from happening it was necessary to go to the help of France. Germany's invasion of neutral Belgium, which threatened the security of the English Channel, helped to convince the British Parliament and people that the government had no choice but to declare war.

THE FIRST WORLD WAR AND THE PARIS PEACE SETTLEMENT 3

3.2 Why the Schlieffen Plan failed

If the Schlieffen Plan (see above) had succeeded, the First World War would probably have been over in a matter of weeks. Once France had been defeated, Germany would have had little to fear. The British army at the beginning of the war was far too small to pose any threat to Germany's control of the continental mainland. The Russian army, though enormous, was also no match for the better organised and better equipped German forces (as subsequent events were to show). The Schlieffen Plan, however, failed and as a result the war dragged on for over four years. These are some of the reasons for its failure:

1 Russia mobilised its forces faster than Germany had expected. This meant that troops had to be transferred to the Eastern Front earlier than intended.
2 The German invasion of France via Belgium, though amazingly rapid, was not as rapid as had been hoped. The Belgians put up more resistance than anticipated. Britain also entered the war, something the Schlieffen Plan had not allowed for. The British Expeditionary Force (BEF) was very small, but it played an important role in slowing down the German advance at the *battle of Mons* (August) and in halting it altogether at the *battle of the Marne* (September).
3 The two sides were more evenly matched than the Germans had thought. As a result a military stalemate soon set in on the Western Front. This stalemate lasted for most of the rest of the war.

3.3 The Western Front, 1914–17

Military stalemate along the Western Front took the form of *trench warfare*. By the end of 1914 the two sides were dug in along the whole length of the Front from the English Channel to the Swiss border. Despite many attempts and despite heavy loss of life, the position of the opposing armies hardly changed during the following three years. The *reasons for this stalemate* include (a) the fact that the two sides were fairly evenly matched, (b) the nature of trench warfare which, by sheltering the defenders, made attack much more difficult than defence, and (c) the use of modern weapons and techniques of warfare that further strengthened the position of the defenders. These weapons and techniques included reliable machine guns and the use of barbed wire defences.

Military commanders on both sides made many attempts to break out of this stalemate. These attempts, however, consisted mostly of futile offensives which gained very little land and led to the deaths of hundreds of thousands of soldiers. Among such battles were those of *the Somme* (1916), *Verdun* (1917), and *Passchendaele* (1917). 60,000 British soldiers were killed on the first day of the battle of the Somme alone. In the battle of Verdun the Germans lost 281,000 men and the French 315,000. In all three countries a whole generation of young men was wiped out – to no apparent purpose. Those who survived did so in appalling conditions, especially in the winter months when large parts of the Front were turned into a sea of mud. Conditions in the trenches are often vividly described in diaries, poems and letters, as well as in memoirs written later on. These show clearly how the early enthusiasm for war soon turned to bitterness and disillusionment.

THE FIRST WORLD WAR AND THE PARIS PEACE SETTLEMENT 3

3.4 The Eastern Front

Fighting on the Eastern Front was between Russia on the one hand and Germany and Austria-Hungary on the other. Despite some initial successes, the Russians were soon heavily defeated by better-trained and better-equipped German forces in the battles of *Tannenberg* (1914) and *the Masurian Lakes* (1915). In the course of 1915 and 1916 the Russians were driven further and further eastwards, with large numbers of their soldiers being killed, wounded or taken prisoner. The Russian army was more successful against the Austrians. None of Russia's efforts, however, succeeded in halting the continuing loss of many of its western provinces. Russia's defeats in the war were a major cause of both the Revolution of February 1917 which overthrew the Tsar (Emperor) and the Revolution of October 1917 which brought the Bolsheviks to power (see Chapter 4). As a result of the Bolshevik Revolution, Russia withdrew altogether from the war, making peace with Germany at the *Treaty of Brest-Litovsk* (March 1918). This treaty handed over to Germany large parts of the Russian empire.

THE FIRST WORLD WAR AND THE PARIS PEACE SETTLEMENT 3

3.5 Other theatres of war

The Balkans, Gallipoli and Salonika

In 1915, as a way of trying to break out of the stalemate on the Western Front, Britain sent an expedition to the *Gallipoli* peninsula in an attempt to gain control of the Dardanelles, the straits linking the Mediterranean and the Black Sea. This, they hoped, would knock Turkey (an ally of Germany) out of the war, as well as reducing pressure on Serbia and making it easier to send supplies to Russia. The expedition was a complete failure, the Turks having received plenty of warning of what was intended. Some of the troops withdrawn from Gallipoli were sent instead to *Salonika* in Greece, in the hope that they might be able to link up with the Serbians, who were now facing attack from both Austria and Bulgaria. The Salonika bridgehead, however, failed completely to prevent Serbia's collapse which took place shortly afterwards.

The Italian Front

Although a member of the Triple Alliance before the war, Italy joined the war in 1915 on the side of the Allies. The Italian government had been encouraged by the promise of substantial territorial gains at Austria's expense. Italian forces had little success in the war, suffering a major defeat at the hands of the Austrians and Germans at the *battle of Caporetto* in 1917. It was not until the *battle of Vittorio Veneto* in 1918 that the Italian army began to have some success against the invading forces.

The war in the Middle East

British forces attacked the Turks in two places in the Middle East: in Mesopotamia, where an expedition was sent to protect oil supplies in the Persian Gulf; and in British-controlled Egypt, which the Turks had invaded. In Mesopotamia the British were besieged and defeated by Turkish forces at Kut in 1916. Another expedition was more successful and by the end of the war the British were in control of the whole of Mesopotamia. In Egypt the British repelled the Turkish invasion, thus removing any threat to the Suez Canal. British agents such as T. E. Lawrence (Lawrence of Arabia) encouraged the Arabs to rebel against Turkish rule. The Arab revolt, together with victories by the British army, meant that by the end of the war most of Palestine and Syria were in British hands (see Chapter 17).

The war in the colonies

There was relatively little fighting outside Europe and the Middle East. Unlike the Second World War, which was more genuinely a *world* war, the First World War was mainly a European affair. Most of Germany's colonies in Africa, the Far East and the Pacific were soon taken over by Britain, France and their allies. Britain's control of the seas prevented Germany from communicating with its overseas possessions and from sending out reinforcements. The only colony in which the Germans were able to put up an effective resistance was German East Africa (now Tanzania), where German forces were still fighting in 1918.

The war at sea

In surface ships the British navy was superior to the German navy. For most of the war German ships played a fairly limited role, confined to port for fear of being sunk by the British. Those German ships operating outside Europe were eventually tracked down and destroyed in the course of 1914 and 1915. In the early stages of the war, however, the German navy succeeded in launching a number of attacks on English east coast towns, such as Scarborough. In 1916 it also fought the only major naval battle of the war, the *battle of Jutland*, an indecisive encounter from which the Germans retreated but in which the British suffered heavier losses.

Britain's control of the seas enabled it to blockade German ports and to restrict Germany's access to vital war materials. Germany retaliated, however, by submarine (or U-boat) warfare which in 1917 caused major damage to merchant shipping, seriously threatening Britain's ability to carry on fighting. At the height of its U-boat campaign, Germany declared 'unrestricted' submarine warfare, sinking all vessels supplying Britain, whether armed or unarmed, neutral or belonging to the Allies. This 'unrestricted' submarine warfare was one of the major causes of the USA's entry into the war on the side of the Allies (see 3.6 below). The use of the convoy system (merchant ships travelling together protected by destroyers) eventually greatly reduced the number of British losses.

New methods of fighting

The First World War saw the introduction of many new methods of fighting. As a result of the industrial revolution of the nineteenth century, countries such as Britain and Germany had the technological skills to enable them to devise new and more deadly methods of warfare. These included more accurate machine guns, flame-throwers, poison gases and explosive mines. Aeroplanes also came to be used increasingly for fighting as well as for reconnaissance. A major innovation, first introduced in 1916, was the tank. This played an important role in the later stages of the war on the Western Front, helping armies to break out of the stalemate of trench warfare.

THE FIRST WORLD WAR AND THE PARIS PEACE SETTLEMENT 3

3.6 Why Germany lost the war

In the spring of 1918 Germany launched a major offensive on the Western Front, using troops that had been released by the ending of the war in the east (see 3.4 above). Initially this offensive was successful. In July, however, the Allies counter-attacked and for the first time the Germans began to be pushed back all along the front. By the autumn many of the German-occupied areas of France and Belgium had been re-conquered, though Germany itself had not been invaded. On *11 November 1918* the Germans agreed to an *armistice*, accepting harsh terms which included the surrender of the whole German fleet. Why did this happen? Why did the Germans accept defeat when their army was still intact and their country unoccupied? These are some possible reasons:

1 *The USA had entered the war in the spring of 1917*, partly as a result of the campaign of 'unrestricted' submarine warfare mentioned above. US troops did not play a major part in the actual fighting. Their presence, however, strengthened the morale of the Allies and weakened that of Germany. As more and more US men and supplies crossed the Atlantic, the prospect of an eventual German defeat reduced Germany's will to resist.

2 *The Allied blockade* of Germany was having more and more effect, limiting Germany's access to both war materials and food supplies.
3 There was *growing discontent within Germany*, caused both by the defeats of 1918 and by food shortages. Left-wing groups seized the opportunity to attack the *autocratic* (p. 195) government of the Kaiser (Emperor). Leading figures in the German army feared that if Germany did not leave the war the country might experience a revolution similar to the one that had taken place in Russia the previous year (Chapter 4). In an attempt to avoid such a revolution Germany's political leaders persuaded the Kaiser to abdicate his throne. Many Germans wished to end the war in order to be able to concentrate on the country's internal problems.
4 Germany's ally *Austria–Hungary was also being defeated*, both in the Balkans (where the Salonika army was at last advancing) and on the Italian front. Under the pressure of defeat the Austrian empire itself began to split up, its various racial groups clamouring for their independence.

Germany's military leaders felt that they had little choice but to sign the armistice. Their hope was that by agreeing to terms at this stage they would secure a better deal from the Allies. They were to be bitterly disappointed.

3.7 The Home Front in Britain

As a 'total war', the First World War caused major changes within Britain itself. These included:

1 *Greater government control of the economy*. Measures such as the *nationalisation* (p. 196) of the coal industry were needed to mobilise the country's resources to fight a 'total war'. The government also introduced *rationing* of many commodities in order to ensure that priority was given to the needs of the armed forces.
2 A sharp rise in both *taxation* and *government borrowing*, in order to pay for the war.
3 The introduction of *military conscription* in 1916, when the government could no longer recruit enough volunteer soldiers.
4 *The increasing employment of women* in jobs traditionally reserved for men. The war was also a major reason why in 1918 women were given the vote in parliamentary elections for the first time.
5 *A growth in trade union membership and in real wages* (i.e. what people can buy with the money they earn). The war in many ways strengthened the position of the working class in Britain. Labour was scarce and therefore workers were able to demand and receive higher wages. There was also a

growing feeling that governments would have to be more responsive to the needs of ordinary people. It was impossible, many felt, to demand such huge sacrifices without the promise of something in return. Hopes were raised by the war, only to be disappointed during the depression years of the 1920s and 1930s (see Chapter 9).

THE FIRST WORLD WAR AND THE PARIS PEACE SETTLEMENT 3

3.8 The Paris peace settlement

The Allies met in Paris to decide the fate of the defeated powers. President Woodrow Wilson of the USA was anxious that the peace settlement should be on the basis of the 14 Points that he had laid down as war aims. One of the most important of these was the right to *self-determination* (p. 32). Wilson wanted a settlement that would not leave the defeated powers feeling too resentful. He was often opposed, however, by Britain and France, whose governments were concerned above all to ensure that Germany should not recover its position as the dominant power in continental Europe. The eventual settlement was therefore a compromise between these different aims.

The Treaty of Versailles

This was the treaty imposed on Germany. These were its main terms:

1 It was a *Diktat* (a dictated peace). Germany was not represented at the peace conference and was forced to accept the terms.

2 *Germany lost substantial amounts of territory in Europe*: Alsace and Lorraine to France; Eupen and Malmèdy to Belgium; northern Schleswig to Denmark; the Polish Corridor and upper Silesia to the new state of Poland; the port of Danzig, to be administered by the new League of Nations. Some of these were lost after *plebiscites* (p. 32). Others, however, were transferred in order to weaken Germany or strengthen its neighbours and without the inhabitants being consulted. Many Germans, for example in Alsace-Lorraine and the Polish Corridor, now found themselves under foreign rule.

3 *Germany lost all of its overseas colonies.* These were given to Britain, France and their allies as *mandates* under the supervision of the League of Nations (p. 173).

4 *Germany was forbidden to unite with German-speaking Austria* – another breach of the principle of self-determination.

5 *Germany was forced to disarm* in the hope that it would never again be in a position to threaten the peace of Europe. It was to have no airforce or

submarines, a tiny navy and an army restricted to 100,000 men. Conscription was banned, so that Germany would be unable to build up a large reserve of trained soldiers. The Rhineland was to be permanently demilitarised (stripped of all troops and fortifications), and occupied for 15 years by Allied troops.

6 Germany was declared to be guilty of causing the war. As a result of this *war guilt clause*, Germany was obliged to pay *reparations* to the Allies (compensation for the losses suffered during the war). These were eventually fixed at 6,600 million pounds, an enormous sum that Germany was likely to have to keep on paying for the rest of the century. The coal-producing area of the Saar was also to be handed over for a period of 15 years as part of this compensation.

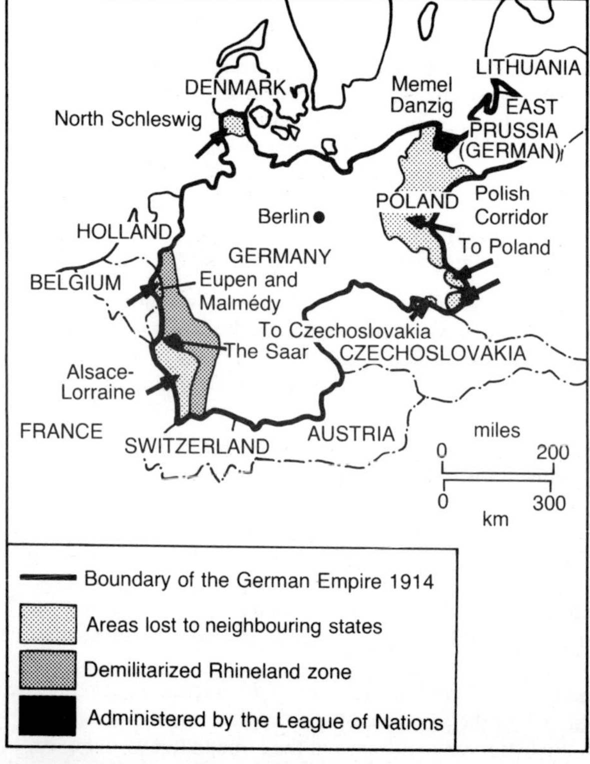

Germany's territorial losses in Europe at the Treaty of Versailles, 1919

Central and Eastern Europe after the First World War

The treaties of St Germain and the Trianon

These were the treaties imposed on the former Austro-Hungarian empire. This empire had now split up into its various parts, with new states being formed in Austria, Hungary, Poland, Czechoslovakia and Yugoslavia. Austria and Hungary, as the leaders of the old empire, were treated as defeated powers. They were forced to accept the collapse of the empire and the loss of lands to neighbouring states such as Romania (which acquired Transylvania) and Italy (which acquired South Tyrol, Trentino and Istria). They were also obliged to pay reparations, though never in fact did so.

Treaties were also signed with Germany's other allies – *Bulgaria* (the Treaty of Neuilly) and *Turkey* (the treaties of Sèvres in 1920 and Lausanne in 1923). Bulgaria lost land to Greece and Turkey was forced to accept the loss of all its possessions in the Middle East (outside Asia Minor).

The effects of this Paris peace settlement were far-reaching. You can read about some of these in many of the chapters that follow, especially Chapters 5, 6, and 7. The League of Nations, which was also established as a result of the Paris peace conference, is discussed in Chapter 18.

THE FIRST WORLD WAR AND THE PARIS PEACE SETTLEMENT 3

3.9 Key historical terms

Alliance system An *alliance* is an agreement or understanding between powers by which they commit themselves to cooperate with each other in various ways. Most of the Great Powers of Europe signed such alliances during the years before 1914. States have continued to sign alliances with each other throughout the twentieth century (see Chapters 7, 10 and 13 especially). Most alliances are *defensive*, i.e. they involve a commitment to go to the defence of an ally if, in certain circumstances, it is attacked by another power. Some alliances have been public; others, including some of the ones signed before the First World War, were secret. This *secret diplomacy* was often criticised after the war as one of the causes of tension between the powers. An *alliance system* is a situation in which there are a number of groups of allied powers, as in Europe before the First World War where the Triple Alliance was ranged against the Triple Entente (p. 21 above).

Self-determination This means the right of peoples to decide upon (determine) their own fate. It was one of the war aims laid down by President Wilson of the USA. It was intended to refer in particular to the many racial and national groups in Europe who at that time were living under foreign rule. Many of these groups, for example Poles and Czechs, seized the opportunity of the collapse of the Austrian and Russian empires at the end of the First World War to gain or regain their independence. In other areas the postwar treaties laid down that *plebiscites* (a popular vote) should be held to determine which state a group of people wished to join. In some cases, however, the right of self-determination was ignored (see 3.8 above).

Other key terms that you need to understand in this topic include *autocratic* (p. 195), *mandates* (p. 173), *nationalism* (p. 56), *nationalisation* (p. 196), *reparations* (p. 30), *total war* (p. 20), and *trench warfare* (p. 24).

3.10 Questions

Evidence questions

Study the leaflet below and on p. 34 issued in Britain in December 1917 and then answer the following questions.

(i) Explain in your own words the meaning of (a) *utmost economy in the use of all kinds of food* and (b) *sedentary work*. (2)

(ii) Do you learn anything from this source about the diet of British people during the First World War? Give reasons for your answer, referring in detail to the source. (4)

(iii) Does this source tell you anything about the impact of the war on the position of women? Explain your answer. (3)

(iv) Referring both to the source and to your own knowledge, explain why these restrictions were introduced. (6)

THE RATIONS.

1 The position of the Food supply is such that the UTMOST ECONOMY IN THE USE OF ALL KINDS OF FOOD must be observed by all classes and by all persons.

2 In particular it is necessary that the strictest economy should be practised in the use of the staple foods: *bread, flour and other cereals; meat; butter, margarine and lard; and sugar.*

3 The weekly rations of these staple foods, which are stated in the following table for different classes of adults according to their sex and occupation, should on no account be exceeded.

4 Children should receive their reasonable rations of these foods.

Their individual needs differ so greatly that no definite ration is laid down for them.

ADULT RATIONS PER HEAD PER WEEK.

Class	Bread.		Other cereals.	Meat.		Butter, Margarine, Lard, Oils and Fats.	Sugar.
	lb.	oz.	oz.	lb.	oz.	oz.	oz.
MEN.							
1. Men on very heavy industrial work or on agricultural work.	8	0					
2. Men on ordinary industrial or other manual work.	7	0					
3. Men unoccupied or on sedentary work.	4	8					
WOMEN.			12	2	0	4	8
4. Women on heavy industrial work or on agricultural work.	5	0					
5. Women on ordinary industrial work or in domestic service.	4	0					
6. Women unoccupied or on sedentary work.	3	8					

Essay question

Why were so many Germans deeply resentful about the terms of the Treaty of Versailles? Your answer might refer to some of the following points: a dictated peace; losses of territory; self-determination; reparations; disarmament; the attitudes of the Allied powers. (15)

RUSSIA 1917–39

4.1 Russia before the Revolution

4

At the beginning of the twentieth century Russia was a vast empire ruled in a traditional way by a *Tsar* (or Emperor), with most of its people earning their living on the land. By 1939 it had become the world's first Communist state, with a ruthless dictator and an industrialised economy. This chapter looks at how and why this transformation took place.

Russia in the early years of the twentieth century

In order to understand how Russia developed during these years it is important to know what kind of country it was at the beginning of the twentieth century. These were some of its main features:

1 The Russian Empire was the *largest country in the world*. Its territories stretched from the Baltic in the west to the Pacific in the east. Its inhabitants were of *many different races*, Russians forming less than half of the total population.

2 The Empire was an *autocracy* (p. 195) ruled by Tsar Nicholas II. Although revolutions in 1905 had forced Nicholas to call a *Duma* or parliament, this had little power. There was censorship of the press and opponents of the regime were kept in prison without trial.

3 Russia was a very divided society with a huge gulf between the rich and the poor. The wealthiest and most powerful class was the *aristocracy*, many of whose members owned large landed estates. It was this class that controlled most of the important jobs in the government and the armed forces. Beneath the aristocracy was a small but increasingly prosperous *middle class*. The vast majority of the population, however, were poor peasants and town workers. The *peasants* were no longer owned by their masters, as they had been until the 1860s, but still in many cases lived in conditions of great poverty. Some of them greatly resented the fact that so much land was still owned by the aristocracy. Peasant violence, directed against landowners and government officials, was common during the years before 1914. Many *town workers* were also discontented. Russia was beginning its *Industrial Revolution* (p. 45) at this time and conditions in many of the new factories and workshops were appalling. Strikes were common, though the authorities did their best to prevent workers from forming trade unions.

4 *Opposition to Tsarist rule* had been growing during the last quarter of the nineteenth century. It continued to grow during the early years of the twentieth century, leading to the revolutions of 1905 mentioned above. Opponents of Tsarism can be divided into a number of different groups:

(i) *Liberals* Some members of the aristocracy and the middle class disliked Tsarist rule because it was repressive and often incompetent. These people mostly wanted a *constitutional monarchy*, in which the Tsar would hand over most of his powers to an elected parliament.

Other opponents demanded much more fundamental changes and were prepared to use violence in order to obtain them. These included:

(ii) *Social Revolutionaries* These were revolutionary socialists who wanted to confiscate the lands of the aristocracy and divide them up among the peasants. Their main support was among the peasantry. They engaged in many violent acts such as the assassination of leading officials.

(iii) *Social Democrats* or *Marxists* This was another group of revolutionary socialists. Their ideas, however, were rather different and they depended mostly on the support of the town workers rather than the peasants. Social Democrats followed the teachings of *Karl Marx* (1818–83), a German thinker who was the father of modern communism. Marx believed that the workers would eventually rise up in a violent revolution, overthrow their masters and establish a new form of society called *socialism* in which there would be no private wealth. You can read more about Marx's ideas on pp. 45–46.

In 1903 the Social Democrats had split into two groups: the *Mensheviks* and the *Bolsheviks*. Both groups followed Marx, but differed from each other in these ways:

(a) The Bolsheviks favoured a much more *authoritarian* party in which everyone obeyed orders without question.

(b) The Bolsheviks believed that they could speed up the course of history and bring the revolution nearer by their own actions. The Mensheviks, however, believed that revolution would only happen when the conditions were ready for it. Mensheviks therefore were prepared to wait whereas Bolsheviks wanted immediate action.

(c) Bolsheviks and Mensheviks had much in common and many of their disagreements were largely a question of rivalries between their leaders. Mensheviks particularly resented the authoritarian way in which *Lenin*, the Bolshevik leader, tried to run the party.

RUSSIA 1917–39
4.2 The causes of the Russian Revolution 4

Despite all the discontent and opposition mentioned above, Russia in 1914 did not seem ready for revolution. None of the revolutionary parties was organised to take over power. Many of their leaders were in prison or exile. It was the outbreak of the First World War that gave them the opportunity for which they had been waiting. You can read about Russia's part in the First World War in Chapter 3.

Why the First World War led to the outbreak of the Russian Revolution

1 As you can read in Chapter 3, *Russian forces were badly defeated* by Germany in the war. Russia lost large amounts of territory. Defeat was blamed on the Tsar's ministers and, after 1914, when he took over as Commander in Chief, on the Tsar himself. In the Tsar's absence power fell into the hands of the Empress Alexandra. The Empress was under the influence of a disreputable holy man called Rasputin and many of the ministers whom she appointed were both incompetent and corrupt. Rasputin's murder in 1916 did little to relieve the situation.

2 The war led to *great suffering among soldiers in the Russian army*. 14 million were drafted into the army. More than 1 million of these were killed, more than 4 million were wounded, and about 3 million were taken prisoner. Most soldiers were desperately anxious for the war to end. Morale was low, especially among young military recruits, many of whom were stationed in towns such as the capital Petrograd. Soldiers such as these had no desire to end up in the same way as all the others. They were to play an important part in the events of the Revolution.

3 The war had also caused *great suffering for civilians*. Food supplies to the towns were disrupted. There was also a serious shortage of accommodation in the towns as refugees flocked there from the conquered provinces and as peasants came to work in factories producing war materials. Conditions became so bad that finally, in February 1917, workers in Petrograd took to the streets.

RUSSIA 1917–39
4.3 The Revolutions of 1917 **4**

The February Revolution of 1917

Russia experienced two revolutions in 1917. It is important not to get them confused. The first or February Revolution was a spontaneous affair that no one had organised. Workers took to the streets and soldiers (for the reasons mentioned above) refused to disperse them when ordered to do so. Unable to suppress the revolt, the leading generals of the Russian army decided that they would have to persuade the Tsar to abdicate (give up his throne). This they were able to do with little difficulty. Russia thus became a *republic*.

The Provisional Government

The Tsar was replaced by a Provisional Government which ruled Russia from February until October 1917. The members of this government were from the middle and upper classes. They were mostly liberals who saw their job as taking control of the country until such time as a Constituent Assembly, elected by the Russian people, could meet to decide on the country's future form of government. In May 1917 the liberal *Prince Lvov* was replaced as leader of the Provisional Government by *Alexander Kerensky*, a Menshevik. Although at first popular, the Provisional Government had many weaknesses. These weaknesses help to explain why later in the year the Provisional Government was overthrown in the second or Bolshevik Revolution of October 1917.

Weaknesses of the Provisional Government

1 Its insistence on continuing the war. This made it very unpopular. Soldiers deserted or refused to obey their officers.

2 Its failure to make any decisions about the redistribution of the big estates. Peasants became impatient. They felt that this government was no more concerned with their interests than the previous one had been.

3 The Provisional Government's authority was challenged by another body set up at the time of the February Revolution. This was the *Petrograd Soviet*, a committee of workers, soldiers and socialist politicians. Similar *soviets* were set up in other cities. The Provisional Government was only able to govern with their cooperation.

4 The growth in Bolshevik influence. At first the soviets were mostly under the control of Mensheviks and Social Revolutionaries, many of whom were prepared to work with the Provisional Government. After the return from exile of the Bolshevik leader Lenin in April 1917, Bolshevik influence in the soviets began to increase. Lenin refused to cooperate with the Provisional Government and in his *April theses* (or statements) demanded 'All power to the soviets' and 'Peace, bread and land'. More and more town workers joined the Bolshevik party. The position of the Bolsheviks was also strengthened in the summer of 1917 by *an attempted right-wing coup* organised by *General Kornilov*. This further emphasised the weakness of the Provisional Government.

The Bolshevik Revolution, October 1917

Having gained control of both the Petrograd and Moscow soviets, the Bolsheviks decided in the autumn of 1917 that the time had come to seize power. Unlike the February Revolution, the Bolshevik or October Revolution was carefully planned. Bolshevik *Red Guards*, commanded by *Trotsky*, Chairman of the Petrograd Soviet, occupied key posts in the capital. Surrounded in its headquarters in the Winter Palace, the Provisional Government surrendered with little resistance. The world's first Communist government had come to power.

4.4 Russia under Bolshevik rule, 1917–24

The Bolsheviks who took over control of Russia in October 1917 were a small dedicated group of professional revolutionaries. They had the support of many town workers, especially in large cities such as Petrograd and Moscow. They were also popular with many of the soldiers of the Russian army. They did not, however, have the support of the majority of the Russian people. The next few years saw a struggle for power within Russia, with the Bolsheviks determined to hold on to the authority they had acquired in October 1917. These were some of the main developments within Russia during these years:

1 The establishment of a Bolshevik dictatorship Elections for a Constituent Assembly had already been planned before the October Revolution. They were held in November 1917. The Bolsheviks only obtained 25% of the vote. With his usual ruthlessness, Lenin closed down the Assembly by force. It had met for only one day. Elsewhere in Russia the Bolsheviks tried to establish their authority wherever they could, frequently using force against their opponents. A secret police known as the *Cheka* was set up, which disposed of anyone suspected of hostility to the new regime. All other political parties were banned.

2 The Treaty of Brest-Litovsk, 1918 True to his promise, Lenin withdrew Russia from the First World War. By the Treaty of Brest-Litovsk Russia lost vast territories to the Germans, together with one-third of its population. In this way Lenin was able to concentrate on his many problems at home.

3 The Russian Civil Wars and the **Wars of Intervention, 1918–21** So great was the opposition to the Bolshevik Revolution that civil wars soon broke out all over Russia. On the one side were the Bolsheviks or *Reds*. On the other side were the *Whites*, a varied group of liberals, Tsarists, Mensheviks and Social Revolutionaries. The situation was further complicated by the involvement of a number of foreign powers, such as Britain, France, Japan, Poland and the USA, who intervened on the side of the Whites.

The aim of the Reds was to survive. The aim of the Whites was to overthrow Bolshevism. The aims of the foreign powers were varied: to defeat communism; to gain lands; to bring Russia back into the First World War.

After a bitter struggle, in which there was great suffering and loss of life, the Reds finally won the civil wars. These are some of the reasons for their victory:

(i) The Whites lost support because they were associated with unpopular foreign invaders.

(ii) The Whites operated around the fringes of the Russian empire while the Reds controlled the centre. This meant that the Reds could move troops quickly to where they were needed.

(iii) The Red Army was built up by Trotsky into a very efficient force.

(iv) The Whites often quarrelled among themselves and lacked a strong overall leader.

(v) The Whites failed to win the support of the peasants. Few peasants had much love for the Bolsheviks, but they often seemed the lesser of two evils.

4 Bolshevik economic policies 1918–24 In order to fight the civil wars Lenin had adopted the economic policy known as *War Communism*. This involved (a) the requisitioning (or seizing) of grain from the peasants, (b) a ban on private trade, and (c) the *nationalisation* (p. 196) of all businesses employing more than ten people. Such a policy was in keeping with the socialist principles of the Bolsheviks. In some ways it was a success (i.e. in enabling the Bolsheviks to feed both the Red Army and the workers in the towns). Eventually, however, it had very damaging consequences. Peasants were angered by the seizure of their crops. Some rebelled. Others simply grew less food. This, together with the civil wars and a drought in 1921, led to an appalling *famine* in which millions lost their lives. Even among Bolshevik supporters there was growing discontent, with strikes in the cities and a *revolt* in 1921 by the sailors of the *Kronstadt naval base*. Lenin was finally convinced that War Communism would have to be abandoned.

The new economic measures that Lenin introduced in 1921 were known as the *New Economic Policy* (NEP). These included: (a) peasants were now allowed to keep most of their crops, thus giving them an incentive to produce more; (b) small businesses were once again permitted; but (c) all major industries remained under state control. The NEP was intended as a temporary measure, until such time as Russia was ready for full-scale socialism. It was certainly successful in leading to an increase in both agricultural and industrial production.

The death of Lenin, 1924

Lenin, the creator of communist Russia, died in 1924, having previously suffered a series of strokes. There was no one obvious successor and the following years saw a power struggle between various rivals.

RUSSIA 1917–39
4.5 Russia under Stalin **4**

The eventual victor in this power struggle was Stalin. By 1929 he was the undisputed ruler of the USSR, having disposed of all his main rivals. Few, if any, would have predicted this in 1924, at which time he was rarely in the public eye. These are some of the reasons for Stalin's success:

1 Stalin had the great advantage of being *General Secretary of the Communist Party*. This meant that many party officials owed their jobs to him and therefore voted in the way he wanted at party congresses.
2 Stalin was absolutely single-minded in his pursuit of power. Unlike Trotsky, his main rival, he was quite happy to change his position and support things that he had previously opposed, if it was in his interests to do so.
3 Stalin's opponents were divided among themselves and unable to form a united front against him.
4 Stalin was very skilful in playing off his opponents against each other.
5 In the course of their quarrel Stalin and Trotsky developed some major differences of opinion about the future development of the USSR. Trotsky felt that Russia's duty was to lead a *world-wide revolution*. Only once this had come about would it be possible to establish a genuinely socialist state in Russia. Stalin on the other hand felt that Russia should concentrate on establishing its own socialist society, without outside help. This policy of *socialism in one country* had more popular appeal and undoubtedly helped Stalin in his rise to power.

Stalin therefore succeeded in disposing of his rivals. Trotsky, for example, was deprived of his command of the Red Army, removed from the *politburo* (the ruling body of the Communist Party), expelled from the Party, exiled to Central Asia, and finally in 1929 deported from the USSR altogether. He continued to denounce 'Stalinism' from exile, until his death in Mexico at the hands of one of Stalin's agents in 1940.

Stalin's domestic policies, 1929–39

Economic policies

Having firmly established his authority, Stalin turned his attention to making 'Socialism in One Country' a reality. His aim was to make the USSR one of the leading industrial nations in the world and to do this in the shortest time possible. The method he adopted was that of the *Five Year Plan*. This was a set of targets, laid down by the government, for huge increases in economic production, to be met within a five-year period. Three Five-Year Plans were launched during these years: in 1928, 1932 and 1938.

Industrialisation (turning a largely agricultural country into a largely industrial one) involved changes to both industry and agriculture. *Industry* had to be expanded and modernised. At the same time *agriculture* had to be reorganised in order to (a) free workers for the factories and (b) produce a food surplus that could be exported to other countries, thus earning money to finance industrial development.

Industry

The Five-Year Plans concentrated on heavy industry in order to give the USSR a strong basis for further economic growth. The three main lines of development were:

1 **Iron and steel** Huge new steel plants were built and production increased dramatically. One of the biggest plants was at Magnitogorsk in the Ural mountains.
2 **Power** To keep the new factories going, more power had to be generated. Priority was given to oil and coal production and to the development of electricity.
3 **Communications** Roads, canals and railways were built in many parts of the USSR, with the intention of providing the fast communications needed in a modern economy. Projects included the Baltic-White Sea Canal and the Turkestan–Siberia railway.

Although they did not reach all of their targets, the Five-Year Plans were spectacularly successful in bringing about a huge and rapid increase in industrial production. The tables opposite show the extent of this success.

These achievements were particularly impressive at a time when the rest of the world was in a state of economic depression. They enabled Russia to defeat Germany in the Second World War (see Chapter 8). They also help to explain why Russia is the superpower that it is today.

The Russian people, however, paid a heavy price for their country's industrialisation. Conditions at work were often appalling, pay was low and many basic goods were in short supply. The Five-Year Plans paid little or no attention to *consumer goods* on the grounds that these would have to wait until heavy industry had been established. Standards of living were on average worse than they had been before the Revolution. It was not until long after the Second World War that the people of the USSR saw any benefit to themselves from the sacrifices they had been forced to make during the 1930s.

Agriculture

Stalin's policy was to *collectivise* Russian agriculture, i.e. to group small farms into larger units (known as *collective farms*) run by party officials. This policy was bitterly opposed by the wealthier peasants or *kulaks* who resisted by destroying animals and crops. Stalin responded with great ruthlessness, systematically eliminating the kulaks as a class. Millions – possibly as many as 11 million during the years 1930–37 – were killed, deported to labour camps or allowed to starve to death. An appalling famine spread throughout southern Russia in 1932–33. Agricultural production slumped and it was not until the late 1930s that it returned to the level that it had been before collectivisation. In the long term, however, by

Production figures compiled from official Soviet statistics

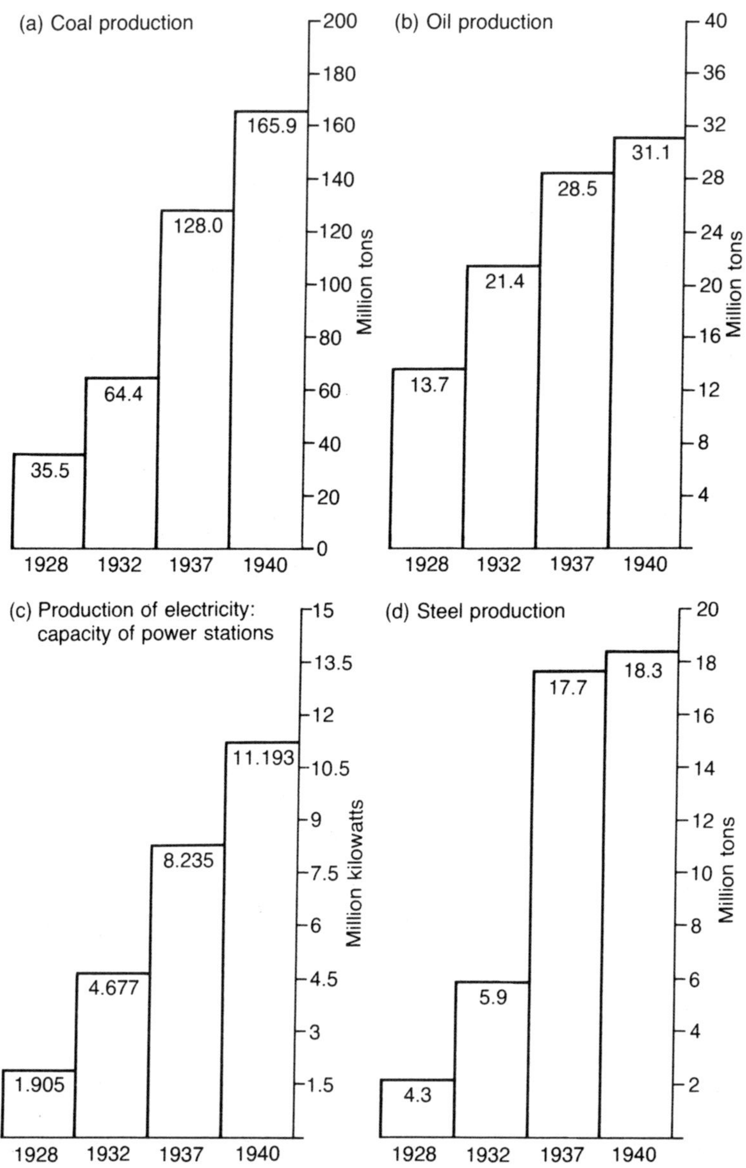

permitting the introduction of tractors and combine harvesters, collective farms reduced the number of workers needed in the countryside, thus freeing them for work in the factories.

Stalin's purges

Stalin's rule during the 1930s was a *totalitarian dictatorship* (p. 65) based on fear and terror. No one was safe. Anyone was liable to be seized in the middle of the night, tortured, shot, kept in prison without trial or sent to a labour camp. It was not even necessary to have said or done anything that might be considered hostile to the government. As a result of these 'purges', as they were called, at least 1 million were executed and over 10 million sent to camps.

Stalin's reasons for embarking on this reign of terror included:

(a) Fear of possible rivals, e.g. former party leaders, many of whom were forced to confess to imaginary crimes in 'show trials'.
(b) The desire to terrorise the Russian people into doing exactly what they were told at a time of rapid economic change.
(c) Because in the end the terror acquired a momentum of its own which it was difficult to stop.

Effects of the purges

These included:

(a) Making Stalin the absolutely unchallenged leader of the USSR. Coinciding with the purges was a *personality cult* of Stalin the hero and saviour of the nation.
(b) Removing many of the country's ablest people. The purge of the Red Army left the country's armed forces in a very weak state.
(c) Causing immense misery, suffering and death for millions – in human terms by far the most important effect.

Stalin's foreign policies, 1924–39

Stalin's main wish in his foreign policy was for Russia to be left alone. His aim was to avoid foreign commitments in order to give the USSR time to build up its own strength. This *isolationist* policy persisted well into the 1930s. The rise of Hitler in Germany (see Chapters 6 and 7) led him to modify this policy in various respects, for example by:

(a) Joining the League of Nations in 1934.
(b) Signing defence treaties (directed against Germany) with France and Czechoslovakia in 1935.
(c) Giving active support to the anti-Fascist forces in the Spanish Civil War of 1936–39 (see Chapter 7).

Stalin, however, was deeply suspicious of Britain and France, fearing that they would be unreliable allies against Nazi Germany. It was partly because of this that he finally concluded that the safest policy would be to come to terms with Hitler. He did so in the *Nazi-Soviet Pact* of August 1939, which you can read about on p. 71. This agreement with Russia's arch-enemy shocked many communists. From Stalin's point of view, however, it had enormous advantages, (a) in giving Russia time to build up its forces, and (b) in securing for Russia vast territories that it had lost at the end of the First World War. In Chapter 8 you can read about the effects of this agreement and how in 1941 it came to an end, plunging the USSR into a devastating war.

RUSSIA 1917–39 4
4.6 Key historical terms

Aristocracy Nobility or upper class. The term usually applies to a class of landowners with titles (e.g. 'prince', 'duke', etc.) that are passed on from one generation to another. (N.B. Not all rich people are aristocrats and not all aristocrats are necessarily rich.)

Industrial revolution/industrialisation A big growth in industrial production together with changes in the way that industry is organised. In a country experiencing an industrial revolution industry usually replaces land as the main source of wealth. An industrial revolution may take place in different ways, e.g. according to plans laid down by a government (as in Stalin's Russia) or in an unplanned spontaneous way (as in Britain in the late eighteenth and early nineteenth centuries).

Marxism The ideas of the nineteenth-century German thinker Karl Marx. These ideas are the basis of twentieth-century communism. Marx believed that he had discovered the laws that control the development of societies. According to these laws every society passes through three stages:

(i) *feudalism*, in which land is the source of wealth and power rests with the big landowners;
(ii) *capitalism*, in which trade and industry are the main source of wealth and power rests with the middle classes; and
(iii) *socialism*, in which there is no longer any private property and power rests with the people.

The change from one stage to another will come about in each case as a result of a *violent revolution*. Marx believed that these revolutions would inevitably take place and that the whole world would eventually become socialist. He had very little to say about what socialism would actually be like. In its early stages there would have to be some kind of *dictatorship of the proletariat* (town workers) until such time as all the enemies of socialism had been disposed of. Followers of Marx therefore have the following attitudes: a dislike of capitalism/private enterprise/private property; willingness to support the use of violence; hostility to religion (disliked as a way of keeping the masses under control); a commitment to what they think are the interests of the working class.

Partly because Marx was often vague about what socialism would be like, Marxists have often disagreed in their interpretation of his ideas. Many Marxists call themselves *Marxist-Leninists* because they follow the particular ways in which Lenin applied Marx's ideas in practice. The main features of *Leninism* are:

(i) A belief that the revolution should be led by a revolutionary party.
(ii) A belief that the course of history can be speeded up, for example that a country can pass almost directly from feudalism to socialism (as Leninists claim happened in Russia).

It is very important that you understand what Marxism involves. It has had a tremendous impact on the twentieth-century world and will be mentioned again and again in this book.

Middle class The class of people in the middle ranks of society, i.e. people who are neither *aristocrats* (see above) on the one hand nor *working-class* on the other. The term 'middle class' covers a wide range of people and is often used to mean different things. People who are almost always described as middle-class include lawyers, factory-owners, doctors, teachers, owners of small businesses, shopkeepers, etc. People refer to different sections of the middle class by terms such as *upper middle class* (e.g. lawyers), *lower middle class* (e.g. small shopkeepers), etc.

Other terms that you need in order to understand the developments described in this chapter include *authoritarian* (p. 195), *autocrat* (p. 195), *civil war* (p. 195), *consumer goods* (p. 195), *coup* (p. 195), *constitutional monarchy* (p. 195), *isolationist* (p. 196), *liberals*(pp. 55–56), *nationalisation* (p. 196), *republic* (p. 197), *totalitarian dictatorship* (p. 65).

Source-based questions

Study the Soviet production figures on p. 43 and then answer the questions below.

(i) Give reasons for the rapid growth in production shown in these tables. (6)
(ii) Why was Stalin so concerned to increase steel production? (3)
(iii) What were the effects on the Russian people of the developments shown in the tables? (6)

Evidence questions

Study the extract and photograph below, both of which refer to collectivisation during the early 1930s, and then answer the questions that follow.

> Trainloads of deported peasants left for the icy north, the forests, the steppes, the deserts. These were whole populations, denuded of everything; the old folk starved to death in mid-journey, new-born babies were buried on the banks of the roadside, and each wilderness had its crop of little crosses of boughs or white wood. Other populations, dragging all their mean possessions on wagons, rushed across the frontiers of Poland, Rumania, and China and crossed them – by no means intact, to be sure – in spite of the machine guns.
>
> (V. Serge, *Memoirs of a Revolutionary 1901–41*, 1963)

Peasants queuing to join a collective farm

(i) Why was it possible to publish this photograph in the USSR in the 1930s, but impossible to publish accounts such as the one in the extract? (4)

(ii) What questions would you need to ask in order to test whether or not the account in the extract was an accurate one? (5)

(iii) 'Photographs never lie'. Do you agree? Give reasons for your answer, making reference both to the photograph on p. 47 and to other photographs in this book. (6)

Essay questions

(i) Why did some peasants support the collectivisation of Soviet agriculture in the early 1930s?

(ii) Why did some peasants oppose it?

(iii) It has been suggested that some peasants 'neither supported nor opposed collectivisation'. Why might this have been?

MUSSOLINI AND THE RISE OF FASCISM IN ITALY

5

5.1 Fascism

Perhaps the most important development in European history during the interwar years was the rise of Fascism. Almost every European country had a Fascist movement of one kind or another. This chapter and Chapter 6 examine the growth of Fascism in Italy and Germany. These were the two countries in which Fascist parties came to power before 1939.

Before looking at how and why Fascists first gained power in Italy, it is important to understand what *Fascism* means. It is a difficult term to define, partly because Fascists were often very vague about what they believed.

These are some of the main features of Fascism as it developed in Italy after the First World War:

1 Intense nationalism A belief that loyalty to the nation was more important than loyalty to other groups such as the Church or the family. Nationalism also meant that the interests of the nation came before the interests of other nations. In practice this usually meant an aggressive foreign policy.

2 A belief in 'strong' government Fascists believed in autocratic or dictatorial government. They were therefore opposed to *democracy* and *liberalism*. Fascists believed that the state should be under the control of one strong ruler. In Italy he was known as *Il Duce* (i.e. the leader).

3 A dislike of communism and socialism Fascists were very hostile to communism partly because communists put first the interests of the working class. This went against their idea that what mattered above all was the nation.

4 Concern for social reform In Italy and Germany Fascists, especially in the early years, were often very critical of existing society. They demanded, for example, that the rich should be taxed more heavily and that wealth should be redistributed. Once in power Fascists rarely did very much along these lines, but the demand for these changes was sometimes an important part of their appeal.

5 Racism One aspect of Fascism that was important in Germany, though not in Italy, was the belief that some races were in themselves superior or inferior to other races. You can read more about Nazi ideas on race in Chapter 6.

5.2 Mussolini's rise to power

The rise of Mussolini and his Fascist supporters was very rapid. Within three years of the establishment of the Fascist party in 1919 Mussolini had become Chancellor (or Prime Minister) of Italy. Why did this happen? These are some of the main reasons:

1 Italy at the end of the First World War was a *parliamentary democracy* (p. 64). The Italian parliament was composed of a large number of political parties, none of which had a majority of seats. Governments were *coalitions* (p. 195). Most of these governments were weak and short-lived. Italy gave the impression of being badly governed. Mussolini's stress on restoring strong government was therefore very attractive to many Italian people.

2 Italian democracy was particularly weak because the two main parties – the *Roman Catholic Popular Party* and the *Socialists* – refused to form part of any of the postwar governments. Power rested therefore with the various small liberal parties, whose leaders attempted to govern without the support of most members of the Italian parliament.

3 Italy after the end of the First World War also experienced many economic problems, with high levels of *unemployment*. Although the economy had begun to improve by 1921, the Fascists were able to convince many people that economic recovery would only be possible with the kind of strong government that they were intending to provide.

4 *Economic problems* led to a great deal of unrest in the immediate postwar years. There were strikes in factories as well as attempts in the countryside to take land away from the big landowners. Many working-class Italians supported socialist demands for the abolition of private property and the redistribution of wealth. This greatly alarmed people such as industrialists and landowners, many of whom turned to the Fascists in the hope that they would succeed in getting rid of socialism once and for all. Money from people like this greatly strengthened the Fascists in their campaigns. The *fear of socialism* was also strong among many of Italy's Roman Catholics who had seen the anti-religious measures taken by the new communist government in Russia and were alarmed at the prospect of a communist revolution in their own country.

5 There was also much discontent in Italy about the way the country had been treated at the Paris peace conference at the end of the First World War. Italy gained far less than either the government or most of the Italian people had expected. Mussolini promised that a Fascist government would adopt a much more assertive and successful foreign policy.

6 The Fascists adapted their message to what they felt people wanted to hear. For example, in some places they were hostile to the Church or to the

monarchy whereas elsewhere or at different times they took a completely opposite line. The fact that they contradicted themselves did not appear to matter. Their advantage over other parties was that they seemed energetic and determined to succeed.

7 *Black-shirted* Fascist squads used violence against other parties, breaking up political meetings and beating up their opponents. This strengthened the impression that the government was not in control of the country. The Fascists often cleverly blamed this violence on their opponents.

8 In 1921 Mussolini was able to enter into an agreement with *Giolitti*, one of the liberal leaders, to campaign together in the general election of that year. This made the Fascist party more respectable. It also helped the Fascists to secure 35 seats in the Italian parliament.

9 In 1922 the Fascists were still only a small party with little prospect of coming to power by peaceful means. Mussolini, however, without using force, managed to persuade and threaten the King to make him Chancellor. This was only possible because the King himself could see some advantages in having a Fascist government and because the existing government was so weak that it was powerless to persuade the King to act otherwise. Mussolini later claimed that the Fascists had seized power by marching on Rome. This is not what happened. The Fascists threatened to do so, but knew that if the army and police had stood up to them they would quickly have been defeated. Mussolini had bluffed his way to power – and his bluff had not been called.

MUSSOLINI AND THE RISE OF FASCISM IN ITALY 5

5.3 The consolidation of Mussolini's power, 1922–29

When Mussolini became Chancellor in 1922 he was still in quite a weak position. The Fascists had very few seats in the parliament and Mussolini's cabinet contained many non-Fascists. Mussolini's aim was to remove obstacles to his power in whatever way he could. These are some of the ways in which he managed to achieve this:

1923: The *Acerbo Law*, by which the party that gained most votes in a general election was to be given two-thirds of the seats in the parliament.

1924: Fascists won a two-thirds majority of both votes and seats. Mussolini was therefore in a position to pass any laws he wished. In the same year one of Mussolini's main opponents, the socialist deputy Matteotti, was kidnapped and murdered. Mussolini eventually accepted responsibility for this and as a result most of the other parties withdrew from the parliament. This simply played into Mussolini's hands.

1926: All other political parties were banned.
During the years after 1923 Mussolini also established a secret political police, imposed censorship of the press and took over control of local government.
1929: Mussolini signed the *Lateran treaties* and *concordat* with the Roman Catholic Church. This ended more than half a century of conflict between the Church and the Italian state. In return for recognising the state of Italy, the Roman Catholic Church was accepted as the country's official church. Given that most Italians were Roman Catholics, these agreements were very useful in winning increased support for Mussolini.

MUSSOLINI AND THE RISE OF FASCISM IN ITALY

5.4 Mussolini's domestic and foreign policies 5

Economic and social policies

As with other aspects of his policies, Mussolini often did not have very clear plans about the economic and social changes that he wished to introduce in Italy. These, however, are some of the policies that he adopted:

1 Although strongly supporting private enterprise, especially at first, Mussolini was also keen to strengthen government control over the economy. During the 1930s he attempted to establish what he called the **Corporate State**. According to this, the country's economic life was controlled by various Corporations. Each Corporation would be organised by representatives of employers and workers who would work together in a cooperative spirit. On paper it sounded a good idea. In practice the Corporate State was largely a device for increasing government control and for ensuring that workers did as they were told. Wages were fixed and strikes were forbidden.

2 Economic self-sufficiency One of Mussolini's aims was to make Italy self-sufficient, i.e. not dependent on imports from other countries. One way of doing this, during the 1930s, was to encourage the production of grain, often at the expense of traditional Italian crops such as grapes and olives. This *battle for grain*, as it was known, was not very successful, leading to increased prices at home and a decline in Italian exports to other countries.

3 Public works Much money was spent on reclaiming land, erecting public buildings and constructing roads. This helped to create jobs, but otherwise brought few benefits to the Italian people. Unemployment and poverty remained high, especially in the impoverished south of the country.

4 Battle for births As a way of boosting the country's prestige, Mussolini was keen during the early 1930s to increase Italy's population. This 'battle

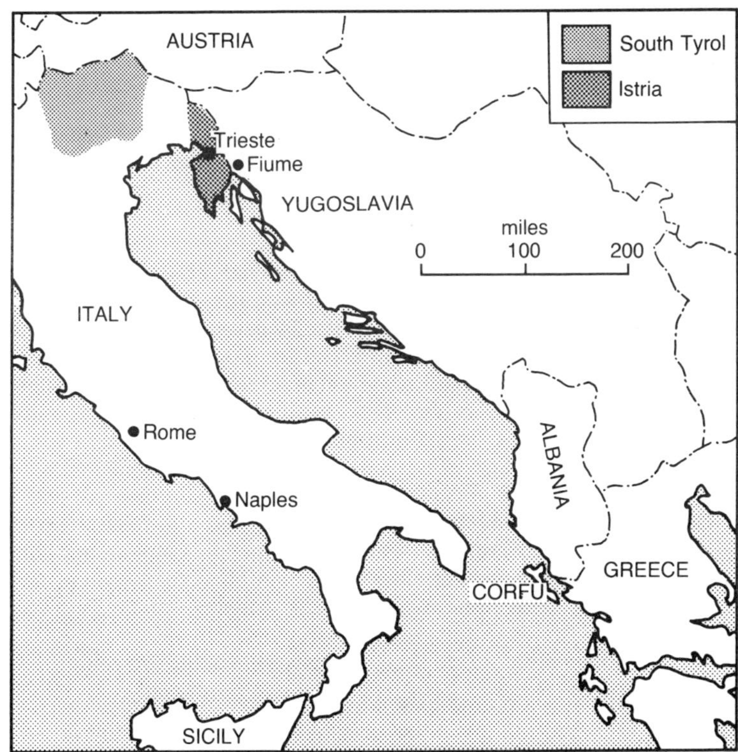

The Adriatic

for births' involved prizes and tax concessions for large families. It was ill-advised at a time of increasing unemployment. It was also unsuccessful.

Mussolini's foreign policies

In foreign affairs Mussolini's main aim was to increase Italy's prestige in the eyes of other nations. He often talked about restoring Italy to the greatness that it had in Roman times. Apart from this, he had few precise aims.

The Adriatic

Italy had particular interests in the area of the Adriatic. Mussolini was active in this area:

(i) in the *Corfu incident* of *1923* when Italian forces occupied the Greek island of Corfu in protest about a dispute between the two countries. Mussolini ignored the procedures for settling disputes laid down by the

League of Nations. Greece was forced to pay compensation and the Italian forces eventually withdrew.
(ii) in *Fiume*, a town claimed by both Italy and Yugoslavia which Mussolini managed to acquire for Italy in 1924.
(iii) in *Albania*, a small country that fell increasingly under Italian influence and which was eventually invaded by Mussolini's forces in the spring of 1939.

Relations with other major powers (to 1935)
Until the mid-1930s Mussolini remained on reasonably friendly terms with Britain and France, the countries that had been Italy's allies in the First World War. Like Britain and France, Mussolini had no wish to see a strong Germany once again dominating central Europe. For this reason he did his utmost in 1934 to prevent a possible German takeover of Austria (rushing Italian troops to the Austrian border as a warning to Hitler). In 1935 he also joined with Britain and France in a protest known as the *Stresa Front* against the ways in which Hitler was beginning to rearm Germany in defiance of the Treaty of Versailles.

The Stresa Front, however, did not last. Italy began to draw closer to Germany. The two governments shared similar political views. They both had grievances against the Versailles settlement. Mussolini hoped that by attaching Italy to Germany he might be able to share in Germany's growing success.

Two developments hastened the coming together of the two countries:

1 Mussolini's attack on the East African country of *Abyssinia* in 1935. Mussolini launched this attack in order to extend Italy's empire in East Africa and as a way of distracting attention from economic problems at home. Unlike Britain, France and the League of Nations, Germany refused to condemn what Mussolini had done.
2 Italy's help to the Nationalists in the *Spanish Civil War* of 1936–39. Both Hitler and Mussolini gave financial and military aid to Franco's Nationalist forces in Spain. In doing so they were breaking non-intervention agreements that Britain and France were trying to enforce. This further weakened Mussolini's ties with his former allies and brought him closer to Hitler.

In 1936 Hitler and Mussolini made an agreement which came to be known as the *Rome–Berlin Axis*. This was followed in 1937 by the *Anti-Comintern Pact*, signed by Germany, Italy and Japan. As an indication of Italy's new friendship with Germany, Mussolini made no objection in 1938 when German troops invaded Austria. In the following year the two dictators signed the *Pact of Steel*, by which Mussolini committed Italy to fighting alongside Germany in any general European war.

MUSSOLINI AND THE RISE OF FASCISM IN ITALY
5.5 The Second World War and the collapse of Fascism **5**

Mussolini was slow to enter the Second World War, despite his commitments in the Pact of Steel. When he did so, in June 1940, Italian forces had little success. Hitler was forced to reinforce the Italians both in Greece (which Mussolini attacked in October 1940) and in North Africa (where the Italian army came into conflict with British forces based in Egypt). The defeat of the Italian and German forces in North Africa in 1942–43 (pp. 80–81) led to an Anglo-American invasion of Sicily in July 1943.

Italy's defeat and the failure of Mussolini's foreign policy prompted the Italian army and the King to get rid of the Duce. *Mussolini was dismissed* and a new Italian government made peace with the Allies. Italy's war, however, was by no means over. German forces occupied the country and put up severe resistance to the continued advance of the Allies. Mussolini was rescued from imprisonment and for a time acted as a puppet ruler of a small Fascist republic in the north of the country.

Italy was finally liberated in the spring of 1945. Mussolini was captured and shot by *partisans*. When his body was strung up outside a garage in Milan crowds came to jeer and spit at it. They may well have been the same people who, ten years earlier, greeted him with cheers and smiles.

MUSSOLINI AND THE RISE OF FASCISM IN ITALY
5.6 Key historical terms **5**

In order to understand the rise of Fascism in Italy it is important that you grasp the meaning of each of the following terms:

Fascism This is obviously the most important. It is defined on p. 49.

Communism and **Socialism** These are important because they are what Fascism, for some of the time, was reacting against. Fascists disliked communism because it placed the interests of one class before the interests of the nation. Many Fascist supporters also had a lot to lose from any attempt to abolish private property. Fascism, however, was influenced by communism and socialism in a number of ways; for example, in its stress on government control of the economy and in its concern (at least in its early years) with social reform. You can find a full definition of communism and socialism on pp. 45–46 and 197.

Liberalism Fascists were also reacting against this. Liberals believe in human freedoms such as freedom of the press, freedom of speech, the right to form associations such as trade unions and political parties, etc. They tend to be supporters of *democracy*, i.e. they believe that people should have a say in how they are governed. None of this was part of Fascism. To Fascists the individual was much less important than the nation. Fascists believed that people should do as they were told. They were often even more contemptuous of liberals than they were of socialists. They felt them to be weak and ineffective.

Nationalism This was a crucial feature of Fascism and an important reason for its appeal. Fascists felt that the nation came first. Its interests came before those of any group within the nation. Its interests also came before those of any other nation.

Other important terms are *Corporate State* (p. 52), *public works* (p. 197), and *economic self-sufficiency* (p. 52).

MUSSOLINI AND THE RISE OF FASCISM IN ITALY 5

5.7 Questions

Essay questions

(i) Many Italians were very discontented with the state of their country during the years immediately after the end of the First World War. Explain why they were discontented and show how Mussolini was able to use this discontent in his rise to power during the years 1919–22. (15)

(ii) 'Mussolini's domestic policies brought little benefit to the Italian people.' Give an account of Mussolini's domestic policies, showing to what extent you agree with this statement. (15)

GERMANY 1919–39: THE WEIMAR REPUBLIC AND THE RISE OF HITLER 6

Germany's defeat in the First World War led to the abdication of the Kaiser (Emperor) and to the formation of a German republic. This republic, known as the Weimar Republic, lasted from 1919 until 1933, in which year it was replaced by Hitler and the National Socialists (Nazis). This chapter examines Germany's experiences under both regimes: *Weimar Germany* (1919–33) and *Nazi Germany* (from 1933 until the outbreak of the Second World War in 1939).

The Versailles settlement and its effects on Germany

The terms of the Treaty of Versailles as they affected Germany are listed on pp. 29–30. Before reading the rest of this chapter remind yourself what these terms were. They had a major impact on Germany and help to explain much of what happened in the country during the following twenty years. These are some of the effects of the Versailles settlement on Germany:

1 Many Germans greatly resented the Versailles settlement. Although Germany's democratic politicians had had no choice but to accept the settlement, they were widely blamed for having done so. In the eyes of many Germans the Weimar Republic was associated from the very beginning with defeat and humiliation.
2 The Versailles settlement caused many economic problems for Germany. The country lost some of its best resources (e.g. in the Saar and in Alsace-Lorraine). At the same time it had to pay *reparations* to the Allies. These economic problems made many Germans discontented with a government which seemed unable to solve them.
3 Most German politicians wanted to modify the Versailles settlement, though found it very difficult to do so. When times were bad, parties such as the Nazis found it easy to win support by denouncing Weimar for its failure in this respect.

GERMANY 1919–39: THE WEIMAR REPUBLIC AND THE RISE OF HITLER

6.1 The Weimar Republic, 1919–24 6

During its early years the government of Weimar Germany experienced many problems. These were some of the main ones:

1 The Weimar *constitution* (p. 195), under which the republic was governed, was a very democratic one. All adult Germans were able to vote at regular intervals both for their President (head of state) and for their representatives in the *Reichstag* (lower house of the German parliament). Problems arose because of the system of *proportional representation* that

was used for Reichstag elections. Under this system a party received the same percentage of seats in the parliament as it had received votes in the election. Although this meant that the Reichstag was more likely to reflect the views of the people, it had two disadvantages:

(a) it encouraged the formation of a lot of small parties, most of which were able to secure at least a few seats in the Reichstag. Some of these parties had very extreme views and would probably not have managed to survive under a system of representation such as the one used in Britain.

(b) because there were so many parties in the Reichstag, no single party was ever able to secure an overall majority. Most governments, therefore, were *coalitions* (p. 195). These were sometimes, though by no means always, both weak and short-lived.

2 During its early years there were attempts to overthrow the republic. Some of these were made by the extreme left; others by the extreme right. Attempts by the *extreme left* included the Spartacist uprising in Berlin and the proclamation of a 'soviet' government in Munich, both in 1919.

3 The threat from the *extreme right* was more serious, partly because extreme right-wing parties sometimes had supporters in high places (e.g. in the civil service, the army and the courts). There were many political assassinations during these years, most of them the work of the extreme right. Few of the assassins were ever punished. The government also had to contend with unofficial right-wing armed forces known as *Freikorps*. One group of these attempted to seize control of Berlin in the *Kapp putsch* of 1920. Another party of the extreme right – the National Socialist party – staged a similar putsch in Munich in 1923.

4 Parties of both the extreme left and the extreme right received more support during these years partly because of the economic problems experienced by Germany at the time. As in other European countries, the end of the First World War led to a drop in economic production and thus to an increase in unemployment. Many ex-soldiers returned home to find that there was no work for them.

The *reparations* imposed by the Treaty of Versailles made the situation much worse. By 1923 the German government was no longer able to meet these payments. In protest against this non-payment the French sent troops into the *Ruhr*, the centre of Germany's heavy industry. The effects on the German economy were devastating. The rate of *inflation*, which was already on the increase, now got completely out of hand. The German mark ceased to have any value. Standards of living fell and life savings were wiped out at a stroke. It was at this point that Hitler staged his unsuccessful putsch in Munich.

5 The French invasion of the Ruhr in 1923 highlighted another problem facing Weimar governments after 1919 – that of *diplomatic isolation*. For some years after the end of the First World War Germany continued to have strained relations with its former enemies. On the German side there

was great resentment about the Versailles settlement. On the side of Britain and France there was continuing suspicion of German intentions. Germany's isolation was heightened by its exclusion from the League of Nations (pp. 172–75). The only country with which it succeeded in improving relations during these years was Russia, which since the Bolshevik Revolution was also isolated from the rest of the world. The two countries signed the *Treaty of Rapallo* in 1922, by which diplomatic relations were restored.

6.2 Weimar: the years of recovery, 1924–29

Despite all the problems mentioned above, the Weimar Republic survived. During the mid-1920s it even appeared to flourish. Part of the credit for this must go to *Gustav Stresemann* who was either Chancellor or Foreign Minister throughout the years 1923–29. Stresemann was also greatly helped by the *economic recovery* of those years, a recovery which his own policies helped to assist. These were some of the successes of Weimar during the mid-1920s:

1 *The withdrawal of French troops from the Ruhr* in return for a promise that Germany would resume reparations payments.

2 The negotiation of a new reparations settlement known as the *Dawes Plan* (1924). This extended the period over which reparations had to be paid. It also provided for US loans to help Germany keep up with the payments.

3 The withdrawal of the old German currency and its replacement with the new *Rentenmarks*.

4 *Falling unemployment*, as a result of the economic recovery mentioned above.

5 *A decline in support for extremist parties*.

6 *Improved relations with other countries*. Stresemann made a big effort to restore relations with Germany's former enemies. His successes included:

- (i) The *Locarno treaties of 1925*, by which Germany accepted the changes to its western frontiers that had been imposed by the Treaty of Versailles.
- (ii) *Germany's admission to the League of Nations in 1926*.
- (iii) An agreement in 1929 that the Allies would withdraw their troops from the Rhineland in the following year (i.e. five years earlier than stipulated in the Treaty of Versailles).
- (iv) A new scheme for reparations payments known as the *Young Plan* (1929), by which the total payment was greatly reduced.

GERMANY 1919–39: THE WEIMAR REPUBLIC AND THE RISE OF HITLER

6.3 The collapse of Weimar Germany, 1929–33 — 6

Weimar's years of recovery came to an abrupt end in October 1929 with the *Wall Street Crash* (see p. 112), an event which coincided with the death of Stresemann. US loans and investments were recalled. The demand for German goods abroad fell dramatically. Factories were closed down and workers laid off. The situation was soon far worse than it had been in the early 1920s. This time there was no inflation, but there was *massive unemployment* on a scale previously unknown. As in the years after 1919 economic problems soon led to political problems. Old resentments about the Weimar Republic reappeared and support for extremist parties, both of the left and the right, once again increased.

As a result of these and other problems the Weimar Republic eventually collapsed and in 1933 was replaced by a very different kind of regime led by Adolf Hitler.

GERMANY 1919–39: THE WEIMAR REPUBLIC AND THE RISE OF HITLER

6.4 Hitler and the National Socialist party — 6

Hitler was born in Austria in 1889 and continued to live in that country until just before the First World War. It was while living in the Austrian capital Vienna that he picked up many of the ideas that were later associated with National Socialism: a dislike of democracy; an intense German nationalism; and a hatred of the Jews. Hitler moved to Germany in 1913 and served in the German army during the First World War.

It was only after the end of the war that Hitler became involved in politics. He joined and soon took charge of a small party known as the *National Socialist German Workers' Party*. It was a *nationalist* party in its demand that Germany recover the power and prestige it had lost through defeat in the war. It was a *socialist* party in that it attacked the rich in various ways, for example, by demanding the abolition of income that was unearned. The combination of nationalism and a kind of socialism was unusual.

Hitler first came to prominence in 1923 when he attempted to seize control of Munich (the *Munich putsch*) at the time of the French invasion of the Ruhr. The attempt was a dismal failure, but Hitler's subsequent trial brought him a great deal of publicity. His brief imprisonment gave him time to write *Mein Kampf*, an account of his political views.

Hitler's experience in 1923 convinced him that he would only manage to come to power by peaceful means. For the rest of the 1920s he concentrated on strengthening the organisation of his party in various ways. These included: developing the Nazi youth movement; forming new branches of the party; establishing a Nazi trade union; holding impressive rallies. The Nazis won very few seats in Reichstag elections during the prosperous years of the mid-1920s, but were in a strong position to take advantage of the situation that developed after the Wall Street Crash of 1929.

The table on p. 65 shows how support for the Nazis grew during the years 1930–33. Why was there such a dramatic growth in this support?

GERMANY 1919–39: THE WEIMAR REPUBLIC AND THE RISE OF HITLER

6.5 Why Hitler rose to power, 1929–33

6

These are some of the main reasons for the rise of Hitler and the Nazis:

1 The *economic problems*, and especially *unemployment*, mentioned above. None of the German governments of these years seemed capable of reducing unemployment. The Nazis promised to do so.

2 Governments during the years 1929–32 were often *weak coalitions*, preoccupied with their own survival. The two parties that were most committed to the survival of Weimar, the Social Democratic Party and the Catholic Centre Party, could not agree with each other and played little part in the governments of those years.

3 Democracy had begun to crumble in Germany even before Hitler took over. A number of governments during these years took advantage of one of the articles of the Weimar constitution that permitted them to bypass the Reichstag and *rule by decree*. This was a precedent that Hitler was soon to follow.

4 The Nazis used very effective methods of *propaganda* in order to win support. Hitler encouraged people to feel that under a Nazi government Germany would be great and prosperous once again. He also encouraged them to blame many of their problems on the Jews. Hitler was a very able speaker. He also made good use of newspapers and newsreels, as well as organising *rallies* with floodlights, marches and stirring music.

5 Hitler managed to obtain the backing of some wealthy German industrialists who provided money for Nazi funds. Like many other Germans they were alarmed by the growth in support for communism that took place after 1929 (see table on p. 65). A strong government such as the one promised by Hitler seemed the best way of protecting the existing capitalist system.

6 Other right-wing politicians thought that they could use Hitler to promote their own interests and then get rid of him once he had served his purpose. Such a politician was Von Papen who played an important part in

undermining the government that was in power at the end of 1932. Both President Hindenburg and some of the leading generals of the German army also viewed Hitler in a similar way.

7 In the last resort, however, President Hindenburg had little choice but to make Hitler Chancellor. As you can see from the table on p. 65, the Nazis were the *largest single party in the Reichstag* – even though they never obtained an absolute majority of either votes or seats.

GERMANY 1919–39: THE WEIMAR REPUBLIC AND THE RISE OF HITLER 6

6.6 Hitler establishes his dictatorship, 1933–34

When Hitler was appointed Chancellor in January 1933 it was as the head of a coalition government. There were more non-Nazis in this government than there were Nazis. Hitler's aim was to move as quickly as possible to a situation in which he had supreme power. These are the steps by which he did this:

(i) *1933 Reichstag election*. Hitler called yet another election in the hope that he would obtain an overall majority. During the campaign he took full advantage of his new position (e.g. intimidating his opponents, censoring the press, etc).

(ii) A week before the election the Reichstag building in Berlin went up in flames. This *Reichstag fire* was blamed on the communists, even though it was almost certainly the work of the Nazis themselves. It provided Hitler with an excuse to issue an emergency decree suspending all the liberties guaranteed by the constitution.

(iii) Despite all his advantages, Hitler did not secure the huge majority for which he had been hoping. His aim now was to persuade and threaten the Reichstag to give up its powers. To achieve this it would have to pass an *Enabling Act*, giving him unlimited power. To obtain the necessary two-thirds majority Hitler (a) excluded the communist deputies from the Reichstag, (b) persuaded the Catholic Centre party to vote for the Act in return for vague promises of concessions, and (c) used the votes of his allies, the conservative Nationalist party.

(iv) After the Enabling Act Hitler took decisive action against his opponents, flinging them into prison and into concentration camps. *All other political parties were banned*. Press, radio and cinema were subjected to total Nazi control.

(v) In 1934 Hitler turned his SS (protective squads) against his own stormtroopers (the SA). In the *Night of the Long Knives* many SA leaders were shot. Hitler was determined to crush the least sign of resistance to his absolute control of both the party and the state.

(vi) In August 1934 *President Hindenburg died.* Hitler replaced him as both President and Commander in Chief of the armed forces. The power of Hitler – or the *Führer* (leader), as he was known – was now supreme.

GERMANY 1919–39: THE WEIMAR REPUBLIC AND THE RISE OF HITLER

6.7 Hitler's domestic policies, 1933–39 **6**

The Nazi regime was a *totalitarian dictatorship*. Hitler's government aimed to influence all aspects of people's lives, including their thoughts. The methods used were (i) terror, (ii) propaganda and (iii) close government control. In addition to those mentioned in the section above, the Nazis strengthened their dictatorship in each of the following ways:

1 Control of the young Hitler realised that it was vital to influence the minds of young people. These were the future citizens of the thousand year Reich (Empire) he was trying to establish. Education was strictly controlled by the state. All boys and girls were also encouraged to join the *Hitler Youth*, an organisation divided up into various sections according to age. The Hitler Youth *indoctrinated* its members with all the attitudes that the Nazis wanted to foster: obedience to the Führer; a willingness to die for the Fatherland; a hatred of the Jews, etc.

2 Hitler and the Christian churches As a totalitarian dictator, Hitler could not bear to think that people might have loyalties that were as important or more important than their loyalty to him or to the German state. Hitler therefore distrusted the Christian churches because he feared that they might weaken his authority. He did not feel strong enough to ban them altogether, trying instead to bring them more and more under government control. With the Protestant churches – to which most Germans belonged – he had considerable success, establishing a new Reich Church with a Nazi bishop at its head. He was less successful with the Roman Catholic Church, though many of Germany's Roman Catholics seemed quite happy with the Nazi regime.

A minority of both Protestants and Roman Catholics denounced Nazism as anti-Christian. Many were to pay for their opposition with their lives.

3 Hitler's economic policies As a party bitterly opposed to communism, the Nazis had no wish to abolish the *capitalist system of private enterprise* (privately owned businesses, private land ownership, etc.) that they had inherited. Hitler was keen, however, for the state to exercise close control over the workings of the economy. The state also employed people directly in a way it had never done before, i.e. in various schemes of *public works* such as road building and slum clearance. Partly as a result of measures such as these, the number of unemployed fell dramatically: from 6 million in

1933 to 2.5 million in 1935. The apparent success of Hitler's economic policies was one reason why the Nazis continued to receive the enthusiastic support of many German people.

4 Hitler and the Jews For the Nazis the Jews were a useful scapegoat for Germany's problems. They also believed that the Jews were racially inferior. After 1933 Hitler systematically persecuted Germany's large Jewish population, humiliating them in innumerable ways, taking away their jobs and closing down their businesses. In the *Nuremberg laws* of 1935 they were forbidden to marry non-Jews and deprived of all their rights as German citizens. In 1938 there was a particularly appalling wave of *anti-Semitic violence* that spread across the whole country. The Final Solution – the planned extermination of the Jews – did not take place until after the outbreak of the Second World War. But the way for it had already been well prepared.

Other chapters of this book that deal with Hitler and the Nazis are Chapter 7 (Hitler's foreign policies 1933–39) and Chapter 8 (the Second World War).

GERMANY 1919–39: THE WEIMAR REPUBLIC AND THE RISE OF HITLER 6
6.4 Key historical terms

National Socialism (or **Nazism**) In order to understand the ideas and attitudes of the Nazis you will need to re-read the section on Fascism on p. 49. German National Socialism was by no means the same as Italian Fascism. Most of the attitudes described on p. 49 were, however, shared by Hitler. Nazis differed from Italian Fascists in their greater concern for racial issues, and in particular in their intense *anti-Semitism*. Nazis were also more preoccupied with foreign affairs, obsessed with their plans to make Germany once again the greatest power in Europe.

Parliamentary democracy 'Democracy' means rule by the people. 'Parliamentary democracy' means the people are able to influence the way in which they are governed by electing representatives to sit in a parliament. There are different kinds of parliamentary democracy in different countries, for example Britain, the USA and Weimar Germany all had parliamentary democracies in the interwar years but each was organised in a different way. Weimar Germany, for example, unlike Britain, had a system of *proportional representation*. Parliamentary democracy is a completely different kind of government from Fascism or National Socialism. Fascists and Nazis regarded parliamentary democracy as weak and worthy only of contempt. For Fascist views on *liberalism* – often closely associated with parliamentary democracy – see pp. 55–56.

Totalitarian dictatorship A 'dictatorship' is a government in which the ruler (or dictator) has complete power. A '*totalitarian* dictatorship' is one which controls all aspects of people's lives. Nazi Germany and Stalin's Russia (Chapter 4) were both totalitarian dictatorships. Mussolini tried to establish a similar kind of regime in Italy, though with considerably less success.

Other key terms you need to understand for this topic are *constitution*, *propaganda*, *coalition*, and *anti-Semitism* (see Glossary).

GERMANY 1919–39: THE WEIMAR REPUBLIC AND THE RISE OF HITLER

6.9 Questions

6

Source-based questions

Study the table below and then answer *all* the questions that follow.

Total numbers of votes obtained by major political parties in elections in the Reichstag, 1924–32. (The figures in brackets represent the percentage of the total votes that was obtained by each party.)

	May 1924	*December 1924*	*May 1928*	*September 1930*	*July 1932*	*November 1932*
National Socialist German Workers Party (Nazi Party)	1 918 000 (6·6%)	908 000 (3%)	810 000 (2·6%)	6 407 000 (18·3%)	13 779 000 (37·3%)	11 737 000 (33·1%)
German Nationalist People's Party (Conservative)	5 696 000 (19·5%)	6 209 000 (20·5%)	4 382 000 (14·2%)	2 458 000 (7%)	2 187 000 (5·9%)	3 131 000 (8·8%)
Centre Party (Roman Catholic)	3 914 000 (13·4%)	4 121 000 (13·6%)	3 712 000 (12·1%)	4 127 000 (11·8%)	4 589 000 (12·4%)	4 230 000 (11·9%)
Social Democratic Party	6 009 000 (20·5%)	7 886 000 (26%)	9 153 000 (29·8%)	8 576 000 (24·5%)	7 960 000 (21·6%)	7 251 000 (20·4%)
Communist Party	3 693 000 (12·6%)	2 712 000 (9%)	3 265 000 (10·6%)	4 590 000 (13·1%)	5 370 000 (14·3%)	5 980 000 (16·9%)

(i) Using the information in the table, describe in your own words the changing fortunes of (a) the Social Democratic Party and (b) the Communist Party during the years 1924–32. In the case of each party give reasons for any changes that you notice. (8)

(ii) How would you account for the growth in the Nazi vote during the years 1930–32? (8)

(iii) Hitler came to power in 1933 with the support of many, if not most, German people. How successful was Hitler in keeping this support during the years 1933–39, and for what reasons? (9)

Evidence questions

Study this German cartoon of 1934 and then answer the questions that follow. The figure on the left, shown leaning on Hitler, represents Germany (Deutschland). The words on the banner mean 'Loyalty, Honour and Order'.

(i) Which political party do you think was responsible for this cartoon? Give reasons for your answer. (3)

(ii) What impression is the cartoonist trying to give of Hitler? Referring in detail to the cartoon, describe the methods he uses to put this impression across. (7)

(iii) What did the party responsible for this cartoon mean by the three slogans on the banner? (5)

INTERNATIONAL RELATIONS DURING THE 1920s AND 1930s 7
7.1 International relations during the 1920s

You can read about some aspects of international relations during the 1920s in other sections of this book, (for example pp. 53–54 Italy's foreign policies, p. 59 Germany's foreign policies, p. 115 US foreign policies, and p. 174 the League of Nations).

In Europe international relations during these years were dominated by the Paris peace settlement that you read about on pp. 29–31. The Allies, and especially Britain and France, were anxious above all to maintain this settlement. Other powers, such as Germany and Italy, were looking for opportunities to change it. On the whole Britain and France were successful. The map of Europe in 1930 differed little from that of 1920 and most of the other provisions of the peace settlement were also still intact.

In the course of the 1920s there was a marked improvement in relations between Britain and France on the one hand and their former enemies, especially Germany, on the other. This was shown most strikingly in the *Locarno treaties of 1925* (p. 59) and in *Germany's admission to the League of Nations in 1926*. In other ways too the 1920s seemed to offer the prospect of improved relations between powers. Some of the international agreements that were signed during these years include:

1921–22 The Washington Agreements These concerned (a) an agreement between the USA, Britain, France and Japan to recognise each other's rights and possessions in the Pacific, and (b) an agreement between Britain, the USA, Japan, France and Italy to limit naval forces. The naval agreement was followed up in 1930 by a further agreement (the *London Naval Agreement*) signed by the USA, Britain and Japan.

1928 The Kellogg–Briand Pact This came about as the result of an initiative by Briand, the French Foreign Minister, who had played a major part in improving relations with Germany. It was a pact to renounce the use of war and was signed by 65 countries. At the time it seemed a major step towards ensuring world peace. Events were soon to show how ill-founded these hopes were.

INTERNATIONAL RELATIONS DURING THE 1920s AND 1930s 7
7.2 The causes of the Second World War in Europe

In order to understand why the Second World War broke out in 1939, you will need to study the foreign policies pursued by Hitler after he came to power in Germany in 1933. It was Hitler's actions that were mainly responsible for the war. From the moment he came to power Hitler looked for every opportunity to break the Versailles settlement. His aim was to make Germany once again a great power. For years he met with little resistance from Britain and France, the powers most committed to upholding the Versailles settlement. As you can read below, their policy of *appeasement* allowed him to make spectacular gains in rapid succession.

Appeasement This is a term often associated with Neville Chamberlain, British Prime Minister from 1937 to 1940. In fact it was a policy that was well-established years before Chamberlain came to power. It dominated British and French policy towards Germany throughout the years after 1933. *Appeasement* means making concessions to other powers in order to avoid conflict and war. Some of the reasons why British and French governments adopted this policy were as follows:

(i) Many British politicians felt that the Treaty of Versailles had been harsh on Germany and therefore sympathised with some of Hitler's demands.
(ii) Many British and French politicians mistakenly treated Hitler as if he were a reasonable man who would stop making demands once a few of Germany's main grievances had been met.
(iii) Some politicians in both Britain and France were much more hostile to communism than to Fascism or Nazism. Hitler's fierce anti-communist views were thus a point in his favour.
(iv) Memories of the First World War were still fresh. People in Britain and France were keen to avoid another war at all cost.
(v) The British government had enough problems to cope with in its empire. The last thing it wanted was conflict in Europe as well.

During the years 1933–39 Hitler expanded German power in each of the following ways:

1933: *Hitler withdrew Germany both from a major Disarmament Conference organised by the League of Nations and then from the League itself.* This action in effect announced that Germany would no longer be bound by treaty restrictions. Hitler embarked on a major programme of *rearmament*.
1935: *Hitler announced the reintroduction of conscription* (which had been banned by the Treaty of Versailles). Britain, France and Italy formed the Stresa Front to oppose this revival of German power, but otherwise took no action. In the same year the people of the *Saar*, ruled by the League since 1919, voted to unite once again with Germany.
1936: *German troops marched into the Rhineland*, an area that had been demilitarised by the Treaty of Versailles. In the same year Hitler drew closer to Italy, for the reasons described on p. 54. This *Rome–Berlin Axis*, as it was known, was extended in 1937 when Germany, Italy and Japan signed the *Anti-Comintern Pact*, a joint declaration against communism.

1936–39: Despite having signed an agreement not to intervene, Germany became involved in the *Spanish Civil War* in support of Franco's Nationalist forces. The Spanish Civil War was a bitter internal struggle between *Republicans* (liberals, socialists, communists, and Basque and Catalan separatists) and *Nationalists* (backed by large sections of the middle and upper classes, the armed forces and the Roman Catholic Church, as well as by Spanish Fascists).

German intervention in the Spanish Civil War had these effects:

(a) It helped Franco to win the war.
(b) It gave German armed forces useful practice, e.g. in the bombing of civilian targets from the air.
(c) It brought Germany and Italy closer together (Italian forces also having been sent to help the Nationalists).
(d) It led to worsening relations with the USSR, which sent help to the Republicans, and with Britain and France, which were trying to enforce the agreement made by the powers not to intervene.

March 1938: Hitler marched into Austria and proclaimed the *Anschluss* (the union of Austria and Germany). This had been expressly forbidden by the Treaty of Versailles. As on previous occasions Britain and France protested, but took no action.

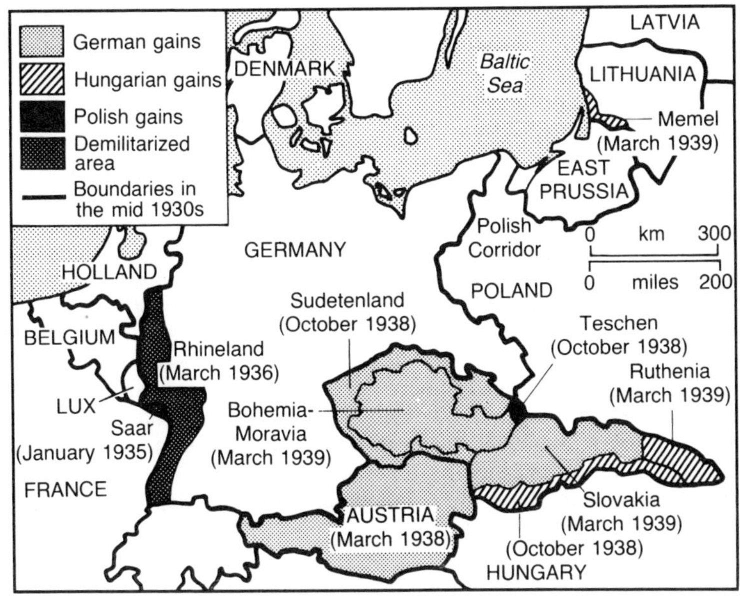

Germany and its neighbours before the Second World War

September 1938: Hitler deliberately provoked a crisis involving the *Sudetenland*. This was a German-speaking province of Czechoslovakia, some of whose inhabitants wanted to join with Germany. However, in the past it had never formed part of Germany. As you can see from the map on p. 69, the Anschluss had greatly weakened Czechoslovakia's position, the western part of the country now being surrounded by German territory. Hitler was also able to take advantage of the many racial tensions that existed within Czechoslovakia (for example, between Czechs and Slovaks).

Hitler probably did not have a very precise idea of what he hoped to gain from this crisis. He created the situation and then waited to see what would develop. The initiative to avoid major conflicts and to reach some kind of settlement came from the British government. Chamberlain, the British Prime Minister, was anxious that the situation should not develop into a war. In the course of September he made three visits to Germany:

(a) to *Berchtesgaden*, where Hitler threatened war if the Sudetenland was not allowed to transfer to Germany;
(b) to *Godesberg*, where Hitler rejected Chamberlain's concession that areas of the Sudetenland with a German population of more than 50% should be transferred to Germany. Hitler now demanded the whole of the Sudetenland, without delay.
(c) to *Munich*, where a four-power conference of Britain, France, Germany and Italy decided Czechoslovakia's fate. Britain and France agreed to almost all of Hitler's demands and within days the German army occupied the Sudetenland. Both Hitler and Chamberlain, for very different reasons, were delighted with this settlement. The Czechoslovak government was not even consulted.

March 1939: Despite solemn promises made in September 1938, *German troops took over the rest of Czechoslovakia*. This was the first non-German territory that Hitler had acquired. Britain and France now realised that Hitler's ambitions were far greater than they had thought. In the same month German troops seized *Memel* (see map on p. 69), a former German area which had been part of Lithuania since the end of the First World War.

The end of appeasement

As a response to the German occupation of Czechoslovakia, Britain and France guaranteed to support Poland – Hitler's next most likely victim – in the event of an attack. Similar guarantees were given to Romania and Greece, countries alarmed by the actions of Hitler's ally Mussolini in seizing Albania in March 1939. Britain and France also speeded up their programmes of *rearmament*.

Poland and the coming of war, September 1939

Hitler's next move was to try and regain the *Polish Corridor* (see map on

p. 69), an area containing many Germans which had been lost at Versailles, and *Danzig*, a city that had been taken from Germany and placed under international control. He may have expected to make his gains without war, but was certainly prepared to go to war if it was necessary.

In order to isolate Poland, Hitler negotiated an agreement with his arch-enemy the USSR. This *Nazi–Soviet Pact of August 1939* took the world by surprise. The USSR promised to remain neutral in the event of a war between Germany and Poland and in a secret agreement the two countries arranged to divide Poland between them. Britain and France had tried to negotiate an agreement with the USSR, but failed to convince Stalin that they were sufficiently serious in their desire to stand up to Hitler.

Poland refused to give way to Hitler's demands. Hitler therefore ordered a full-scale attack. Britain and France kept their promise to Poland and on 3 September both countries declared war on Germany. The Second World War had begun.

INTERNATIONAL RELATIONS DURING THE 1920s AND 1930s 7
7.3 Key historical terms

The most important term you need to understand in this chapter is *appeasement*. This was discussed on p. 68. Other terms include *conscription* (p. 195), *disarmament* (p. 196), *demilitarisation/remilitarisation* (p. 195), and *rearmament* (p. 197).

INTERNATIONAL RELATIONS DURING THE 1920s AND 1930s 7
7.4 Questions

Essay questions

(i) The following factors all played a part in the outbreak of the Second World War:

The ideas of National Socialism
Hitler's attempts to expand Germany's frontiers in 1938–39
Anglo-French appeasement
The attitude of the USSR

Using these factors, explain why the Second World War broke out in September 1939. (25)

(ii) Why did governments in Britain and France adopt a policy of appeasement towards Germany and Italy during the 1930s? (15)

Evidence questions

Study Sources A, B, C, D and E, and then answer the questions that follow.

Source A: a British newspaper cartoon published shortly after the signing of the Munich agreement in September 1939. The three figures (from left to right) represent Chamberlain, Mussolini and Hitler.

EUROPE'S AUCTIONEER
"—And, of course, this one for you, Sir."

Source B: from an unpublished letter by Geoffrey Dawson, Editor of *The Times*, 23 May 1937:

> I should like to get going with the Germans. I simply cannot understand why they should apparently be so much annoyed with *The Times* at this moment. I spend my nights in taking out anything which I think will hurt their susceptibilities and in dropping in little things which are intended to soothe them.

Source C: from a speech, given in Berlin, by the British Ambassador to Germany, Sir Nevile Henderson, 1 June 1937:

> . . . far too many people have an *erroneous* conception of what the National Socialist regime really stands for. Otherwise they would lay less stress on Nazi dictatorship and much more emphasis on the great social experiment which is being tried out . . .

erroneous: mistaken

Source D: from the official German record of a meeting on 19 November 1937 between Hitler and Lord Halifax, an unofficial representative of the British government:

> In spite of (some) difficulties, he (Halifax) recognised that Hitler had not only performed great services in Germany but also, as he would no doubt feel, had been able, by preventing the entry of communism into his own country, to bar its passage further west.

Source E: from an article by Lady Londonderry, written in February 1937:

> I was prepared to find Herr Hitler as he is invariably represented in our daily Press – a fierce, fighting type of *swashbuckler*. But on our meeting I discovered that this impression was far removed from the truth . . . From the Führer's own lips I learned of the great desire for friendship with the English . . . Surely this offer of friendship merits acceptance in the spirit in which it has been made, instead of the rather suspicious view of our Foreign Office with its (pro-French) bias appears to take it.

swashbuckler: a swaggering ruffian

(i) Sources A and B suggest different attitudes on the part of the British press towards Hitler. What do you learn from Sources A and B about how the British press responded to Hitler? (4)

(ii) Which other source tells you something about the attitudes of the British press? Explain in your own words what it tells you. (2)

(iii) What do you learn from these sources about the attitude of the British government towards Hitler? Refer in detail to the sources in support of your answer. (4)

(iv) How valuable are these sources to someone studying appeasement during the 1930s? Explain your answer. (4)

(v) Do you think Source A gives an accurate impression of Chamberlain's policy towards Germany during the years 1937–38? Explain your answer, referring to your background knowledge. (6)

THE SECOND WORLD WAR IN EUROPE 8

This chapter examines the events of the Second World War in Europe, the kind of war it was, and its short-term effects. You can read about the causes of this war in Chapter 7 and about the war in the Far East in Chapter 10.

Total war

One of the basic features of the Second World War that you need to understand is that it was a *total war*. By this is meant a war in which the resources of the countries involved are mobilised to their utmost, i.e. a war in which vast numbers of men and women are conscripted for military service or for work in war-related industries and a war in which civilians are exposed to the effects of fighting (for example, through the use of bombing from the air). The Second World War was much more of a total war than the First. This was partly because of the new methods of fighting that it involved (i.e. the use of *blitzkrieg* (see below) and of aerial bombardment).

THE SECOND WORLD WAR IN EUROPE 8

8.1 The war in the East, 1939

As described in Chapter 7 (p. 71), the Second World War began with *Hitler's invasion of Poland in September 1939*. Poland was conquered in less than one month, despite fierce resistance. The Polish armed forces were no match for Germany's tanks, aeroplanes and motorised infantry. Hitler's rapid success was largely due to his use of the tactics of *blitzkrieg* (or 'lightning war'). Blitzkrieg usually involved the following stages:

(a) *Dive-bombers attack* from the air, e.g. railway junctions, bridges, airfields, in order to *destroy communications*;
(b) *paratroopers* are then dropped to secure key positions;
(c) these are closely followed by *fast-moving columns of tanks*, and
(d) *motorised infantry*, moving fast on lorries and motorbikes.

Blitzkrieg was used to great effect by Germany in most of its campaigns during the next two years. It was also used by Germany's ally Japan in the Far East.

At the same time as the Germans took over the western parts of Poland, the USSR took over the east. This had been agreed between the two countries in the Nazi-Soviet Pact of August 1939 (p. 71). The USSR also forced the Baltic states of *Estonia*, *Latvia* and *Lithuania* to sign treaties which in effect put an end to their independence. The USSR thus regained many of the territories that it had lost at the end of the First World War. *Finland* refused to sign such a treaty and a brief war between Finland and the USSR followed during the winter of 1939–40. The Finns lost and had to hand over territories to the USSR.

Poland suffered enormously at the hands of the occupying forces. German rule in Poland has been described as 'mass murder', with the systematic extermination both of Poland's large Jewish population and of any Poles thought capable of organising resistance to German rule. Between 1939 and 1944 the Germans killed one-fifth of the Polish population.

THE SECOND WORLD WAR IN EUROPE 8

8.2 German conquests in western Europe

While a full-scale war was raging in the east, very little was happening in the west. Britain and France were not equipped for an offensive war and Hitler had no desire to become involved at a time when he was fully occupied elsewhere. This was the period of the so-called *Phoney War* in the west. It did not last. In the spring of 1940 Hitler launched a massive attack on western Europe with the intention of bringing the whole area under German control. The main stages of this attack were: *the occupation of Norway and Denmark*, in order to secure Germany's northern flank; *the conquest of the Low Countries*; and *the invasion and rapid defeat of France*. The whole operation, using blitzkrieg tactics, took only three months. In every case the German armed forces had overwhelming superiority in numbers, equipment and tactics. British forces were sent to France, but only in small numbers. They were unable to halt the German advance, but successfully evacuated their troops from the beaches of Dunkirk.

The German occupation of France

On 14 June the Germans entered Paris. The French government had already left, moving southwards – first to Tours and then, as the German advance continued, to Bordeaux in the south-west. The French Prime Minister resigned, handing over to Marshal Pétain, an elderly First World War veteran. Pétain then signed an armistice with the Germans. By its terms the Germans were to occupy the whole of northern France and the Atlantic coast down to the Spanish frontier. In the rest of the country Pétain's right-wing government was to rule (based at the spa town of Vichy), under close German supervision.

German plans to defeat Britain

At the end of June 1940 Britain was the only enemy of the Germans that remained undefeated. Hitler's thoughts now concentrated on *Operation Sea Lion*, his plan for the invasion of England. As a first step towards this the Germans had to gain control of the air over the English Channel. The Luftwaffe (German airforce) launched successful attacks on British air bases, destroying many planes. They then changed their tactics, attacking cities and factories instead. This was probably a mistake and in the airborne *Battle of Britain* that followed the Luftwaffe suffered heavier losses than the RAF. Although the so-called *Blitz* on British cities continued throughout the winter of 1940–41, German air superiority had not been achieved. Operation Sea Lion was called off.

THE SECOND WORLD WAR IN EUROPE
8.3 The war in North Africa and the Balkans, 1940–41 8

Having failed to defeat Britain, Hitler decided that his next target would be the USSR. Expansion eastwards had always been his main concern. An attack on the USSR was therefore planned for the spring of 1941.

In the meantime Hitler had to send help to his ally Mussolini who had belatedly entered the war on Germany's side in June 1940. This help was needed:

(a) In *North Africa* where Italian forces based in Libya (an Italian colony) had attacked the British in Egypt, only to be driven back; and
(b) In *the Balkans* where Italy had launched an unsuccessful offensive against Greece, which was supported in its struggle by the British.

Hitler sent troops to both areas. In North Africa German troops, under Field-Marshal Rommel, succeeded in driving the British once again back into Egypt. In the Balkans Germany had to fight its way through Yugoslavia, which had refused to cooperate, in order to link up with the Italians. A quick victory against the Yugoslavs was soon followed by the collapse of Greece. British forces withdrew to the Greek island of Crete, which also fell shortly afterwards as a result of an airborne German invasion. Hitler had gained further spectacular victories. His diversion into the Balkans, however, had delayed his invasion of the USSR by a vital few weeks.

THE SECOND WORLD WAR IN EUROPE
8.4 Operation Barbarossa: the German attack on the USSR, 1941 8

The German attack on the USSR in June 1941 involved 4 million men along a front that stretched from the Baltic to the Black Sea. Using blitzkrieg tactics once again, the Germans advanced with amazing speed, capturing whole provinces in a matter of days. Vast numbers of Soviet troops were taken prisoner. Hitler, however, failed to capture either Moscow, the capital, or Leningrad, before winter set in.

The offensive was resumed in the spring of 1942, when the Germans once again swept all before them, moving this time in the direction of the Caspian Sea. The USSR, however, did not surrender and a large part of Germany's resources continued to be tied up in this theatre of the war.

THE SECOND WORLD WAR IN EUROPE 8
8.5 Europe under Nazi rule

The map on p. 78 shows you the extent of Germany's vast empire. Since the time of the Romans no single power had controlled so much of Europe. German authority was exercised in a number of ways:

(a) Direct German rule, e.g. in Poland and the USSR.
(b) Through local Fascist groups cooperating with the Germans, e.g. in Norway.
(c) Through governments that were nominally independent, but in fact had little choice about what they could do, e.g. Bulgaria and Romania.

The Nazis ruthlessly exploited this vast empire in their own interests. Hitler was only interested in his new possessions as sources of raw materials and labour that could be used to Germany's benefit. Millions were forced to work as slave labourers in Germany. Attempts at opposition were suppressed with great brutality. Conditions were worst in the German-occupied areas of eastern Europe, where millions were simply shot or allowed to die as a way of forcing these countries to submit to German control.

The Holocaust

Hitler's conquests gave him control over most of Europe's large Jewish population. He seized the opportunity to carry through what he termed the 'Final Solution to the Jewish problem', the systematic mass murder of Europe's Jews. 6 million Jews were killed during these years. Many were simply lined up and shot. Others were beaten and tortured to death. Some were buried or burnt alive. Large numbers died of starvation or exhaustion: on death-marches or in deportation trains. Most were taken to extermination camps and gassed. The 'Final Solution' was organised with ruthless efficiency – even the shoes of murdered children were carefully sorted and sent back in trainloads to Germany for use by German families. Hitler's obsession with the Final Solution was total. Even during the last stages of the war it was often given priority. All this is very difficult to explain. The following figures for numbers of Jews killed speak for themselves: Poland

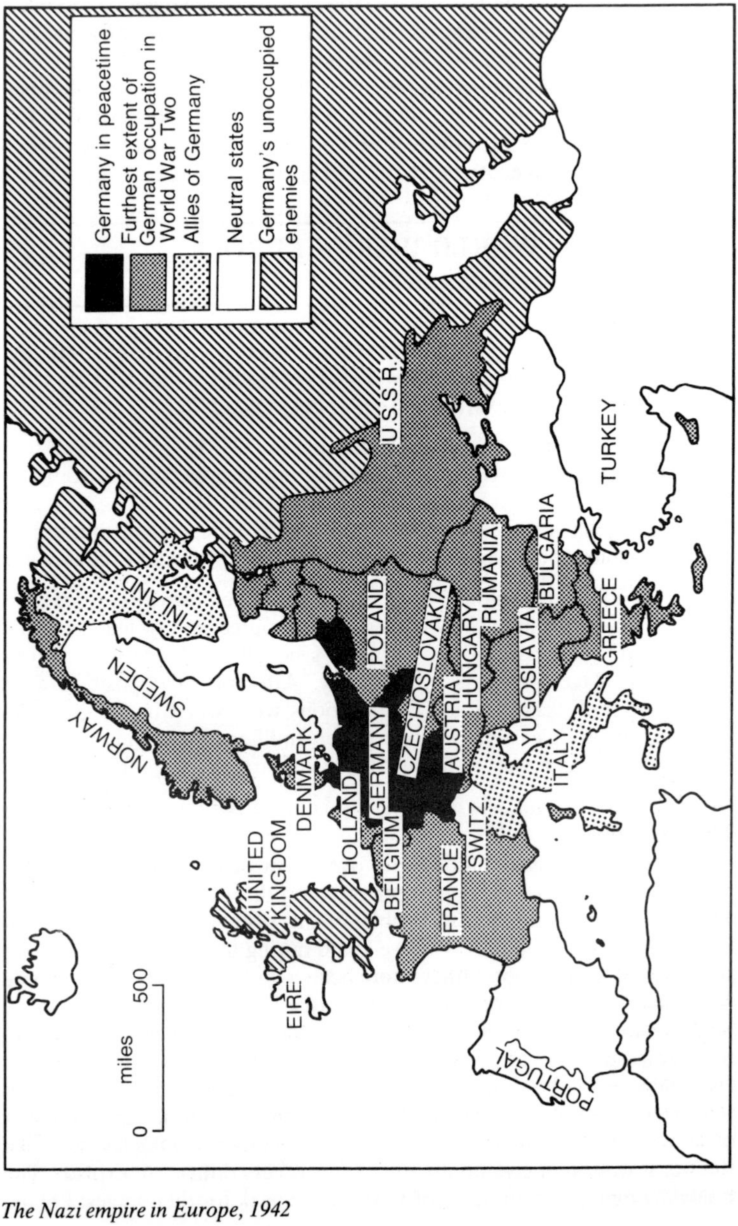

The Nazi empire in Europe, 1942

(2 600 000); USSR (750 000); Hungary (700 000); Romania (500 000); Germany (180 000); France (65 000) . . . the list could go on and on.

Many others also perished in the concentration and extermination camps. Other victims of the Nazis included large numbers of Poles and Russians, German and other opponents of Nazism, gypsies, and homosexuals.

THE SECOND WORLD WAR IN EUROPE 8

8.6 The Home Front in Britain

Britain's experience of the Second World War was very different in that its territory (with the exception of the Channel Islands) was never occupied by the Germans. The war, however, had a major impact on the lives of ordinary British people. Compare the effects mentioned below with the effects of the First World War described on pp. 28–29.

1 *The Blitz of 1940–41* (p. 76) led to civilian deaths (though far fewer than in other European countries) and to extensive damage to housing in many cities.

2 The prospect of German aerial attacks led to a massive programme of *evacuation*, mostly of children, from the cities. As well as the effects on the children themselves, evacuation brought home to many people the social problems of Britain's inner cities, by showing them for the first time what the lives of the very poor were really like.

3 Partly because of German submarine attacks on shipping coming to Britain, foodstuffs and other materials were in short supply. Many basic items were *rationed* throughout the war years.

4 War had a major impact on the lives of British *women*. Many took on jobs previously reserved for men. Others played an important part in the armed forces. Whether this created more equal opportunities for women in the long term is, however, less certain.

5 In order to fight a total war, the government was forced to exercise *control over the country's economy* in a way that it had never done in peacetime. The extent of this control was even greater than in the First World War. The policies of *nationalisation* adopted by the postwar Labour government (p. 196) were therefore a continuation of what had happened during the war.

6 The sacrifices of the war years made people determined that, once the war had ended, there should be no return to the poverty and unemployment of the 1920s and 1930s. From an early stage in the war, plans therefore were made for what was called postwar *reconstruction*. One of the most influential of these was the Beveridge Report of December 1942. This Report was one of the major influences on the *welfare state* that was established after 1945.

8.7 The decline and fall of Nazism

Until 1942 Hitler's forces seemed unbeatable. Only Britain, with its island position, and the USSR, with its vast size, population and resources, proved impossible to conquer. In 1942 the tide began to turn. There were three main reasons for this:

(a) The Germans had taken on far more territories than they could cope with.
(b) The USSR managed to recover from its losses, build up its stock of war materials and strike back against the German forces.
(c) In December 1941 the USA (p. 97) entered the war and in the following year began to make a major contribution to the war effort in Europe and North Africa.

Faced with two powers as strong as the USA and the USSR, Hitler's eventual defeat seemed more and more certain.

The following were crucial turning-points in the war:

The battle of Stalingrad (September 1942–January 1943): a long and bitter struggle between the Germans and the Russians, ending in the capture of an entire German army. After Stalingrad, German forces began to be pushed back westwards. By the spring of 1944 Soviet forces had recaptured most of the lands lost in 1941–42. From there they went on to *liberate* most of the countries of eastern Europe and the Balkans and in 1945 were poised to invade Germany itself.
The battle of El Alamein (October 1942): a major German defeat in North Africa at the hands of the British. German and Italian forces were driven westwards across Libya. In the following month British and US forces landed in the French colonies of Morocco and Algeria (see map on p. 81) and began to advance from the other side. By May 1943 the Germans and Italians had been driven out of the whole of North Africa. This then led to an Allied invasion of Sicily in July 1943 and to a slow Allied advance northwards up the Italian peninsula.
The D-Day landings (June 1944): the Anglo-American invasion of northern France, which marked the opening of a Second Front in western Europe. The invasion was superbly organised and took the Germans by surprise. Allied troops moved eastwards across France, entering Paris in August. The Germans put up strong resistance, for example in the Ardennes area of Belgium, but were pushed steadily back towards Germany itself. By March 1945 Allied forces had crossed the Rhine.

Germany's defeat and surrender

With Anglo-American forces advancing across Germany from the west and Soviet forces invading from the east, Hitler accepted Germany's defeat. After handing over power to one of his military leaders, he killed himself in

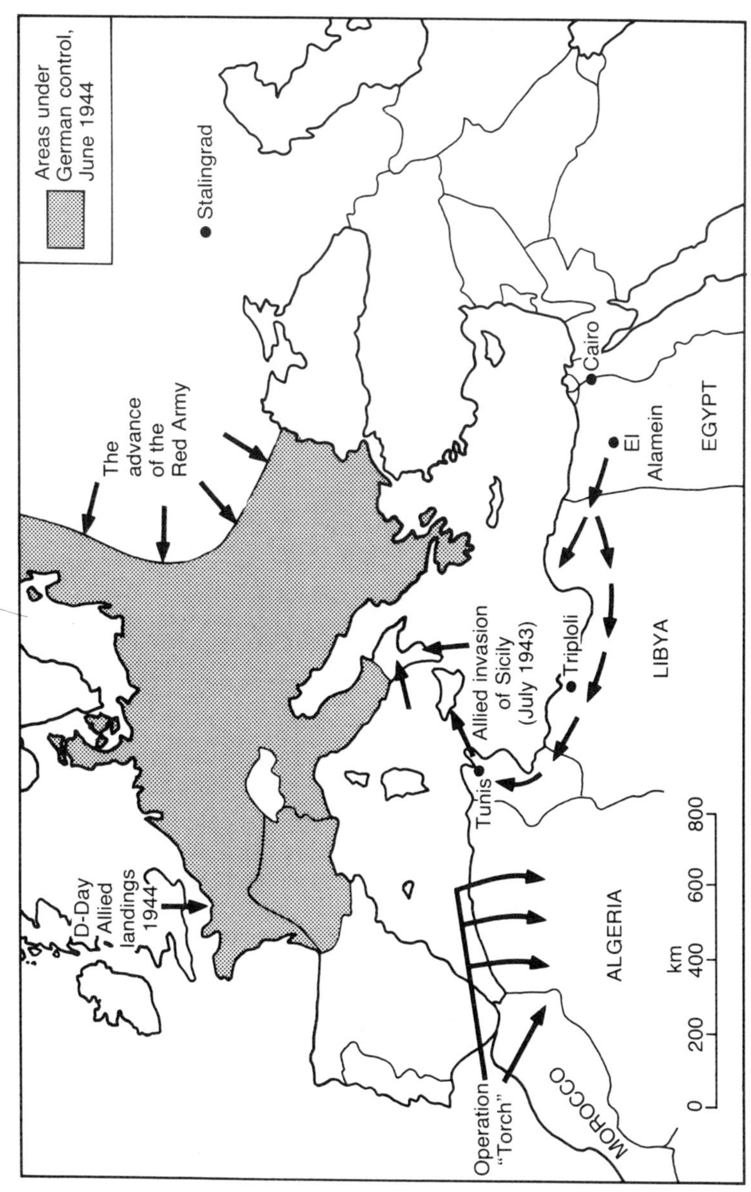

Decline and fall of Nazism, 1942–45

his underground headquarters in Berlin. A few weeks later the German authorities surrendered unconditionally.

In the Far East the war continued for a further few months. You can read about the war in the Far East in Chapter 10.

THE SECOND WORLD WAR IN EUROPE 8.8 Key historical terms — 8

Terms you need to understand for this topic include *total war* (p. 74), *blitzkrieg* (p. 74), and *Holocaust* (p. 77). Also important are:

Collaboration A term used to describe willing cooperation with German authorities during the Second World War. *Collaborators* were often severely punished after the end of the war.
Genocide The deliberate killing of a whole race of people. This is what the Nazis tried to do with their 'Final Solution'.
(The) Resistance Those who actively resisted German rule during the Second World War. Resistance movements played an important part in weakening German power in a number of occupied countries.

THE SECOND WORLD WAR IN EUROPE 8.9 Questions — 8

Evidence questions

Study the photograph on p. 83 and the extract below and then answer the questions that follow. The extract was written by a former member of the British Army Film Unit, set up during the Second World War.

> Audience reactions to *Desert Victory* were, generally, very good, especially amongst women who, apart from the many actually seeing their men-folk, were made more aware of the realities of warfare. But there were always the critics; those with enough technical knowledge to point out the fact that the night sequences could only have been filmed in a studio. Perfectly true – they were. This took place at Pinewood Studios whilst I and 35 other trainees were being put through our paces . . . But this artistic licence was necessary to create the full impact of Montgomery's enormous attack. What some people may not realise is that many later film sequences and stills pictures were studiously faked and passed off as the real thing. Naturally, this did not have the approval of a large number of other members . . . However, it was an order that was handed down by a higher authority . . .
>
> (Ian Grant, *Cameramen at War*, 1980)

(i) Describe in your own words what the extract tells you about the film *Desert Victory*. (3)

(ii) Do you think that this extract is likely to be a reliable source of information about the work of the British Army Film Unit? Explain your answer. (3)

(iii) Do you learn anything from the photograph about the battle of El Alamein? Give reasons for your answer. (3)

(iv) Do these sources suggest that the British Army was concerned to give the public a true impression of what was happening in the war? Explain your answer. (4)

BRITAIN DURING THE TWENTIETH CENTURY 9

Some GCSE modern world history syllabuses do not include the study of specific developments in British history. Even where it is included, only limited aspects are prescribed for study. The topics below are those listed in GCSE world history syllabuses. This chapter does not therefore attempt to cover all the major developments in the history of Britain during the twentieth century.

Sections 9.1, 9.2, 9.3 and 9.4 relate to the domestic policies of British governments during the years 1905–51. They are concerned with the economic and social policies of these governments and with the ways in which governments responded in different (and sometimes similar) ways to the country's social and economic problems. One of the main themes is the way in which governments took on more and more powers, providing more services for the British people and acquiring greater control over the British economy.

BRITAIN DURING THE TWENTIETH CENTURY

9.1 Liberal governments, 1905–15 9

Governments during the nineteenth century had taken many measures to tackle the social problems thrown up by the *Industrial Revolution* (p. 45). These included provision for better public health, restrictions on the employment of women and children, and free state education at elementary level. The general view of the role of government, however, was that it should only do what was absolutely essential. People, including the poor, were expected to provide for themselves. This *laissez-faire* ('leave things alone') view of the state's role was still dominant at the beginning of the twentieth century. One of the most important developments of the first half of the century was the way this view came to be challenged.

The first occasion on which it was challenged was during the Liberal governments of 1905–15. These governments were responsible for various measures that helped to lay the foundations of the modern *welfare state* (p. 9). There are a number of reasons why greater welfare provision should have been made at this time. These include:

(a) The publication at the end of the nineteenth century of reports which showed that extreme poverty was still a major problem, despite the general rise in the country's standard of living.
(b) A growing realisation that in a democracy (which Britain had only recently become) governments could not afford to ignore the interests of those who held a majority of the votes.

(c) The growth in support for the new *Labour Party*, which greatly increased its number of seats in the 1906 election. Some Liberals feared that the working classes would increasingly support the Labour Party unless the Liberals could also show themselves to be a party of reform.
(d) The example of other countries, such as Germany, which had already introduced major measures of welfare provision.

Liberal welfare reforms included the following:

1 The **Workmen's Compensation Act** (1906), increasing the liability of employers in cases of injury to their workers.
2 The **Old Age Pensions Act** (1908), introducing non-contributory old age pensions to people over 70 if their income each week was below a certain amount.
3 The establishment of **Labour Exchanges** (1909), to collect information about jobs that were available.
4 The **National Insurance Act** (1911). This was a major scheme under which (a) most of the working population was compulsorily insured against sickness and (b) workers in the building and engineering trades were insured against unemployment. The scheme was financed by contributions from the employer, the worker and the state.

In order to pay for some of these measures the Chancellor of the Exchequer, David Lloyd George, introduced a radical '*People's Budget*' in 1909. This increased income tax and death duties, imposed a new super-tax on the very rich, and introduced new taxes on the value of land. It was bitterly opposed and eventually rejected by the House of Lords, where the Conservatives had a huge majority. This had never happened before, as finance bills were normally passed automatically by the Lords after approval in the Commons. After a general election in which the Liberals were returned to power, the government introduced a Parliament Bill to curb the powers of the House of Lords. The Lords, however, rejected this as well and it was only after a further general election, together with threats to create large numbers of Liberal peers, that the Parliament Bill finally became law. The *Parliament Act* (1911) had three main clauses:

(a) The Lords lost its power to delay money bills.
(b) If a bill was passed by the Commons in three successive sessions, the Lords no longer had the power to *veto* it (in other words the House of Lords lost its power of *absolute veto*).
(c) The maximum length of a parliament was reduced from seven years to five.

The Liberals and the trade unions

The early twentieth century saw an increase in both the membership and power of trade unions. Like the growth of the Labour Party, this was a way in which the British working classes were beginning to demand improvements in their way of life. Trade unions were especially active during the years immediately before the outbreak of the First World War. This can partly be explained by the fact that real wages during this period (i.e. what people could buy with the money they earned) were either declining or failing to rise. In 1911, for example, there were big strikes among dockers, seamen and railway workers. These were followed in 1912 by a further dockers' strike and by a national strike of coal miners. Industrial unrest continued right up to the outbreak of war in 1914.

The Liberal government was anxious to win the support of trade unionists. Its two most important measures were the Trade Disputes Act of 1906 and the Trade Union Act of 1913. The *Trade Disputes Act* (1906) laid down that unions were not legally responsible for business losses incurred as a result of a strike. This reversed a court decision in the Taff Vale case of 1901. Unions were therefore free to strike without being sued for damages by employers.

It was a legal decision that also led to the *Trade Union Act of 1913*. This was the Osborne judgement of 1909 which ruled that unions could not require their members to make a contribution to the funds of a political party. This judgement threatened the existence of the Labour Party, many of whose MPs were funded by trade unions. The Trade Union Act of 1913 modified this judgement, permitting unions to raise money for political purposes but giving members the right to 'contract out' if they wished to do so.

BRITAIN DURING THE TWENTIETH CENTURY 9

9.2 The General Strike (1926)

You can read about the effects of the First World War on British society in Section 3.7. One effect had been to interrupt trade between Britain and some of its trading partners. Some of the overseas markets lost during the war were never recovered. Countries either developed industries of their own or began to trade elsewhere (e.g. with the USA). In the early 1920s this led to an *economic recession* (p. 196) and to the loss of large numbers of jobs. By the end of 1921 over 2 million people were unemployed.

Particularly badly affected was the coal industry. Faced with declining demand for British coal abroad, mineowners in 1925 proposed a reduction in miners' wages and an increase in the length of their working day. Predictably, this greatly angered the miners, many of whom were already strongly opposed to private ownership of the mines and had been agitating for them to be *nationalised*. The miners' union threatened to strike if the mineowners' conditions were imposed. This threat received the backing of other unions and of the Trades Union Congress (TUC).

Baldwin, the Prime Minister, tried to defuse the situation by appointing the *Samuel Commission* to investigate conditions in the coal industry. Despite recommending nationalisation in the long-term, the commission supported the mineowners' demand for an immediate reduction in wages. This the miners could not accept, insisting that there should be 'not a penny off the pay, not a minute on the day'. Encouraged by promises of support from other unions, the miners came out on strike at the end of April 1926. A few days later the TUC declared a *General Strike*, i.e. a stoppage of work by workers of all unions.

The strike, in which most working people took part, lasted for only nine days. It failed for the following reasons:

(a) The TUC lacked the financial resources to mount a lengthy strike.
(b) The TUC was worried by the government claim that a general strike was illegal.
(c) The government was successful in keeping many essential services running, thus reducing the strike's effectiveness.

The TUC therefore agreed to a compromise formula and called off the General Strike – to the immense anger of the miners who felt that they had been betrayed. The miners' strike continued until the end of the year, when desperation finally forced them back to work on the mineowners' terms.

The failure of the General Strike weakened the trade union movement. Trade union membership fell during the following years. Unions were also weakened by the government's *Trade Disputes Act of 1927* which (i) declared general strikes illegal and (ii) insisted that workers who wished part of their union subscription to go to the support of the Labour Party should 'contract in' rather than 'contract out'. This second clause was designed to weaken the Labour Party. It remained a major grievance until finally repealed by a Labour government in 1946.

BRITAIN DURING THE TWENTIETH CENTURY

9.3 Developments during the years 1929–39

9

The Labour government of 1929–31

The 1920s saw major changes in British politics. Perhaps the most important was the decline of the Liberals and the rise of the Labour Party. Labour's promise of radical social reforms attracted more and more support from working-class voters. The Liberals were also much weakened by divisions among their leaders.

Labour formed a government for the first time in 1924, under Ramsay MacDonald. This, however, was a minority government (i.e. Labour did not have a majority of seats in the House of Commons) and was only short-lived. In the general election of 1929 Labour did very much better, winning more seats than the Conservatives. Stanley Baldwin, Conservative Prime Minister since 1924, resigned and MacDonald became Prime Minister for the second time. This *second Labour government (1929–31)*, however, was also a minority government. Although Labour had more seats than the Conservatives, it could still be defeated by a combined vote of Conservatives and Liberals. This greatly restricted Labour's freedom of action. A number of measures of social reform were introduced, for example, a Coal Mines Act that reduced hours of work for coal miners. Many measures, however, failed to get through Parliament.

One reason for Labour's success in the general election of 1929 had been the high level of unemployment. Unemployment continued to rise throughout the period of the second Labour government. This was largely a result of the worldwide *economic recession* that followed the Wall Street Crash of 1929 (p. 112). By the end of 1930 two and a half million people were out of work. The government seemed helpless in the face of these growing economic problems.

The formation of the National Government, 1931

In 1931 the recession turned into a major financial crisis. Foreign investors, worried about the state of the British economy, began to withdraw money from the country. The Bank of England urged the government to accept a recent report by the *May Committee*, which had recommended heavy cuts in government expenditure, especially expenditure on the dole (money paid to the unemployed). By reducing expenditure and balancing the budget, the Bank hoped to restore foreign confidence in Britain's financial stability. Labour ministers were so divided about what should be done that in the end they resigned. Most were not prepared to accept heavy cuts in the dole. Ramsay MacDonald, however, agreed to remain in office as head of a new *National Government* consisting of representatives of the three major parties. This government proceeded to make the cuts in expenditure that had been recommended. MacDonald's action appalled most members of the Labour Party. He was accused of 'betrayal' and expelled from the party.

The National Government and economic recovery

Britain was ruled by National Governments throughout the 1930s, headed first by MacDonald (1931–35) and then by the Conservatives Baldwin (1935–37) and Neville Chamberlain (1937–40). The major problem facing these governments was unemployment. This remained high throughout the

1930s. The numbers out of work did, however, go down – from nearly 3 million in 1931 to 1 million in 1939. Government policies contributed to this economic recovery in a number of ways:

(a) *Higher tariffs were imposed on imported goods.* This helped to protect British industry from foreign competition.
(b) *Interest rates were kept low.* This helped people to borrow cheaply in order to expand their businesses. The effects of this were particularly noticeable in the building industry, which experienced a boom during the 1930s with many new houses being built.
(c) Although its activities cannot compare with Roosevelt's New Deal in the USA, *the National Government became more involved in the running of the economy* – as a way of trying to stimulate economic growth. Government measures included subsidies to shipbuilding and agriculture, the creation of marketing boards for various agricultural products, as well as closer government control of coal mining and air transport.

Government policies, however, were only one factor in promoting economic recovery. Many of the economic developments of the 1930s (e.g. the growth of the car industry) happened independently of government initiative. Economic recovery was also largely confined to the south-east of England and to the English Midlands. While new industries thrived (e.g. the car industry and light industries based on electric power), Britain's traditional industries declined. Areas such as central Scotland, South Wales, and the north of England that were heavily dependent on these industries (i.e. shipbuilding, coal, iron and steel, and cotton textiles) had a very different experience of the 1930s. For people in these areas the Thirties was the decade of high unemployment, hunger marches and the means test (the latter a test imposed by the government which meant that unemployed men lost part of their benefit if other members of their family were at work).

The Abdication crisis, 1936

A minor episode in the 1930s, but one which attracted a lot of attention at the time, was the Abdication crisis of 1936. This was brought about by the prospect of a marriage between King Edward VIII, who had come to the throne early in 1936 on the death of his father George V, and an American divorcee. Baldwin, the Prime Minister, strongly opposed the marriage. It was felt that most people in the country probably shared his opinion. Edward VIII was therefore persuaded to resign in favour of his younger brother, who succeeded as George VI. The consequences of this change of monarch were of little significance. In a *constitutional monarchy* (p. 195) like Britain's the monarch was a figurehead with little or no political power.

9.4 The Labour governments of 1945–51

You can read in Section 8.6 about the effects of the Second World War on Britain. One of these effects was to bring to power in 1945 a Labour government committed to a major programme of social reform. This was the first occasion on which Labour had an overall majority in the House of Commons. The changes brought about by Labour during the following few years were of two main kinds: a major increase in welfare provision and an increased role for the state in the running of the economy. These changes represented an important stage in the growth of state power in twentieth-century Britain. They took further – and in some cases very much further – the measures, described above, that had been introduced by the Liberal governments before the First World War and by the National Governments of the 1930s.

The Welfare State

Labour built upon the foundations of the welfare state laid by the Liberals before 1914. Memories of the suffering and hardship of the 1920s and 1930s made the government determined to protect people against the worst effects of poverty, sickness, old age and unemployment. These were the main features of the 'welfare state' as it was established at that time:

(a) *Family Allowances*, introduced in 1946.
(b) The *National Insurance Act* of 1946 which required everyone to take part in a contributory insurance scheme which entitled people to sickness, unemployment and maternity benefits, as well as retirement and widows' pensions.
(c) *National Assistance* payments to those not covered by the national insurance scheme.
(d) The *National Health Service* (1946) which provided everyone with free health care.

Nationalised industries

During the Second World War the government had controlled most aspects of the country's economy. The Labour Party, with its *socialist* beliefs (p. 197), was keen to continue this control after the end of the war. A major programme of *nationalisation* (p. 196) was therefore introduced. Industries nationalised during these years included coal, electricity, gas, public transport, civil aviation and iron and steel. Britain became a *mixed economy* (i.e. with large areas of economic life under both state and private control).

Despite opposition at the time, most of these postwar Labour reforms were retained by Conservative governments during the 1950s, 1960s and 1970s. These were the years of *consensus politics* in which both parties shared similar fundamental views about social and economic policy.

BRITAIN DURING THE TWENTIETH CENTURY
9.5 Britain's changing world role since 1945 — 9

Most aspects of this GCSE topic are described elsewhere in this book. The main themes of the topic are: (i) the loss of Britain's overseas colonies, discussed in Chapters 14, 15 and 16; (ii) Britain's alliance with the USA, discussed in Chapter 13; and (iii) Britain's relationship with Europe, leading up to Britain's entry into the European Community in 1973 (Chapter 18). You should also study the part played by Britain in the Suez crisis of 1956 (Chapter 17). The main emphasis in this topic is the way in which the British government accepted the loss of its empire and came to realise that its future lay in close economic cooperation with western Europe rather than in any attempt to try and save something of the empire through the Commonwealth.

BRITAIN DURING THE TWENTIETH CENTURY
9.6 Key historical terms — 9

Welfare state A state in which the government makes provision for all major aspects of the welfare of its people. These usually include insurance against sickness, unemployment and old age; assistance to those who are unable to provide for themselves; free education; free health care. The creation of a welfare state was a demand of the Labour Party from its foundation onwards. Once established after 1945 it was also accepted as a permanent feature of British life by the Conservatives. This persisted until the 1980s when some sections of the Conservative Party began to challenge some aspects of the welfare state. Similar welfare provision has also been made in some other western democratic states. There has sometimes been considerable controversy about the extent to which welfare provision should be made, for example, in the USA at the time of the New Deal (p. 113–15).

Other key historical terms for this topic include *constitutional monarchy* (p. 195), *economic recession* (p. 196), *industrial revolution* (p. 45), *laissez-faire* (p. 196), *mixed economy* (p. 90), *nationalisation* (p. 196), *socialism* (p. 197), and *veto* (p. 197).

BRITAIN DURING THE TWENTIETH CENTURY
9.7 Questions

9

Essay questions

(i) During the twentieth century British governments have come to play a more and more important role, both in the country's economic life and as the provider of welfare services.

(a) Show how this happened during *one* of the following periods: 1905–14; the 1930s; 1945–51.

(b) Give reasons why this happened, referring in particular to the period you have chosen. (20)

(ii) Which was more important to British governments during the 1960s and early 1970s – the British Commonwealth or membership of the European Community? Explain your answer. (20)

THE RISE OF JAPAN AND THE SECOND WORLD WAR IN THE FAR EAST 10

10.1 Japan in the early twentieth century

In the late nineteenth and early twentieth centuries Japan experienced many changes, both in the kind of country it was and in its relations with the outside world. In order to understand why this relatively small country has played such an important part in the history of Asia and the Pacific during the twentieth century, it is essential to know something about these changes. These are some of the main developments taking place in Japan at that time:

1 *Rapid economic change.* As a result of growing contacts with economically more advanced countries in Europe and North America, Japan's economy was booming. New industries, such as shipbuilding, were developing. Agriculture was being modernised. The population was growing fast. These developments were speeded up by the First World War, which gave Japan the opportunity to supply goods that Europe was no longer able to produce.

2 The development of a modern economy similar to that of western countries led also to a great deal of westernisation in the way of life of the Japanese people. *Westernisation* means the adoption of customs similar to those in western countries, for example, western dress or western methods of education.

3 Part of westernisation was a change in the way in which Japan was governed, i.e. the introduction of a *Diet* or parliament. In practice, however, the Diet's powers were very limited. Japan continued to be ruled by officials and by members of the old upper class, acting in the name of the Emperor. The Emperor played only a limited part in the country's government, but was still regarded as divine (godlike) and therefore worshipped by his people.

4 Many Japanese felt that westernisation was necessary to enable Japan to compete with the rich and powerful countries of Europe and North America. Others wished to preserve the distinctive Japanese way of life and were fiercely hostile to foreign influences. This intense *nationalism* was particularly strong in the Japanese army.

5 As a more 'developed' country than its neighbours, *Japan's influence in the Far East* had been growing for some time. The Japanese government was keen to take advantage of the weakness of neighbouring China. During the First World War China was forced to accept Japanese advisers and to grant special rights to the Japanese in the northern province of Manchuria (see map on p. 94).

THE RISE OF JAPAN AND THE SECOND WORLD WAR IN THE FAR EAST 10

10.2 Why Japan became an expansionist power in the 1930s

'Expansionist' means extending power, usually by taking over other countries or provinces. This is what Japan began to do in the 1930s. It continued to act in this way in the early 1940s, thus causing the outbreak of the Second World War in the Far East. Why did this happen?

(i) As Japan's population and industries grew, the country became more and more dependent on imports of raw materials and of foodstuffs. Building an empire might give them access to supplies of both food and raw materials.

(ii) Like Germany, Japan suffered from the effects of the *Great Depression* that followed the Wall Street Crash of 1929 (p. 112). The demand for Japanese silk and cotton textiles fell. As a result Japan was short of money with which to buy imported food. Foreign conquests might help to make the country *self-sufficient.*

(iii) During the 1920s many Japanese felt increasingly resentful towards other countries. Some of the reasons for this were:

- (a) Resentment that the *Covenant of the League of Nations did not include the declaration of racial equality requested by the Japanese.* Many Japanese felt that Europeans and Americans looked down on them as inferior.
- (b) Resentment at the *Washington Naval Agreement of 1922* (p. 67), which limited the size of Japan's navy by comparison with that of Britain and the USA.
- (c) Resentment at new *immigration restrictions in the USA*, which discriminated against Japanese immigrants.
- (d) Resentment at the way other countries increased their import duties on Japanese goods at the time of the Great Depression.

(iv) There was much pressure on the government from nationalist groups within Japan. Some of these groups, or 'patriotic societies' as they were called, had close links with the army.

THE RISE OF JAPAN AND THE SECOND WORLD WAR IN THE FAR EAST 10

10.3 Japanese expansion during the 1930s

Manchuria, 1931

Japan had been closely involved in the Chinese province of Manchuria for many years. It had its own base at Port Arthur, together with extensive economic interests and an army (the Kwantung Army) permanently stationed there to protect its rights. In 1931 it seized the whole province and placed it under the control of a Chinese puppet ruler. The initiative for this action came from the Kwantung Army. The government in Tokyo was powerless to control the situation and had to accept what had happened. China appealed to the League of Nations, which eventually condemned Japan but failed to take *sanctions* (p. 172).

Britain and the USA, both of which had strong economic links with China, disapproved of Japan's actions. Ties with these countries were therefore weakened. Later in the 1930s Japan drew closer to Germany and Italy, for example in the *Anti-Comintern Pact* of 1937 directed against the USSR. Japan, Italy and Germany were similar in that they wished to upset the existing state of affairs.

During the 1930s Japan's economy recovered from the effects of the Great Depression. This helped to make the government more confident of its strength. The population also continued to grow, increasing the pressure for more 'living space' on the Asian mainland.

The Japanese attack on China, 1937

Relations with China deteriorated into full-scale war in 1937. Again the initiative came from the Japanese army on the mainland, using as an excuse a minor clash between Japanese and Chinese forces on the *Marco Polo Bridge* near Peking. By the end of the year vast areas of China were under Japanese control, including Peking, Shanghai and the Chinese capital, Nanking. The Chinese government, however, refused to come to terms with the Japanese. Fighting between the two countries continued throughout the years 1937–45.

Although the Japanese government talked of creating a 'New Order in East Asia' (later known as *The Greater East Asia Co-Prosperity Sphere*), from which all would benefit, in practice it ruthlessly exploited its new empire in its own interests.

THE RISE OF JAPAN AND THE SECOND WORLD WAR IN THE FAR EAST
10.4 War with the USA: Pearl Harbor, 1941 **10**

In a sense the Second World War in the Far East had already begun, i.e. with Japan's attack on China in 1937. The war that broke out with the USA in 1941 was really a continuation of that war. The outbreak of war in Europe in 1939 had opened up new prospects for Japan. The defeat of the Netherlands and France in 1940 left the Dutch East Indies and French Indo-China wide open to attack (see map on p. 96). Britain likewise would

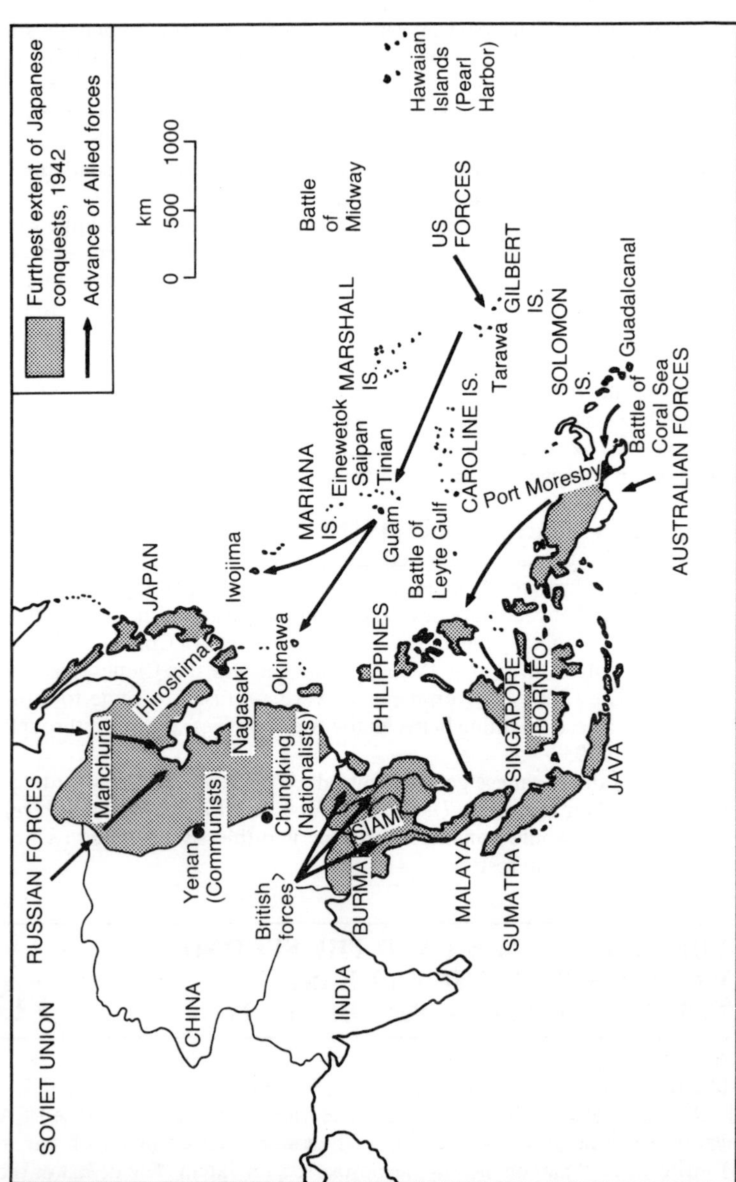

The Japanese empire in 1942

find it harder to hold on to its colonies in Malaya and Burma. All these territories contained raw materials that would be very useful to Japan. The only obstacles to further Japanese expansion were the USA and the USSR. Operation Barbarossa (pp. 76–77) removed any threat from the USSR. That left the USA, with its large navy, its Pacific bases (e.g. the Philippines) and its close connections with the Chinese. If Japan were to dominate the whole of eastern Asia, it would have to challenge the power of the USA.

War with the USA came as a result of a surprise Japanese attack on the US base at *Pearl Harbor* in *Hawaii* in December 1941. This attack badly damaged, but did not destroy, the US Pacific fleet. At the same time Japanese forces landed on the coast of British Malaya. Within six months Japan was in control of all the areas shown on the map opposite: Malaya, parts of Burma, Hong Kong, parts of Thailand, Indo-China, the Philippines, the Dutch East Indies, and most of New Guinea. Japanese tactics, for example the use of *blitzkrieg* (p. 74), were similar in many ways to those used by Hitler in Europe.

THE RISE OF JAPAN AND THE SECOND WORLD WAR IN THE FAR EAST

10

10.5 Reasons for Japan's defeat

The vast Japanese empire that you can see opposite did not last. Slowly but steadily, US forces recovered control of one Japanese conquest after another, meeting fierce Japanese resistance all the way. You can see the various stages of this war on the map.

These are some of the reasons for Japan's eventual defeat:

(i) The attack on Pearl Harbor did not succeed in destroying the US Pacific fleet.

(ii) By attacking the USA, Japan was committing itself to a war with a power that had far greater resources than itself.

(iii) Like the Germans (Chapter 8), the Japanese over-stretched themselves. Once their enemies began to counter-attack, Japan found it difficult to defend and control such a vast area.

(iv) Asian peoples soon turned against the Japanese, realising that they were going to gain little from Japanese rule. Armed resistance in some territories weakened Japanese control.

(v) The US tactic of *island-hopping*, i.e. concentrating on regaining control of key bases, for example those with airfields, proved very effective.

(vi) The USA eventually gained control of the air. This allowed them to inflict extensive damage on Japan itself.

(vii) Despite all the points mentioned above, the Japanese still seemed determined to resist until the very end. The Japanese government only surrendered when the USA dropped *atomic bombs* on the Japanese cities of *Hiroshima* and *Nagasaki* in August 1945. The appalling devastation caused by these bombs finally convinced them that they could not fight on.

THE RISE OF JAPAN AND THE SECOND WORLD WAR IN THE FAR EAST 10

10.6 Key historical terms

Key terms that you can read about elsewhere in this book are *Great Depression* (p. 112), *nationalism* (p. 56), and *sanctions* (p. 172).

Two other terms are very important for an understanding of the developments mentioned in this chapter. These are:

Self-sufficiency A country is *self-sufficient* when it is able to provide for itself out of its own resources, e.g. does not have to depend on imports for essential raw materials and foodstuffs. Some twentieth-century governments have tried to make their countries self-sufficient as a way of making them stronger and more independent. Some have felt that self-sufficiency was particularly important in the event of war. Fascist Italy, Nazi Germany and Japan all adopted a policy of self-sufficiency. In the case of Japan this seemed particularly important as the country was completely dependent on imports for many essential commodities such as iron and oil.

Westernisation The way in which a country becomes more like 'the West', i.e. more like the economically developed countries of Europe and North America. *Westernisation* might involve:

(a) A more western-type of economy (one more geared to trading and profit).
(b) Western styles of dress and behaviour.
(c) A western-type political system (e.g. with an elected parliament).

As the countries of Europe and North America developed closer links in the nineteenth century with the non-western world, so westernisation became more common. It has continued throughout the twentieth century. As in Japan, it has often met with resistance from those who wanted to preserve their own ways of life. The rise in *Islamic fundamentalism* in the Arab world (p. 168) was also a reaction against western influences.

THE RISE OF JAPAN AND THE SECOND WORLD WAR IN THE FAR EAST

10

10.7 Questions

Essay questions

(i) (a) Explain why Japan created an empire in eastern Asia during the 1930s and early 1940s. In the course of your answer refer to the following:

Japan's desire for self-sufficiency
worsening relations with the USA
the patriotic societies
the role of the Japanese army
the impact of the outbreak of war in Europe

(b) Describe the various stages by which this empire was created during the 1930s and early 1940s. (20)

(ii) In August 1945 the USA dropped atomic bombs on the Japanese cities of Hiroshima and Nagasaki.

(a) Describe the effects of these bombs on those cities and their inhabitants.

(b) What arguments have been used both for and against the dropping of these bombs? (20)

Source-based questions

Study the map on p. 96 and then answer the questions below:

(i) Which country ruled the Philippines at the beginning of 1941? (1)
(ii) Which country ruled the Philippines at the beginning of 1942? (1)
(iii) Why were Japanese forces able to capture Singapore in February 1942? (2)
(iv) What happened to halt the Japanese advance in Burma? (2)
(v) Why did the USSR not declare war on Japan until August 1945? (2)
(vi) Why were the Japanese unable to bring an end to the war in China? (3)
(vii) Why did the USA decide to drop atomic bombs on Japan in August 1945? (4)

CHINA IN THE TWENTIETH CENTURY 11
11.1 China in the early twentieth century

In studying twentieth-century world history China is a country that it is impossible to ignore. China is one of the largest countries in the world. Its population is far larger than that of the whole of Europe, more people speaking Mandarin, the main form of Chinese, than any other language in the world. It has also experienced fundamental changes in the course of the twentieth century. Some of these changes have had a major impact on the outside world.

At the beginning of the twentieth century China was ruled by the Manchus, a *dynasty* (line of rulers) that had been in power since the seventeenth century. It was an *autocratic* (p. 195) government, run by a large civil service in the interests of the Emperor and of the landlords who owned most of the country's land. Most Chinese were peasants living under the close authority of their local landlord. Many were extremely poor.

Like Japan (p. 93), China during the nineteenth century had been influenced in many ways by the West. As in Japan, western influences had been both welcomed and resented by different groups of Chinese. Unlike Japan, however, the Chinese government had been unable to stand up to the western powers and compete with them on their own terms. China's economy and armed forces, for example, had not been *modernised* in the way that Japan's had been. As a result China had been forced over the years to make many concessions to European powers, such as giving them special trading rights and allowing them to take over the collection of Chinese customs duties.

Sun Yat-sen and the overthrow of the Manchus

There was growing resentment in China at the way the country was governed. Some educated Chinese felt that the monarchy was incapable of giving China the leadership that it needed. The best-known critic of the regime at the beginning of the century was Sun Yat-sen, a Chinese doctor. Sun was influenced by western ideas, but wished to use them to make China a great power once again. His reform programme was based on what he called the *three People's Principles* of *Nationalism* (freeing China from control by foreign powers), *Democracy* (getting rid of the monarchy), and *Socialism* (social reforms, such as land redistribution, rather than *socialism* as defined on p. 197).

Sun won considerable support, especially in southern China. There were a number of attempted uprisings, culminating in a revolt in the autumn of 1911. The Emperor abdicated and China became a *republic*, with an elected parliament and with Sun Yat-sen as its first President. For Sun's supporters, however, the *1911 revolution* proved a great disappointment. The parliament had little authority. Power soon passed to *Yuan Shih-Kai*, a former

Manchu military commander. Yuan Shih-Kai's rule was very conservative and autocratic. In practice little had changed.

Yuan Shih-Kai's death in 1916 led to a period of confusion and civil war. China broke up into hundreds of small regions, each ruled by a local *warlord*. These warlords often fought among themselves. All this disorder enabled Japan, during the First World War, to make the gains at China's expense that you can read about on p. 93. The main group opposed to the rule of the warlords were the supporters of Sun Yat-sen, who had formed themselves into the *Nationalist* or *Kuomintang* (KMT) *Party*. As an anti-western organisation, these Nationalists received support from the new Bolshevik government in the USSR. Also hostile to the warlords was the *Chinese Communist Party* (CCP), whose ideas were based on those of Marx and Engels (pp. 45–46). Formed in 1921, the CCP was much smaller than the KMT. At first the Kuomintang and the Communists cooperated against the common enemy.

CHINA IN THE TWENTIETH CENTURY
11.2 Civil war between the Kuomintang and the Communists

11

Sun Yat-sen died in 1925. Power within the Kuomintang now passed to *Chiang Kai-shek*, one of the Nationalist military leaders. Chiang Kai-shek conducted a successful campaign in 1926 against the warlords in northern China. These victories encouraged him to turn against his former allies the Communists. Chiang was very hostile to communism. He also had close links with wealthy banking and commercial circles, his wife being a member of one of China's wealthiest banking families. People such as these stood to lose a great deal if communism took hold. In *1927* Chiang and his supporters carried out a ruthless *purge of Communists* in many cities. Large numbers were killed. The rest fled to the interior, finding refuge in the mountains of Hunan and Kiangsi. In 1928 a second campaign against the warlords completed Chiang's success. A new national government was formed at Nanking, with Chiang at its head.

The Nationalists were now in control of most of China. This enabled them to deal more effectively with foreign powers, Chiang succeeding in persuading western powers to give up some of the rights they had acquired in the past. Chiang was therefore applying the first of Sun's three principles, Nationalism. The other two, however, were largely ignored. There was little Democracy in Nationalist China, Chiang ruling in the same *autocratic* way as previous leaders. There was also little Socialism or concern for social reform.

Events of the civil war

The 1927 purge had failed to destroy the Communist Party altogether. In their remote hideout the Communists, under the leadership of Mao Zedong (Mao tse-tung), rebuilt their strength, creating an independent *soviet*-style government. Chiang could not afford to ignore this threat to his authority. In a series of campaigns he attempted to encircle (surround) the Communist forces. These campaigns tied down troops at a time when China was also fighting the Japanese in Manchuria (pp. 94–95).

The encirclement campaigns, as they are called, did not succeed in eliminating the Communists. Mao Zedong, however, decided that it would be safer to try and break out. In 1934 his forces began the *Long March*. This was an amazing feat of endurance, in which only one-third of the retreating Communists survived. Being attacked at every point, and suffering from hunger, cold and disease, the Communists withdrew to the province of Shensi. Here they were safe from further attempts at encirclement. From this base Communist forces carried out increasing numbers of *guerrilla* attacks on the Nationalists and, after 1937, on the Japanese who by this time had launched a full-scale invasion of China (p. 95).

Although Nationalists and Communists sometimes cooperated against the Japanese, the struggle for power within Chinese territory continued. By the end of the war in 1945 the Communists were in a much stronger position than ever before, with a million troops and control over large parts of the country. The civil war resumed with much greater intensity after 1945, continuing until 1949. The Nationalists won some victories at first, but slowly the Communists wore down their resistance. Peking fell and on *1 October 1949* Mao Zedong proclaimed the establishment of the *People's Republic of China*. By the end of that year the whole of mainland China was in Communist hands. Chiang and the Nationalists withdrew to the offshore island of Taiwan where a Nationalist Chinese government has survived until the present day.

Reasons for the Communist victory in the civil war

1 *Guerrilla warfare.* The guerrilla tactics used by the Communists proved very effective. These involved (a) frequent surprise attacks on enemy forces, followed by withdrawal in the event of counter-attacks, (b) avoiding open battles, in order to prevent major losses, and (c) an attempt to win over the local population so that Communist forces could merge back into the community and be fed and supported. Guerillas proved difficult to find or to eliminate. Their attacks slowly weakened the morale and wore down the resistance of the enemy.

2 The Communists succeeded in winning the *support of the peasants* in many of the areas that they controlled. This was partly through careful treatment, for instance rules about not looting, partly through measures of

land reform, and partly (in some cases) through the use of intimidation. Without peasant support guerrilla warfare would have been much less likely to succeed.

3 *The Communists often proved more effective opponents of the Japanese than the Nationalists*. This won them much popular support. At the end of the Second World War the Communists were in a good position to take over from the Japanese in many parts of the country. This gave them the advantage of large quantities of *captured Japanese weapons*.

4 Nationalist troops, especially after 1945, suffered from low morale. Many surrendered to the Communists. This was partly due to the more general unpopularity of the Nationalists. Reasons for this included (a) widespread *corruption* among senior officials, (b) a high rate of *inflation* after 1945, (c) the *brutality* of the KMT secret police, and (d) Chiang's failure to win over the *peasants* by agreeing to land reform.

CHINA IN THE TWENTIETH CENTURY
11.3 Mao Zedong and the creation of a Communist society, 1949–76

11

Chinese communism, like Russian communism, was based on the ideas of Marx, Engels and Lenin. Communism, however, had come to China in a way that none of these thinkers could have envisaged, i.e. with the support of peasants rather than town workers. Marxism therefore had to be adapted in order to fit the rather different conditions of China. In other ways Mao's aims were similar to those of the Bolsheviks in the USSR, which were to create a society without private property or differences in wealth. These are some of the measures that attempted to achieve these aims:

1 **Agrarian Reform Law, 1950** The confiscation and redistribution to peasants of all landlords' land. Peasants were encouraged to denounce landlords. Hundreds of thousands of landlords were put to death.

2 **Collective farms** The 1950 law was only the first step to *collectivisation* (p. 42). More and more collective farms were set up after 1953. These were not always popular with peasants, some of whom now felt that they were losing the land that they had so recently gained.

3 **The First Five-Year Plan, 1953–57** As a Marxist, Mao was keen to *modernise* (p. 196) and therefore to *industrialise* (p. 45) China. He was also keen to make China once again a great power, something that would only be possible if China were economically more developed. The First Five-Year Plan concentrated on heavy industry and power supplies. Most targets were met.

4 A Hundred Flowers, 1956 Mao was concerned that the Communist Party was turning into a group of officials who had lost touch with ordinary people. To safeguard against this he encouraged people to say what they felt about the government. However, this 'let a hundred flowers blossom' campaign led to many criticisms that Mao did not like, e.g. criticisms of the very idea of communism. The campaign was quickly brought to an end.

5 The Great Leap Forward, 1958 This was launched at the beginning of the Second Five Year Plan. It had two main features: (a) further rapid development of heavy industry, but with as many people being involved in this as possible, e.g. through the building of 'backyard' steel furnaces; and (b) the creation of *communes*. These were set up in both towns and rural areas. Each commune would control both the economic life and the government of its area. They were quite large units. In the countryside each might consist of a number of collective farms. They did *not* involve communal living, except sometimes for the unmarried.

In practice the Great Leap Forward was a disappointment. Industry certainly developed, but more modestly than had been hoped. Communes proved a failure and emphasis on them was subsequently reduced.

6 The Cultural Revolution, mid-1960s This was a development that for a few years transformed the everyday lives of millions of Chinese people. The reasons why Mao launched this cultural revolution were as follows:

(i) *to strengthen his position within the Communist Party*. There had been criticisms of Mao because of the problems associated with the Great Leap Forward and because of the split with the USSR which took place at that time (pp. 105–06). The cultural revolution created a powerful new force known as the *Red Guards* whom Mao could use to weaken the power of party officials and to dispose of his enemies.

(ii) *to stop the revolution going stale*. Mao believed that some of the idealism of the early years of the Revolution was beginning to fade. A major aim of the cultural revolution was to whip up enthusiasm, especially among the young. Associated with this was an attack on everything that was thought to be hostile to communism (e.g. western influences, ancient traditions, religious practices, etc).

During the cultural revolution Red Guards – mostly students from schools and universities – demonstrated, chanted slogans, broke into offices and denounced numerous enemies of the state. They were intensely loyal to Mao, who was treated as if he were a god.

The cultural revolution succeeded in removing Mao's enemies. It caused great damage, however, to the Chinese economy as well as to the educational system. Eventually even Mao felt it had gone too far. The army was called in to take over from the Red Guards. By the end of the 1960s the cultural revolution was over.

CHINA IN THE TWENTIETH CENTURY
11.4 China since the death of Mao **11**

Mao died in 1976. For some years after his death there was still no one prepared publicly to criticise his views. There were many, however, who had disliked the oppressive dictatorship and *personality cult* (p. 196) of his later years. At first the criticisms were directed against the so-called 'Gang of Four' who had supposedly ruled badly in Mao's name. Mao's widow, Chiang Ching, was subjected to particularly hostile attacks and was eventually arrested, tried and imprisoned.

The new leader who eventually emerged was *Deng Xiao-ping*. He was very much a *pragmatist*, someone prepared to modify his ideals (i.e. communism) if he felt it would be helpful to do so. Deng believed in allowing more freedom, for example to wear western clothes, take part in religious worship, and produce goods for personal profit. He was also keen to improve relations with the West, something that had already begun during the last years of Mao's rule (see below). Greater freedom caused problems, however, as it had done in Mao's hundred flowers campaign in the 1950s (p. 104). There were signs in the late 1980s that Deng feared he might have gone too far.

CHINA IN THE TWENTIETH CENTURY
11.5 China's foreign policies, 1949 to the present day **11**

China's isolation after 1949

At first, apart from its relationship with the USSR, the Chinese Communist government felt itself to be very isolated in a hostile world. Many powers refused to recognise the Communists as the rulers of China, supporting the Nationalists in Taiwan instead. During the 1950s and 1960s China's place on the Security Council of the United Nations was taken by the Nationalists. The Korean War (1950–53), which you can read about on pp. 125–26, increased this fear of being surrounded by hostile powers.

China and the USSR

The USSR gave substantial aid to China after 1949. Thousands of Soviet technicians played an important part during the 1950s in the development of China's economy. Relations, however, were never smooth and deteriorated further in the late 1950s. Reasons for this included:

(a) *Differences in their interpretation of Marxism*, the Chinese placing more emphasis on the role of the peasants.
(b) *Mao's dislike of the way Stalin's successor Khrushchev denounced Stalin in 1956*, fearing that this admission of error would damage the communist cause.

(c) Mao's attack on the USSR for being *revisionist*, i.e. revising Marx's ideas by suggesting that change could come about by peaceful means rather than by revolution and war.
(d) *Disputes over border areas* between the two countries, e.g. in the area of the Ussuri River, where armed clashes occurred later in 1969.

Public criticisms led in 1960 to the withdrawal of all Russian technicians in China. Relations deteriorated further during the 1960s and at the time of the border clashes in the late 1960s there was even talk of a possible nuclear attack by the USSR on China. Communist parties all over the world were forced to make the choice of following either China or the USSR. This was an important development in that for the first time there were different centres of communism each with its own view of what communism was all about.

Relations with the USA

During the 1950s and 1960s China's relations with the USA were extremely poor. To China the USA was the arch-enemy. This was because the USA:

(a) supported the Nationalists in Taiwan;
(b) opposed Communist China's admission to the UN;
(c) continually interfered in Asian affairs (e.g. in the Korean war of 1950–53, through the anti-communist defence league SEATO, the South East Asia Treaty Organisation, formed in 1954, and in the Vietnam war of the 1960s and 1970s).

In the early 1970s a surprise *rapprochement* (improvement in relations) took place in Chinese–US relations. The reasons for this included (a) US desire to have China's help in bringing the Vietnam war (pp. 127–28) to an end, (b) a common interest in challenging Soviet power, and (c) a US willingness to make concessions (e.g. admitting China to the UN), in order to make the above gains.

This rapprochement took various forms:

A visit of a US table tennis team to China
A visit to China by the US President Richard Nixon
US agreement to support China's admission to the UN in 1971
Improved trading links

After Mao's death some attempts were made to improve relations with the USSR. China, however, carefully refused to commit itself to either the USA or the USSR. This gave the country a new freedom in its foreign affairs.

China's relations with its neighbours

As the largest power in Asia and a former great empire, China has attempted since 1949 to extend its influence over neighbouring states. Its actions have included the following:

the *occupation of Tibet*, an area previously ruled by the Chinese Emperors, in 1950–51;
military support for North Korea in its struggle with South Korea and the United Nations during the Korean War of 1950–53 (pp. 125–26);
border fighting with India in 1962;
military support for the Vietcong and the North Vietnamese in the Vietnam war of the 1960s and 1970s (pp. 105–06).;
military invasion of North Vietnam in 1979, following border disputes between the two countries.

Despite being an *anti-imperialist* power, China has made it quite clear which power it thinks should be the dominant influence in eastern Asia.

CHINA IN THE TWENTIETH CENTURY 11
11.6 Key historical terms

Anti-imperialist 'Imperialism' means the rule of one people by another people, especially when this rule is exercised in the interests of the more powerful group. One example of imperial rule is that of the European powers in their Asian and African colonies at the beginning of the twentieth century. Another example is Chinese rule in Tibet after 1950. An *anti-imperialist* is someone opposed to imperialism. Marxists, such as the Chinese Communists, however, use imperialism in an even looser sense to refer to all *capitalist* states who (supposedly) exploit poorer states in their own interests. Thus, to a Marxist, European states that have lost their colonies are still *imperialist* powers. So too, in their eyes, is the USA.

Guerrilla warfare The nature of guerrilla warfare is discussed on p. 102. It is very important to understand what it involves. As well as being a major factor in the success of the Chinese Communists, it has also played a vital part in the Vietnam war (pp. 105–06), the Cuban revolution (p. 133), the struggle against the Russian-backed regime in Afghanistan (p. 130), and many other twentieth-century conflicts. Its greatest success, however, was in China and Mao Zedong's writings on guerrilla warfare strongly influenced many later guerrilla leaders. One of the features of these writings is their acceptance that revolutionary change can only come about as a result of violence and bloodshed. This fits in with the Marxist belief in violent revolution.

Other important terms include *autocratic* (p. 194), *collectivisation* (p. 42), *commune* (p. 104), *cultural revolution* (p. 104), *dynasty* (p. 100), *indus-*

trialisation (p. 45), *modernisation* (p. 196), *pragmatist* (p. 105), *personality cult* (p. 196), *rapprochement* (p. 106), *republic* (p. 197), *revisionist* (p. 197), and *socialism* (p. 197).

CHINA IN THE TWENTIETH CENTURY 11
11.7 Questions

Evidence question

Study the following extracts from *The Mandate of Heaven, Record of a civil war: China 1945–49*, first published in 1968. The author, John Melby, was a US agent in China after the end of the Second World War. The following extracts are from a diary Melby kept at the time:

> **Chungking, 10 November, 1945** Last night I had a talk with Tillman Burdin of the *New York Times* who has just come back from a visit to Kalgan in the north. According to him the Communists are behaving very well there, being quiet and unobtrusive, and are trying to *conciliate* people who are still suspicious . . .
> **6 December, 1945** I had lunch today with a man named Chun from . . . Kunming. We got to talking about student activities, since during the last couple of days there has been another bad and bloody student strike in Kunming which the Kuomintang is putting down with machine guns . . .
> **20 December, 1945** (At a dinner party tonight) the Chinese interested me most. These men, and others of their rank today, were at one time the flaming revolutionaries of Asia . . . passionately devoted to Dr Sun Yat-sen and what he stood for . . . Now they are sleek, polished, well fed, worldly, cynical, reactionary, interested only in maintaining their own positions.
> **20 June, 1948** One of the principal weaknesses continues to be the unwillingness of the *Generalissimo* to [give up] personal control . . . of every phase of national life . . . Time and again he has promised changes and then done nothing. Time and again he has promised to bring in abler men and then appoints the most incompetent he can find.
> **13 July, 1948** . . . it now looks as though the days of the Government are numbered. Even General Ho Ying-chin, Minister of Defense, says all is lost.

conciliate: please/win over *Generalissimo:* Chiang Kai-shek

(i) Identify the *Government* mentioned in the extract for 13 July, 1948. (1)

(ii) In what ways do the other extracts help to explain the problems that faced this government in 1948? Refer in detail to the extracts in support of your answer. (6)

(iii) Are these extracts likely to give us an accurate impression of what Melby thought about developments in China during these years? Give reasons for your answer. (3)

(iv) Quote one statement of *fact* and one statement of *opinion* to be found in these extracts. (2)

(v) 'US officials after the Second World War were frequently obsessed with the threat from communism.' Was this true of Melby? Explain your answer. (3)

(vi) What do you think is the value of diaries such as this one for someone studying the history of China during the late 1940s? (3)

THE USA: INTERNAL DEVELOPMENTS SINCE 1919 — 12

This chapter examines some of the main issues in the history of the USA since the end of the First World War. It is mainly concerned with internal developments, though Section 12.5 briefly describes US foreign policy during the years 1919–41. Chapters 8, 10 and 13 look at the increasingly important part played by the USA in world affairs since 1941.

A democratic state

The twentieth century has seen major changes in the way of life of the American people, some of which are discussed in this chapter. What has *not* changed, however, is the basis of the US political system. Throughout the twentieth century the USA has continued to be governed under a *constitution* laid down at the time when the country gained its independence, at the end of the eighteenth century. This constitution provides for:

(a) an elected Congress or parliament with two houses (the House of Representatives and the Senate);
(b) a President elected directly by the people;
(c) a balance of power between the *federal* government in Washington and the governments of the various states of the Union.

The way the constitution works in practice has changed, but it has remained the basis of the US political system for over 200 years. It is therefore a *parliamentary democracy* (p. 64) of a particular type.

THE USA: INTERNAL DEVELOPMENTS SINCE 1919 — 12

12.1 The Twenties

Republican policies

During the 1920s and early 1930s the USA was governed by a succession of Republican presidents: Warren Harding (1921–23), Calvin Coolidge (1923–29) and Herbert Hoover (1929–33). The main aim of these Republican governments was to foster the conditions in which US trade and industry would prosper. Standards of living in the USA were already the highest in the world. The aim of the Republicans was to make the country even richer. Their way of trying to do this was through policies of *laissez-faire* (let things alone) and 'rugged individualism' (giving individuals the freedom to prosper – or not to prosper – without government interference). They believed that the secret of the USA's economic success lay in the individual efforts of its people rather than in any government interference.

Laissez-faire, however, did not prevent the US government from actively promoting the country's exports throughout the world. It also did not prevent the imposition of *tariffs*, such as the Fordney-McCumber tariff of 1922, on imported foreign manufactured goods. These were designed to give US manufactured goods a strong advantage within the home market.

Prosperity: the 1920s boom

In many sectors of the US economy the 1920s was a period of boom. Production continued to rise, as did the average standard of living. Methods of *mass production* in factories helped to make available a whole range of products that had a dramatic effect on people's lives: motor cars, radios, washing machines, vacuum cleaners. *Hire purchase* was developed, allowing people to pay for these new products in instalments.

The growth of the *motor car industry* was particularly important, the number of cars in the USA rising from 7 million in 1919 to 24 million ten years later. The effects of this 'automobile revolution' on the USA and on other countries are discussed on p. 185. Two other major new industries of the 1920s were *radio* and *films*. The film industry was based at Hollywood in California, where throughout the interwar years more films were made than in the rest of the world put together.

Poverty: the other side of the 1920s boom

For many people in the USA the 1920s boom meant very little. For these people conditions remained the same or, in some cases, got worse.

Most farmers did not share in the prosperity of the 1920s. At the end of the First World War many countries cut back on their import of US farm produce. Heavy tariffs on foreign goods coming into the USA also discouraged other countries from purchasing US goods. Land fell in value, as did the price of agricultural products.

The USA's 12 million blacks also saw little benefit from the boom. Discrimination against them, especially in the southern states, probably got worse during the 1920s. *Segregation laws* were extended. These restricted where blacks could live, the schools they could attend and the transport facilities they could use. Many still did not have the vote. They were also the victims of racial abuse. One group that was particularly active in the southern states during the 1920s was the *KKK* (*Ku Klux Klan*), an organisation of whites that terrorised anyone who was thought not to be 'pure American'.

Other victims of the KKK included Jews and Roman Catholics, the descendants of immigrants from central and eastern Europe (in the case of Jews) and from southern Europe and Ireland (in the case of Roman Catholics). Discrimination against these groups was part of a general distrust of immigrants that was apparent in some quarters in the 1920s. This distrust led to the passing of an *Immigration Act* in 1921 which introduced a quota system for immigrants. This was extended by later acts during the 1920s and had the effect of greatly reducing the number of immigrants coming into the USA. It also discriminated against particular regions such as eastern Europe, from which fewer immigrants were allowed, and Japan, from which immigration was banned altogether.

One measure of the 1920s which had harmful effects that were not intended was *Prohibition*. Imposed in 1919, this involved a ban on the drinking, manufacturing and importing of alcohol. It was the result of a long anti-alcohol campaign which had received much support from the churches. It proved impossible to enforce and led to a great deal of illegal 'bootlegging' (making or importing illegal liquor) as well as to an increase in crime, with gangsters controlling vast numbers of illegal distilleries and 'speak-easies' (bars). Prohibition eventually came to an end, at least as a *federal* law, in 1933.

THE USA: INTERNATIONAL DEVELOPMENTS SINCE 1919 — 12

12.2 The Wall Street Crash and the Depression

One of the features of the 1920s boom was *speculation* in stocks and shares. As the profits from industry grew and as the standard of living rose, more and more people bought shares in a wide range of companies. The value of many shares rose dramatically. This encouraged people to buy them as a short-term investment (i.e. in the hope that they would be able to sell quickly and make a fast profit). By the end of the 1920s the price of shares was rising to incredible heights and vast sums of money were changing hands every day on the New York stock exchange.

It looked as if nothing could stop the upward movement of share prices. And then on 24 October 1929 the bottom fell out of the market. The value of shares collapsed and thousands of people were ruined. Many people had bought shares on borrowed money. They were now unable to repay these loans, with the result that banks ran out of money and were forced to close. Companies also went bankrupt, throwing out of work large numbers of employees. This *Wall Street Crash*, as it is known, set in motion an economic depression that was to last well into the 1930s and that had repercussions throughout the world (see p. 60 and p. 95).

Speculation in shares was not the only cause of the Depression. US industry had also been *over-producing*, i.e. factories had been making more goods than they could sell. Firms began to lay off workers, with the result that the number of unemployed began to rise. The effect of this was to reduce further the demand for goods, thus encouraging more firms to lay off workers, and so on. High US tariffs also had the effect of reducing demand for US goods abroad.

By 1933 14 million Americans were unemployed. US factories were producing about half the goods they had produced in 1929. US trade had also dropped to a third of what it had been before 1929.

President Hoover hoped that the Depression would not last. He saw no reason to abandon the laissez-faire policies that seemed to have been so effective during the 1920s. Republican measures to deal with the Depression were therefore on a small scale. These included loans to firms to help them avoid bankruptcy and a limited programme of *public works*. Measures such as these had little impact. Public opinion therefore turned against the Republicans and in the *presidential election of 1932* the Democratic candidate Franklin D. Roosevelt won a huge majority. Roosevelt appealed to the electorate because of his energy, his record as an effective Governor of New York, and above all because he promised the US people a *New Deal*, a major programme of reforms to tackle the Depression.

THE USA: INTERNAL DEVELOPMENTS SINCE 1919
12.3 Roosevelt and the New Deal 12

The New Deal had three main aims: (a) *Relief* (short-term measures to help the millions of unemployed); (b) *Recovery* from the effects of the Depression; and (c) *Reform*, in order to make the USA a fairer and juster society. In the early stages of the New Deal priority was given to Relief and Recovery. The second New Deal (1935–39), as it is sometimes known, found more time for Reform. The main features of the New Deal are listed below:

1 The Hundred Days During the first hundred days of his presidency Roosevelt gave priority to

(i) *relief measures*, e.g. cash handouts and work schemes for the unemployed (organised by *FERA*, the Federal Emergency Relief Administration), and

(ii) *restoring people's confidence in the country's banking system*, by closing down all the banks and then reopening the sound ones with government support (Emergency Banking Act of 1933).

Roosevelt also did a great deal to boost public confidence by his 'fireside chats' over the radio.

2 Work for the unemployed A major feature of the New Deal was the creation of millions of new jobs as a way of reducing the number of unemployed. The government now took on the role of employer. It also began to spend huge sums of money. This of course was very different from the policies of laissez-faire pursued by the Republicans.

By creating all these jobs and thus increasing the number of people receiving a wage, Roosevelt hoped to increase demand for goods. As demand increased so factories would produce more, thus employing more workers. These workers would then be able to buy more goods, thus further increasing production, thus creating yet more jobs, and so on. The following diagram will help to make this clear:

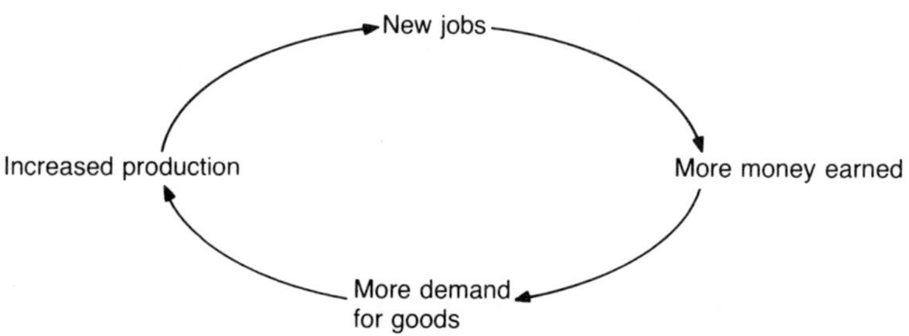

In order to provide employment, Roosevelt established a number of 'alphabet agencies'. These included:

The Public Works Administration (PWA), which employed millions of people building roads, schools, hospitals, etc.;

The Civil Works Administration (CWA), a similar organisation which was taken over in 1935 by a new body called the *Works Progress Administration* (WPA);

The Civilian Conservation Corps (CCC), a scheme for providing jobs for young men, mostly in mountain and forest areas.

3 Assistance to farmers One of the main problems facing US agriculture was over-production. Roosevelt set up the *Agricultural Adjustment Administration* (AAA) to tackle this problem. By paying farmers to produce less, the AAA succeeded in increasing the price of farm produce. By 1937 the total income of US farmers was double what it had been in 1932.

4 Conditions of work One of Roosevelt's main concerns in trying to *reform* US society was his attempt to improve conditions for workers. The *National Recovery Administration* (NRA) drew up a code or set of rules which employers were encouraged to adopt. These included an 8-hour day, a minimum wage and a ban on child labour. The National Industrial Recovery Act of 1933, which set up the NRA, also gave workers the legal right to bargain with their employers through trade unions. This was followed in 1935 by the *Wagner Act* which compelled employers to negotiate on wages and hours with the union to which a majority of their employees belonged. This greatly strengthened the position of US trade unions which, until this time, had been very weak.

5 Social security The *Social Security Act* of 1935 set up, for the first time in the USA, government schemes for old age pensions and unemployment insurance.

The New Deal: support and opposition

In general the New Deal was popular with the American people. This was shown by the large majorities with which Roosevelt was re-elected President in 1936 and 1940 (and again, in wartime, in 1944). Many Americans, however, were very critical. Some felt it gave too much power to the government. Many objected to the increased taxes they had to pay in order to finance Roosevelt's schemes. Employers often resented the growth in the power of trade unions. Some critics on the other hand felt that the New Deal did not go far enough and pointed to its failure to reduce unemployment below 7 million.

In the mid-1930s a number of Roosevelt's laws were brought before the US Supreme Court to test whether they were allowed under the constitution. Most of the judges in the Supreme Court had very conservative views and in a number of decisions condemned some of Roosevelt's agencies, such as the AAA, as unconstitutional (i.e. not in agreement with the constitution). This led to a serious clash between the President and the Supreme Court which was only resolved by the eventual death or resignation of some of the judges and the election of others less hostile to Roosevelt's measures.

THE USA: INTERNAL DEVELOPMENTS SINCE 1919

12.4 US foreign policy, 1919–41

12

US foreign policy during the 1920s and 1930s has often been described as *isolationist*, i.e. the USA is supposed to have cut itself off from the rest of the world in order to concentrate on building up its strength at home. Many developments support this idea. These include: the US decision not to join the League of Nations (p. 175); the imposition of tariffs (p. 111) and restrictions on immigration (p. 111–12); strict *neutrality* during the major conflicts that developed during the 1930s. *In other ways, however, the USA was never completely isolated*. It played a major part in attempts to solve the problem of German reparations after the First World War (p. 59). It took the initiative in the Washington disarmament conference of 1922 (p. 67) and the Kellogg-Briand Pact of 1928 (p. 67). It continued to show an active interest in parts of the world, such as Latin America and the Far East, in which it had strong economic interests as well as territories of its own (such as the Philippines and the Panama Canal Zone).

The USA maintained its policy of neutrality after the outbreak of the Second World War in Europe in 1939. The US government's sympathies, however, were with the victims of German aggression. In 1939 it allowed the British government to buy arms and supplies from the USA on a *cash and carry* basis, that is, that Britain was allowed to buy arms as long as it had the money to pay for them. This was followed in 1940 by an agreement between the US and British governments by which the USA gave Britain 50 destroyers in return for the right to use various British bases in the Americas. In 1941 the *Lend Lease* scheme even went so far as to allow the US government to supply Britain with war materials without charge. In the same year Roosevelt and Churchill, the British Prime Minister, also met to draw up the *Atlantic Charter*, an agreement about the kind of world that the two countries wished to create once the war was over. It was not long before these measures were followed by the US declaration of war on Japan and Germany. You can read about the part played by the USA in the Second World War in Chapters 8 and 11.

THE USA: INTERNAL DEVELOPMENTS SINCE 1919 — 12

12.5 Truman, the Fair Deal and McCarthyism

The Second World War had an enormous impact on the US people. Over 15 million Americans served in the armed forces and over 1 million were killed or wounded. At home, however, many people prospered as a result of the war. The needs of the armed forces boosted industrial production, with the result that wages rose and unemployment virtually ceased. Despite a sharp price rise in 1946, this prosperity continued into the immediate postwar years.

Roosevelt died suddenly in 1945, being replaced by his Vice-President *Harry Truman*. Truman was elected in his own right in 1948, serving as president until the end of his second term in 1952. To a large extent his policies were a continuation of Roosevelt's. His *Fair Deal*, launched in 1945, included measures relating to insurance, social security and housing. These continued the reforms that had been introduced as part of the New Deal. Further reforms were envisaged, but were held up by opposition in Congress from both Republicans and conservative Democrats.

Truman's last years in office were overshadowed by the problem of *McCarthyism*. Senator Joseph McCarthy was a fanatical anti-communist convinced that the USA was being undermined from within by communist sympathisers in high places. His accusations led to the public disgrace of large numbers of people whose only crime was to have liberal or left-wing views that McCarthy and his supporters happened to dislike. McCarthy's success can partly be explained by the onset of the Cold War and in particular by American involvement in the Korean War of 1950–53 (pp. 125–26). This made many Americans feel that their country was under attack. McCarthy eventually went too far with his accusations, causing great resentment among military leaders as a result of attacks on the US army. In 1954 the Senate condemned his activities, after which his influence rapidly diminished.

THE USA: INTERNAL DEVELOPMENTS SINCE 1919

12.6 Eisenhower (1953–60), Kennedy (1961–63) and Johnson (1963–69) — 12

Truman did not stand for re-election in 1952. His successor, the first Republican president since 1932, was *Dwight Eisenhower*, a war hero who had led US forces in the North African and Normandy landings during the Second World War. Eisenhower had very conservative views, being keen to reduce taxes and restrict the kind of government activities that had developed during the periods of the New Deal and the Fair Deal. In practice he had little success with either of these aims. This was partly because welfare provision had become an accepted feature of US life.

The presidential election of 1960 was won by a Democrat, *J. F. Kennedy*. His election was greeted with great enthusiasm by liberal Americans, many of whom hoped that he would embark on a period of reform similar to Roosevelt's New Deal. Kennedy certainly had ambitious plans, for example in the fields of education, medical provision and civil rights (see below). He was able to achieve relatively little, however – mainly as a result of persistent opposition from Congress. His presidency was cut prematurely short in 1963 when he was assassinated on a visit to Dallas.

Kennedy's Vice-President *Lyndon Johnson* took over in 1963. He was elected in his own right the following year, serving as president until 1968. Johnson proved a better manager of Congress than Kennedy and was able in the end to carry through some very substantial reforms. These were mostly along lines already laid down by Kennedy. They included civil rights measures, major education programmes for poor areas, and the introduction of medicare (medical benefits for people over 65).

Throughout the presidencies of Eisenhower, Kennedy and Johnson issues concerning race relations and civil rights played an increasingly important part in US politics. These are considered separately below.

THE USA: INTERNAL DEVELOPMENTS SINCE 1919 12

12.7 Race relations and civil rights since 1945

Pressure for civil rights

At the end of the Second World War conditions for many blacks had improved little since the 1920s. In the southern states they were still subject to segregation laws. Many more now lived in the big cities of the north, to which they had moved in search of employment. Here they often formed a majority of the population in the run-down inner parts of cities. As a group they tended to hold the worst-paid jobs.

The Second World War helped to strengthen the feeling among blacks that they were being treated unjustly. Many black soldiers had fought and lost their lives in the struggle against Nazi racism. This made black people more conscious of the racism that was still widespread within their own society. Educational improvements had also helped to create a much larger educated black middle class, many of whose members were now in a stronger position to organise movements for reform. Blacks also received growing support from many liberal whites.

The civil rights movement

During the 1950s and 1960s a very powerful civil rights movement developed within the USA, committed to struggle until all forms of discrimination had been removed. Most blacks supported moderate leaders such as *Martin Luther King* who adopted tactics of non-violent resistance similar to those used by Gandhi in India (p. 142). King's protests included:

(i) A successful boycott of bus services in Montgomery, Alabama, in 1955, in protest against segregated seating for blacks and whites.
(ii) 'Sit-ins' throughout the south in 1960 in protest against segregation in shops and restaurants.
(iii) The 'freedom rides' of 1961 when supporters travelled all over the south enforcing *de-segregation* of bus station waiting rooms and cafes.
(iv) A peaceful march on Washington in 1963.

As you will read below, these protests were effective in securing major changes in the legal position of blacks. They did little, however, to reduce the huge differences in wealth between the black and white communities. In the 1960s some blacks turned to more violent methods of protest, supporting organisations such as the *Black Panthers* and *Black Muslims* who were opposed to any cooperation with liberal whites. During the mid- and late 1960s there were many riots in cities throughout the USA, especially during the hot summer months.

During the late 1960s and early 1970s other racial minorities also pressed for an improvement in their conditions. Particularly active were the *Amer-*

ican Indians (i.e. the survivors of the original Indian inhabitants of North America) and the *Chicanos* (Spanish Americans).

Civil rights measures

Even before the civil rights movement got under way there had been various attempts to improve the legal position of blacks. *Truman* had been keen to tackle discrimination, but was obstructed by conservative politicians in Congress. He succeeded, however, in ending segregation in the US army. *Eisenhower* was perhaps less interested, though more successful, partly as a result of growing pressure from the civil rights movement. *The Civil Rights Acts of 1957 and 1960* ensured that blacks in southern states were no longer deprived of the vote. Also during Eisenhower's presidency the Supreme Court made a number of decisions declaring illegal various forms of discrimination. The most important of these was a verdict in 1954 declaring segregated schooling illegal. Eisenhower enforced this verdict in 1957 when he sent federal troops to *Little Rock High School in Arkansas* in order to overrule the state governor who was trying to prevent black children from attending the school. Despite this dramatic gesture many southern states continued to defy the Supreme Court's ruling.

Kennedy and *Johnson* were both supporters of the civil rights movement and important changes were made during their presidencies. Kennedy forced Alabama to accept black students at its university. He also appointed blacks to a number of important government posts. Johnson was even more successful in pushing measures through Congress. Perhaps the most important was the *Civil Rights Act of 1964* which banned discrimination in a wide range of public facilities such as hotels and golf clubs.

THE USA: INTERNAL DEVELOPMENTS SINCE 1919 — 12

12.8 Richard Nixon, 1968–74

To many Americans the 1960s seemed a decade of protest and disorder. As well as the activities of militant blacks, there were also protests about US involvement in the Vietnam War (pp. 127–28), student riots, and mounting agitation by groups such as feminists and homosexuals. The hostility of many Americans to movements such as these helps to explain the election of the Republican *Richard Nixon* in 1968. Nixon's commitment to law and order at home won him much support. During his presidency there was also a slackening of the reform measures, such as civil rights, with which Johnson had been associated. The latter part of his presidency, however, was overshadowed by the *Watergate affair*. Nixon and some of his closest supporters were found to be guilty of a variety of illegal actions. Threatened with *impeachment* (being brought to trial on charges of abusing his authority), Nixon became the first US president ever to resign.

Nixon's successors as president have been Gerald Ford (Republican, 1974–76), Jimmy Carter (Democrat, 1977–80), Ronald Reagan (Republican, 1981–88) and George Bush (Republican, 1989–).

THE USA: INTERNAL DEVELOPMENTS SINCE 1919
12.9 Key historical terms 12

Civil rights This term refers to the rights possessed by the citizens of a state or that people feel ought to be possessed by these citizens. In the USA it referred to rights laid down by the constitution, but which in the past had been denied to one section of the community, i.e. the blacks. The main purpose of the civil rights movement of the 1950s and 1960s was to ensure equal treatment for blacks and whites: for example, that both groups should have an equal right to vote, use public facilities, be taught at the same educational establishments, etc.

Other important terms are *constitution* (p. 195), *federal* (p. 180), *isolationist* (p. 115), *laissez-faire* (p. 196), *parliamentary democracy* (p. 64), *public works* (p. 197), *racism* (p. 161) and *rugged individualism* (p. 110).

THE USA: INTERNAL DEVELOPMENTS SINCE 1919
12.10 Questions 12

Source-based questions
Study Sources A and B, both taken in the USA during the 1960s, and then answer the following questions.

(i) Why, during the 1950s and early 1960s, did many people take part in marches such as the one shown in Source A? (6)
(ii) In what ways does Source A illustrate important features of the civil rights movement? (3)
(iii) To what extent, during the 1950s and 1960s, did the civil rights movement achieve its aims? Explain your answer. (6)
(iv) How would you explain the actions of the people shown in Source B? (5)

Source A: a civil rights march

Source B: a demonstration protesting against a civil rights march

THE USA, THE USSR AND THE COLD WAR 13
13.1 The origins of the Cold War

One of the most important themes in twentieth-century world history is the rise to prominence of the two superpowers, the USA and the USSR. In the course of the century they came to replace European states like Britain and France as the new great powers of the world.

Even at the beginning of the century it was apparent that in terms of size, population and resources no European power on its own was able to match them. Their importance, however, was disguised during the interwar years by *isolationist* foreign policies which allowed European states to continue to act as if Europe were still the centre of the world.

A turning-point in the rise of these superpowers was the Second World War. Without American and Russian involvement Germany and Japan would not have been defeated. At the end of the war both states had gained enormously in influence and prestige.

The wartime alliance between the two superpowers did not last for long. Within a short time it had turned into a *Cold War* which, in different forms, has persisted ever since. It is important to be clear what this term means. It refers to the conflict between the West (the USA and its allies) on the one hand and the East (the USSR and its allies) on the other hand. It is called the 'Cold' War because it has been fought mostly with words rather than with weapons.

This chapter looks at the origins of the Cold War, at how it developed in different parts of the world, and at the spheres of influence which the two superpowers have created for themselves.

People have often disagreed about the origins of the Cold War. Politicians on both sides have usually blamed their opponents for the way in which it developed. These are some of the reasons that help to explain it:

1 *The USA and its allies were very suspicious of the intentions of the USSR*. At the end of the war the USSR had set up communist governments in all of the states of eastern Europe. These states became the *satellites* of the USSR, i.e. they were under close Soviet control. The USA and its allies feared that the USSR would try to spread communism throughout western Europe as well. They were determined to prevent this from happening.

2 *The USSR was equally suspicious of the USA*. At the end of the war the USA was the only power to possess atomic weapons. This knowledge created panic throughout the communist world and helps to explain the very tough line taken by the Soviet Union in some of the crises of the late 1940s.

3 A number of clashes in the late 1940s increased tension between the two sides. These helped to turn conflict into a habit. These clashes included:

(i) *Civil war in Greece*. The communists in this civil war were supported by neighbouring communist states and by the USSR. Their opponents,

Central and Eastern Europe after 1945

the royalists, received aid from Britain and the USA. US assistance eventually led to a royalist victory.

(ii) *The Berlin airlift, 1948*. At the end of the war Germany had been divided into occupation zones controlled by Britain, France, the USA and the USSR. The capital, Berlin, which lay deep inside the Soviet zone, was also divided into a western sector controlled by the western powers and an eastern sector controlled by the USSR. The two sides disagreed about the future of Germany. The Russians wished to keep it weak and divided whereas the western powers were wanting to build up the economic strength of their own zones as a way of preventing any further spread of communist influence. Stalin, the Soviet leader, also hoped to force the western powers out of West Berlin. In 1948 he cut off all road and rail links between West Berlin and western Germany. The USA was determined not to let West Berlin fall to communism, fearing that this would be the first step towards the extension of communist control elsewhere in western Europe. Its response was a massive airlift of supplies to West Berlin. A year later Stalin called off the blockade.

The effect of this crisis was to drive the two sides much further apart. Europe was now divided into two hostile camps along a clear demarcation line known as the *Iron Curtain*, with the communist states to the east and the non-communist states to the west. Both sides came to recognise that they had little power to influence events on the other side of the line. As a result many later crises in the Cold War took place in other parts of the world where the demarcation line was not so clear. The one major exception was the crisis over the building of the *Berlin Wall* in 1961, an attempt by the eastern bloc to stop the flow of refugees to the west.

THE USA, THE USSR AND THE COLD WAR 13
13.2 The formation of two power blocs

As a result of the Cold War both the USA and the USSR took various steps to strengthen ties with their allies. In the case of the West these included the following:

1 The Marshall Plan (1947), a scheme to provide US economic aid to western Europe.
2 The Truman Doctrine (1947), a declaration by the USA that it would come to the support of 'free peoples' whenever their freedom was threatened.
3 NATO (the North Atlantic Treaty Organisation), a military alliance of the USA and most of the states of western Europe, formed in 1949. NATO committed the USA to the defence of western Europe. In return the countries of western Europe were expected to support the USA in other parts of the world.

The USSR strengthened its control over the eastern bloc through the formation of the following:

1 Cominform (1947), the Communist Information Bureau whose purpose was to coordinate the activities of the different communist parties.
2 Comecon (1949), the Council for Mutual Economic Assistance which strengthened economic links between the countries of eastern Europe.
3 The Warsaw Pact (1955), a military alliance similar to NATO.

13.3 The Cold War outside Europe

Although it began in Europe, the Cold War was soon no longer confined to that continent. The differences in *ideology* (sets of ideas) between the two superpowers meant that they often took different sides in the many conflicts that have developed throughout the world since 1945. Both the USA and the USSR have been quick to seize opportunities to extend their influence. In doing so they have frequently come into conflict – sometimes directly and sometimes via their allies. You can read about superpower involvement in the Middle East in Chapter 17. This section examines the two major crises of the Cold War in the Far East: the Korean War and the war in Vietnam.

The Korean War (1950–53)

Causes Korea had been occupied by Japan until 1945. After Japan's defeat the country was divided into two occupation zones controlled by the USA and the USSR. A communist government was established in the North and a non-communist government in the South. All peaceful attempts to reunite the country failed. Encouraged by the victory of the communists in neighbouring China (p. 102) and by the withdrawal of US forces from South Korea, the communist North launched a surprise attack on the South in 1950. The US government was determined that South Korea should not fall to communism. It succeeded in persuading the UN Security Council to send an international army to protect the independence of South Korea.

Events Most of the South was soon captured by North Korean forces. The UN army, under the US General MacArthur, counter-attacked and drove the North Koreans back to the 38th parallel (the border between the two parts of the country). At this point the aim of the UN intervention changed – from defending the South to reuniting the whole country under a democratic government. MacArthur's forces swept through North Korea, almost reaching the Yalu River, the border between North Korea and Communist China. This greatly angered the Chinese who now entered the war on the side of North Korea, sweeping MacArthur's forces right back into South Korea. MacArthur again counter-attacked and the war developed into a military stalemate around the 38th parallel.

Consequences The war ended with an armistice in 1953. All attempts to reunite Korea, whether under a communist or a non-communist government, had failed. The war had led to very heavy loss of life, with 3–4 million deaths. Its long-term effect was to create a deep distrust between the USA and Communist China. It also encouraged the USA to strengthen the West's defences in the Far East and the Pacific through the creation in 1954 of *SEATO (South East Asia Treaty Organisation)*, a military alliance of anti-communist states.

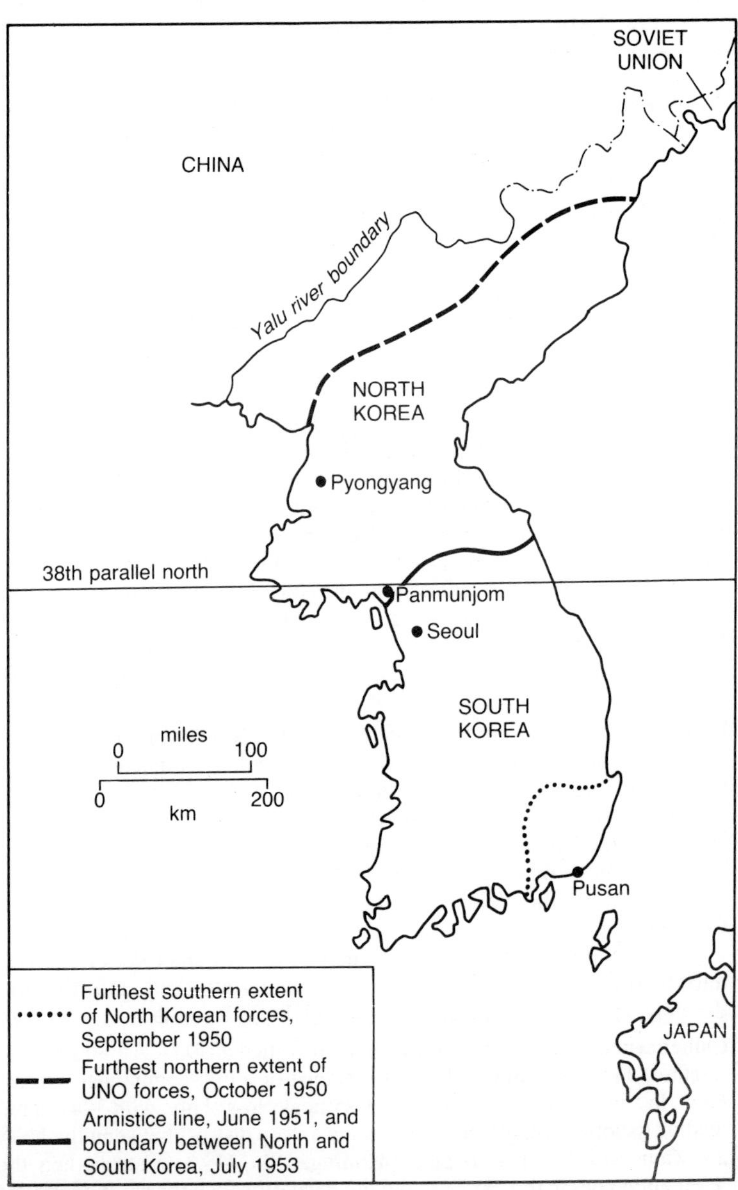

The Korean War

The war in Vietnam

Causes You can read on p. 147 about how the French withdrew from Indo-China in 1954. Independent states were set up in Laos and Cambodia (see map on p. 128). Vietnam was temporarily divided into two parts: communist North Vietnam, under the control of Ho Chi Minh, the leader of the Vietminh forces who had defeated the French, and non-communist South Vietnam. Communist *Vietcong* guerrillas, however, continued to operate in South Vietnam, being supplied with weapons from the North along the so-called Ho Chi Minh trail (see map on p. 128). The USA was alarmed at the prospect of South Vietnam falling to communism, fearing that this would have a *domino-like effect* throughout South East Asia (i.e. that other states as a result would also fall to communism). It gave more and more support to South Vietnam, eventually committing itself in the mid-1960s to a full-scale war against the Vietcong.

Events Despite their superior strength, US and South Vietnamese forces found it impossible to defeat the Vietcong. The USA resorted to direct attacks on North Vietnam, both from the sea and from the air. The methods used by both sides were often appallingly brutal. The USA was criticised throughout the world for its use of napalm bombs (bombs that spray out an inflammable jelly that causes hideous damage to human beings) and chemical sprays.

The successful Tet offensive launched by the Vietcong in 1968 helped to convince the US government that, despite the presence of half a million troops, it was not going to win the war. A new US President, Richard Nixon, embarked on a policy of *vietnamisation*, by which responsibility for the conduct of the war was gradually handed over to the South Vietnamese. Peace talks were held and led in 1973 to a ceasefire. One of the terms of the ceasefire was that US forces should be withdrawn altogether. The ceasefire, however, did not insist on the withdrawal of North Vietnam's forces from South Vietnam. Once the US troops had left, a final North Vietnamese offensive in 1975 had little difficulty in reuniting the country under communist control.

The USA's defeat in the Vietnam war was a major humiliation. Why did it happen? These are some possible reasons:

1 *The USA was fighting a guerrilla army* that merged easily into the civilian population. You can read on p. 102 about the advantages of guerrilla warfare. The strategy of the Vietcong was carefully planned by General Giap, the leader of the North Vietnamese army, who was one of the world's leading experts on guerrilla warfare.
2 *Many peasants willingly supported the Vietcong*. Governments in South Vietnam were often corrupt and dictatorial and did little to promote the interests of the peasants. The Vietcong by contrast promised land reform. They also sometimes terrorised peasants into helping them.

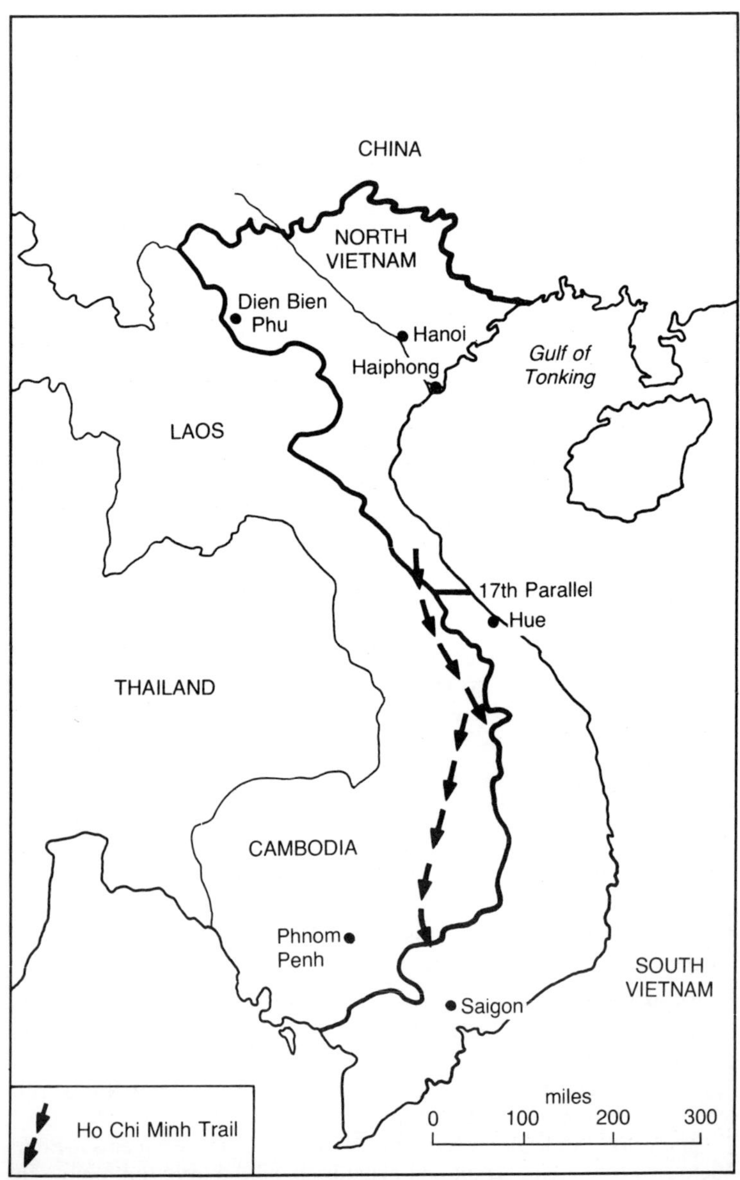

Indochina in the 1960s

3 *The USA was not just fighting the Vietcong*. Throughout the war the Vietcong continued to receive supplies, along the Ho Chi Minh trail, from North Vietnam and (via North Vietnam) from China and the USSR.
4 *US soldiers were often unpopular in Vietnam simply because they were foreigners*. Even some non-communists supported the Vietcong as a way of getting rid of such a large foreign presence in their country.
5 *There was a great deal of opposition to the Vietnam war in the USA*. This, together with the heavy cost of the war at a time of *economic recession*, helped to convince the US government that it was time to withdraw.

THE USA, THE USSR AND THE COLD WAR 13
13.4 Coexistence and detente

The Cold War is not the whole story of relations between the superpowers during the period since the Second World War. Since the late 1950s there have been various attempts both at *coexistence* and at *detente*. *Coexistence*, a word often used during the 1960s, simply means living in peace without making too many attempts to change the situation to the advantage of one side or the other. *Detente*, a word heard more frequently during the 1970s, refers to attempts that have been made actively to improve relations between the two sides.

Reasons why attempts at coexistence began to be made in the late 1950s include:

(i) the death of the Soviet dictator Stalin in 1953 and his eventual replacement by a leader, *Nikita Khrushchev*, who was more willing to talk;

(ii) the realisation by both sides that their power to hurt each other was such that it was in the interest of neither side to intensify the conflict. This realisation was to a large extent a result of the rapid growth in *nuclear weapons* after the Second World War. By the end of the 1950s both sides were able to destroy each other many times over.

These are some of the ways in which attempts were made to pursue coexistence and detente:

1 Summit meetings These meetings between heads of state from the two sides have taken place from time to time since the mid-1950s. They have not always been successful, e.g. the Paris summit of 1960 which collapsed as a result of the shooting down over the USSR of an American U-2 spy plane. The fact that the two sides continue to meet and talk is, however, an important change from the worst days of the Cold War.
2 The Cuban missile crisis of 1962 (see p. 133) led to the establishment of a *'hot-line' telephone and telex link* between the White House in Washington and the Kremlin in Moscow.

3 Arms control and disarmament talks These talks, held since the 1960s, have failed to prevent the rapid growth in the number and capacity of nuclear weapons held by the two superpowers. Agreements, however, have been reached on a variety of issues. These include:

(i) The *Partial Test Ban Treaty* (1963) which banned all nuclear testing under the sea, above ground and in the atmosphere.

(ii) The *Non-Proliferation Treaty* (1968), by which the powers agreed not to help any other countries in the development of nuclear weapons.

(iii) The *SALT 1 agreement of 1972*. This followed some years of Strategic Arms Limitation Talks (SALT) between the USA and the USSR. It imposed certain limitations on the nuclear missile systems that could be used by the two sides.

(iv) The *SALT 2 agreement of 1979*. This extended the provisions of the SALT 1 agreement. It was never, however, formally ratified (approved) by the USA, partly in protest against the Soviet invasion of Afghanistan that took place in the same year.

(v) In the 1980s SALT was replaced by START (Strategic Arms Reduction Talks). Progress at first was slow, but speeded up in the late 1980s with the emergence of a new Soviet leader, Mikhail Gorbachev, who appeared keen to promote detente. An important agreement in 1987 provided for actual *disarmament* (the reduction in the number of weapons) as opposed to just *arms control* (agreed limitations on the development of new weapons).

4 The signing of the **1987 agreement on intermediate nuclear forces** was part of a general improvement in relations between the two superpowers that took place in the late 1980s. This improvement led some observers to hope that a new era in East–West relations had begun. The withdrawal of Soviet troops from Afghanistan (invaded in 1979) helped to reduce one major source of conflict between the two sides.

THE USA, THE USSR AND THE COLD WAR 13
13.5 Spheres of influence

One of the ways in which the two superpowers have managed to coexist is by accepting that there are certain 'spheres of influence' belonging to the other side with which they ought not to interfere. For most of the period since 1945 US governments have accepted that they have little power to influence events in eastern Europe. Similarly the USSR has been reluctant to interfere directly in the Americas, an area of special concern to the USA. The rest of this chapter examines the relationship between the superpowers and these spheres of influence.

The USSR and eastern Europe

At the end of the Second World War the USSR established pro-Soviet communist governments throughout eastern Europe. It has always been one of the main aims of Soviet foreign policy to ensure that the whole of this area remained firmly under its control. On a number of occasions this control has been challenged. The three most troublesome countries, from the Soviet point of view, have been Hungary, Czechoslovakia and Poland.

Hungary, 1956

There was widespread resentment in Hungary at the kind of communist government that had been forced upon the country at the end of the Second World War. The death of Stalin in 1953 and the criticisms of Stalin that began to appear within the USSR encouraged Hungarians to feel that they now had an opportunity to remove their own Stalinist rulers. The Hungarian dictator Rakosi was forced to resign and was replaced by a new government headed by *Imre Nagy*. This new government, though communist, made some fundamental changes, e.g. allowing the establishment of other political parties and withdrawing Hungary from the Warsaw Pact (p. 124). This greatly alarmed the new Soviet leader Khrushchev who feared both that Hungary would be lost as a satellite state and that other eastern European countries might be tempted to follow Hungary's example. A Soviet army was therefore dispatched to Hungary and after a few days of street fighting in Budapest, the capital, succeeded in suppressing this 'Hungarian rising'. A pro-Russian government was established and many of the leaders of the 'rising', including Nagy, were arrested and executed. Both the United Nations and the west had been powerless to intervene on Hungary's behalf.

Czechoslovakia, 1968

Khrushchev's actions in 1956 showed that Stalin's death had made little difference to Soviet foreign policy. Khrushchev's fall from power in 1964 similarly had little effect on Russia's relations with its satellites. This was shown by the Soviet response to developments in Czechoslovakia.

Czechoslovakia since the early 1950s had been under the control of a pro-Soviet dictator, Novotny. Economic problems and mounting discontent in the mid-1960s led in 1968 to his resignation and to the creation of a new government headed by Svoboda (as President) and *Alexander Dubcek* (as First Secretary). Though a communist, Dubcek was anxious to establish what he called 'socialism with a human face'. This involved the release of political prisoners and the relaxation of press censorship. Unlike Nagy, Dubcek had no wish to break altogether with the USSR or to allow non-communist political parties. This, however, did not reassure the government of the USSR which saw Dubcek's reforms as a major threat to its authority in eastern Europe. As in 1956, Soviet troops invaded, this time assisted by troops from other Warsaw Pact countries. The Czechoslovaks did not resist by force of arms, choosing instead to organise a campaign of passive resistance, holding demonstrations and silent protests. Dubcek was arrested and taken to Moscow where he was forced to sign an agreement to abandon most of his reform programme. Opposition to the Soviet occupation continued within Czechoslovakia and eventually Dubcek was removed from office altogether, being replaced by a repressive pro-Soviet regime. Unlike Nagy, however, Dubcek was neither imprisoned nor executed.

Poland

Although never experiencing a full-scale military invasion, Poland has proved the most persistently troublesome of the Soviet Union's eastern European satellites. Poles were traditionally anti-Russian. As Roman Catholics, many were also strongly opposed to a communist government that was actively hostile to religion.

Opposition to the regime has broken out on a number of occasions since 1945. In 1956 strikes led to a change of leadership within the Communist Party, bringing to power *Wladyslaw Gomulka*. During the 1950s and 1960s Gomulka received a certain amount of support at home for sometimes taking an independent line in relations with the USSR. His regime, however, became increasingly unpopular in the 1960s both because of its treatment of opponents and because of its failure to solve Poland's many economic problems. Riots and strikes forced Gomulka to resign in 1970.

His successor, Edward Gierek, was initially more successful, though disturbances continued, for example in 1976 in protest against price rises. In 1980–81 further disturbances led to the emergence of an independent trade union known as *Solidarity*, led by *Lech Walesa*. Encouraged by its success, Solidarity began to make political as well as economic demands. It won so much support that the Polish government seemed to be losing control. In December 1981 the armed forces, under the leadership of *General Jaruzelski*, took over the government, declaring martial law and arresting most of Solidarity's leaders. It is very likely that they were acting under pressure from the USSR. Unlike 1956 and 1968, the USSR did not intervene directly, perhaps fearing a huge upsurge of anti-Soviet feeling within Poland that they would not be able to contain. Many of Solidarity's leaders were eventually released, though tension between the Polish authorities and large sections of the Polish people persisted throughout the 1980s. Strikes and demonstrations broke out once again in various Polish cities in 1988.

The USA and the Americas

There are some similarities between the attitudes of US governments towards the rest of the Americas and those of Soviet governments towards eastern Europe. US governments have certainly regarded central and

South America as areas of special concern and since 1945 have been very anxious to prevent the establishment in the Americas of any communist or left-wing government that might be hostile to US interests. US military forces intervened in a number of central American and Caribbean countries during the interwar years. They have continued to do so since the Second World War: in the *Dominican Republic* in *1965*, to prevent a communist takeover; and in the island of *Grenada* in *1983*, to overthrow an unpopular communist government. They have also interfered in the internal affairs of various countries, giving aid to anti-communist forces in their attempts to overthrow left-wing governments in *Guatemala* (1954), *Cuba* (1961), and *Nicaragua* (1980s).

The USSR has mostly accepted that the Americas are the USA's special sphere of influence. On one occasion, however, it attempted to challenge US power in a very dramatic way. This led to the Cuban missile crisis of 1962.

The Cuban missile crisis, 1962

In 1959, as a result of a revolution led by *Fidel Castro*, the pro-US Cuban dictator Batista was finally overthrown. Castro's government was at first not openly communist, though it had links with the Cuban Communist Party. It may well have been US hostility to the new regime that finally persuaded Castro to identify publicly with communism. The US government was anxious not to lose its influence over the island. It was also concerned at the threat to US economic interests posed by the new regime. US hostility encouraged Castro to establish closer links with the USSR and China – which in its turn further increased the anxiety of the US government.

In 1961 the US President, John F. Kennedy, gave his support to an invasion of Cuba by a group of anti-Castro Cuban exiles. This *Bay of Pigs invasion*, as it is called, was a complete disaster. Its effects, however, were to strengthen even further Cuba's association with the eastern bloc. Khrushchev took advantage of the situation to secure bases on Cuba for Soviet missiles aimed at the USA. When aerial photographs revealed the presence of these bases, the US government was deeply alarmed. The Soviet action was seen as the most serious threat to US security since the beginning of the Cold War. The USSR was formally asked to withdraw all existing missiles and the US navy imposed a blockade of the island in order to prevent the arrival of any new ones. Khrushchev offered to withdraw the missiles on condition that the USA agreed to withdraw its missiles from Turkey, an ally of the USA as close to the Soviet Union as Cuba was to the USA. Kennedy refused. The crisis was a very tense one. For a few days the world seemed to come closer to nuclear war than on any occasion either before or since. At the last minute, with Soviet ships heading towards the US blockade, Khrushchev backed down. It was agreed that all missiles would be withdrawn from Cuba. In return the US government agreed to lift its blockade and promised not to support any more attempts to invade the island.

The Cuban missile crisis of 1962 encouraged the superpowers to consider ways of relieving tension. It led, for example, to the establishment of the 'hot line' mentioned above (p. 129). It also acted as a stimulus to people all over the world to press for disarmament and arms control.

THE USA, THE USSR AND THE COLD WAR 13
13.6 Key historical terms

Important terms include *arms control* (p. 130), *coexistence* (p. 129), *Cold War* (p. 122), *detente* (p. 129), *disarmament* (p. 196), *guerrilla warfare* (p. 107), *Iron Curtain* (p. 124) and *satellite* (p. 122).

THE USA, THE USSR AND THE COLD WAR 13
13.7 Questions

Evidence question

Study Sources A and B, and then answer questions (i) to (iv) which follow.

Source A: from a document prepared by a secret conference of communist leaders in South Vietnam, 1971:

> The General Offensive and Uprising initiated in early spring of 1968 brought serious defeat to the limited war strategy of the US imperialists and forced them to halt their sabotage of North Vietnam, accept the four-sided Paris Conference and *de-escalate* the South Vietnam war.
>
> Although they were on the defensive and defeated, the US imperialists continued to display their obstinacy by resorting to the Vietnamisation plan. The main objectives of this strategy were to increase *pacification activities* . . . consolidate the puppet government . . . and facilitate a gradual troop withdrawal.

de-escalate: reduce/scale down
pacification activities: attempts to stop the fighting in certain parts of South Vietnam by putting an end to guerrilla activity

Source B: from an Address to the Nation given by the US President Richard Nixon in 1972:

> There is only one way to stop the killing. That is to keep the weapons of war out of the hands of the international outlaws of North Vietnam . . . I

therefore concluded that *Hanoi* must be denied the weapons and supplies it needs to continue the aggression. In full coordination with the Republic of Vietnam, I have ordered the following which are being implemented as I am speaking to you.

All entrances to North Vietnamese ports will be mined . . . Rail and all other communications will be cut off . . . Air and naval strikes against military targets in North Vietnam will continue.

Hanoi: the capital of North Vietnam

(i) Using both the sources and your own knowledge, explain in your own words what is meant by each of the following:
The General Offensive and Uprising (Source A);
the Paris Conference (Source A);
Vietnamisation (Source A);
the Republic of Vietnam (Source B).

(ii) What do you learn from Source A about the attitudes of its authors? Refer to the source in support of your answer. (4)

(iii) What do you learn from Source B about Nixon's attitude towards the government of North Vietnam? Refer to the source in support of your answer. (4)

(iv) To what extent do Sources A and B (a) contradict each other and (b) support each other? Explain your answer. (4)

COLONIALISM AND ITS AFTERMATH: AN INTRODUCTION 14

All GCSE world history syllabuses include the study of what is called *decolonisation*. This is the process by which, during the twentieth century, former colonies of European powers have freed themselves from European rule and become independent states. Chapters 15 and 16 look at decolonisation and its consequences in Asia and Africa, the continents where most European colonies were to be found at the beginning of the twentieth century. This introductory chapter looks in general terms at:

(a) the nature of colonial rule
(b) why decolonisation came about
(c) what decolonisation involved
(d) how former colonies have developed since independence.

Even if you are only studying events in one former colony, it is still important to read this chapter as it will help to explain the background to these events.

COLONIALISM AND ITS AFTERMATH: AN INTRODUCTION 14

14.1 Colonialism

At the beginning of the twentieth century most of Africa and large parts of Asia were under European control. You can see these colonies on the maps on p. 144 and p. 151. In addition there were many European colonies in both the West Indies and the Pacific.

Some of these colonies had been under European rule for centuries, in some cases since the European 'voyages of discovery' in the fifteenth and sixteenth centuries. Many had been acquired during the nineteenth century when there had been a rapid expansion of Europe's overseas empires.

Europeans ruled their colonies in different ways. The French, for example, tended to rule their colonies *directly* and to try and impose French customs on the people they ruled. By contrast the British often preferred to leave some power to local rulers (such as the Indian princes) and thus to rule more *indirectly*. Even within one empire the nature of European rule might vary from one colony to another, depending on the circumstances. The British, for example, treated differently colonies in which there were large numbers of European settlers. By the beginning of the twentieth century most British colonies with large numbers of white settlers were already self-governing *Dominions* within the British empire. These included Australia, New Zealand, Canada and South Africa.

At the beginning of the twentieth century few Europeans imagined that their colonies would ever become independent. Although the British had granted self-government to white settlers in colonies such as Australia, non-Europeans were thought to be incapable of governing themselves.

COLONIALISM AND ITS AFTERMATH: AN INTRODUCTION
14.2 Why did decolonisation take place? 14

Europeans were soon to be proved wrong. As the century advanced, pressures for decolonisation increased. By the end of the 1940s most of Europe's Asian colonies had gained their independence. During the 1950s and 1960s colonies in Africa followed suit. Why did this happen? These are some reasons that apply to most colonies:

1 **The effects of two world wars** The two world wars speeded up decolonisation in these ways:

(a) because of their *financial and economic effects on Europe.* Partly because of the world wars, European countries lacked the resources to continue ruling their colonies – especially in the face of growing opposition to colonial rule. This, for example, was an important factor in persuading the British to leave India in 1947 and the Dutch to leave the East Indies (Indonesia) in 1949.

(b) because they helped to spread *ideas that challenged European rule.* In the First World War Britain and France claimed to be fighting for democracy. In the Second World War Britain and its allies talked a great deal about freedom and human rights. Colonial peoples began to ask why all these rights did not also belong to them.

(c) because in the Second World War many European powers either suffered occupation at the hands of the Germans or lost their Asian colonies to the Japanese (see Chapters 8 and 10). Occupied countries such as France and the Netherlands found it difficult to resume control of their colonies once the war had ended. Japan's victories also showed how Europeans could be defeated at the hands of non-Europeans.

(d) because Europeans were forced, during wartime, to make promises in order to keep the support of their colonial peoples; for example, the British promised to give India its independence at the end of the Second World War.

2 **Social and economic developments**

(a) *Education* Some people in the colonies were able to receive a European education. It was often these people who led independence movements. Their education had helped to give them the confidence to challenge European rule.

(b) *European languages* Many colonies consisted of large numbers of different peoples all speaking different languages. The spread of a common European language made it easier for colonial peoples to work together to overthrow European rule.

(c) *Improvements in communications* European rule often meant improved communications, e.g. roads, railways, steamships and (eventually) aeroplanes. This brought different groups of people into contact with each other, encouraging them to think in terms of the country or nation as a whole (e.g. Nigeria) instead of just the tribe.

(d) *Expanding trade* Trade between colonies and their mother country often grew rapidly during the first half of the twentieth century. A few colonies also began to develop industries of their own. These developments encouraged the growth of ports and cities. They also sometimes created a new middle-class group of merchants, bankers and manufacturers. It was often in these cities and among this middle-class group that independence movements first began.

3 The rise of the USA and the USSR The influence of these superpowers increased enormously after the Second World War (see Chapter 13). In the case of both countries, this influence helped to speed up the process of decolonisation. The USSR gave very little practical help to most independence movements, but encouraged them by repeatedly condemning colonialism. According to Marxists, colonialism was simply a *capitalist* trick to obtain cheap raw materials and safe markets for European exports. The USA was also often unsympathetic to European rule, seeing itself as a champion of freedom. Its governments feared that if European powers denied them their independence colonial peoples would turn to communism instead. The USA also stood to gain economically (e.g. by increased trade) from the collapse of the European empires.

4 Imitation Decolonisation in one part of the world often had a big influence on other parts of the world; for example, the achievement of Indian independence in 1947 greatly encouraged nationalist groups in Africa. As more and more countries became independent, the pressure on European powers to withdraw became difficult to resist.

COLONIALISM AND ITS AFTERMATH: AN INTRODUCTION

14.3 How the transfer of power came about

14

Decolonisation took place in many different ways. These are some of the major differences:

(i) In some colonies the transfer of power was sudden, with very little preparation for independence. This was the case in the Belgian Congo, which obtained its independence in 1960 (pp. 156–57). By contrast in many of Britain's African colonies independence was preceded by a period of self-government, which prepared people in the colony for full independence.

(ii) In many colonies independence was achieved without violence. The European power agreed to withdraw, for many of the reasons mentioned earlier in this chapter, without actually being forced to do so. This is what happened in most of Britain's colonies and in France's colonies in west Africa. Elsewhere independence only came after years of armed struggle. This was the case in French Algeria and Indo-China (pp. 156–157) and in all of Portugal's African colonies (p. 157).

(iii) In most colonies independence was achieved without the colony breaking up into a number of different states. In some cases, however, there were major conflicts within the colony which led to a *partition*. This is what happened in British India (divided into India and Pakistan in 1947) and in French Vietnam (divided in 1954 into North Vietnam and South Vietnam).

COLONIALISM AND ITS AFTERMATH: AN INTRODUCTION 14

14.4 Developments since independence

The newly independent states of Asia, Africa and the Caribbean have developed in many different ways. It is not possible to produce a list of developments since independence that would apply to all of them. These, however, are some of the main features to look out for when studying developments in these former colonies:

1 National pride Many newly independent countries were very pleased to be able to govern themselves after years of foreign rule. People in these countries may not always have been better off in terms of standards of living. They may also have disliked some features of their new governments. Most, however, did not regret the ending of colonial rule.

2 Continuing European influences Many countries since independence have been strongly influenced by the way in which they developed in colonial times. European languages were still spoken (e.g. French in west Africa). European political systems continued to be used (e.g. *parliamentary government* in India). Education was still often based, as in many former French colonies, on what happened in colonial times. Economic links with the former mother country were often very strong. In many cases there were also political links through groupings of states such as the *British Commonwealth*, an informal organisation of former British colonies with the British monarch at its head.

3 Conflicts within newly independent states Many colonies had very artificial boundaries that had been drawn up for the convenience of European powers. This often meant that a colony contained a number of different peoples or tribes. It also meant that frontiers sometimes passed through the middle of a tribe's territories, leaving members of the same tribe in two or more different states. After independence this sometimes led to conflicts between different tribes within a state. It also led to border disputes between neighbouring states. You can read about some of these conflicts (e.g. the civil war in Nigeria) in Chapters 15 and 16.

4 Economic developments Former colonies have developed economically in very different ways. Most of these states have tried to *industrialise* (p. 45) and *modernise* (p. 196) their economies, with varying degrees of success. Many have remained what is sometimes called 'under-developed', i.e. largely dependent on agriculture, with few industries and a low standard of living. The problems of poverty and 'under-development' are discussed in Chapter 19.

COLONIALISM AND ITS AFTERMATH: AN INTRODUCTION
14.5 Key historical terms 14

Key terms for this chapter include *capitalist* (p. 195), *colonialism* (p. 195), *decolonisation* (p. 195), *Dominion* (p. 196), *industrialisation* (p. 45), *modernisation* (p. 196), *partition* (p. 196), *parliamentary government* (p. 64), and *under-developed* (p. 187).

COLONIALISM AND ITS AFTERMATH: AN INTRODUCTION
14.6 Questions 14

Essay questions

(i) During the 1940s, 1950s and 1960s most European colonies in Asia and Africa obtained their independence. Reasons why they did so at this time include: the impact of the Second World War; the spread of European political ideas; economic changes within the colonies.

Using these and other reasons, explain why European powers lost their colonies during these years. Illustrate your answer by reference to at least *two* specific colonies. (20)

(ii) Choose *two* colonies that became independent during the 1940s, 1950s and 1960s. Describe the circumstances that led to the achievement of independence in *each* of these colonies. What similarities and/or differences do you notice in the way that these two colonies became independent? (20)

COLONIALISM AND ITS AFTERMATH: ASIA 15

This chapter is mainly concerned with how the Indian subcontinent became independent and how it developed after independence. It is this aspect of decolonisation in Asia that is most frequently studied in GCSE syllabuses. The final part of the chapter looks briefly at decolonisation in other parts of Asia. This chapter should be studied in conjunction with Chapter 14, which examines some of the general reasons why decolonisation took place.

15.1 British India at the beginning of the twentieth century 15

India at the beginning of the century was a vast country with almost as many inhabitants as the whole of Europe put together. These inhabitants were of many different races and religions. Most were Hindus, a religion that divided people into different *castes* or groups. Over one hundred million, however, belonged to other religions, i.e. were *Muslims* (p. 170), Sikhs, Buddhists, Christians, etc. The largest of these other religious groups was the Muslims.

Although India possessed some large and splendid cities, as well as developing industries, most Indians lived in the countryside and worked as farmers. Most were very poor.

British rule in India dated back to the seventeenth and eighteenth centuries. In the early twentieth century India was the largest and most valuable of Britain's overseas possessions. 60% of the country was ruled directly by Britain, through a Viceroy, the British army stationed in India, and the British-staffed Indian Civil Service. The remaining 40% was ruled indirectly by Indian princes who were allies of the British and who received guidance from a British Resident appointed by the Viceroy.

15.2 The growth of Indian nationalism 15

British rule had brought some benefits to the Indians, e.g. improved communications, education and medical care. Indians, however, were treated as inferiors and prevented from having a major say in how their country was governed. As early as 1885 Indian *nationalists* (p. 148) had organised themselves into the *Indian Congress*, an organisation run by wealthy Hindus. The Congress movement demanded greater participation in government. Its impact, however, remained limited until after the First World War.

Amritsar, 1919

Over a million Indians served in the British army during the First World War. Many resented the fact that the British, who preached freedom and democracy in Europe, practised something very different in their own country. Protests and demonstrations took place. At Amritsar in April 1919 British troops opened fire on a political meeting of unarmed civilians, killing almost 400 and wounding 1000. A wave of protest against this 'massacre' swept across India.

Dyarchy

In order to reduce discontent, the British government decided to make some concessions. *The Government of India Act of 1919* set up a new system of administration known as a *dyarchy* (a government of two rulers). Power was to be shared between British officials and assemblies elected by the Indian people. There was to be a national assembly in the capital Delhi, together with provincial assemblies in each of India's provinces. The new system gave a few Indians some experience of government. Most Indians, however, were not allowed to vote. British officials also continued to make all important decisions. Congress was not satisfied and agitation therefore continued.

Gandhi

Mohandas (Mahatma) Gandhi played a major part in the growth of Indian nationalism during the interwar years. It was largely as a result of his efforts that the Indian Congress was transformed into a powerful mass movement. Gandhi's aim was independence. His method was *non-violent passive resistance* (or *satyagraha*). He was totally opposed to the use of force, even against those who used force themselves.

Satyagraha could take many forms, for instance refusing to cooperate with British officials and boycotting British goods. Gandhi encouraged Indians to spin and weave their own clothes so that they would not need to buy imported machine-made clothes from Britain. In the early 1930s he also led a protest against the British government's salt tax by encouraging Indians to make their own salt.

Britain's response

The British government responded to Gandhi's actions in various ways. Gandhi and other Congress leaders were sentenced to prison on a number of occasions. This, however, failed to stop the protests. By the early 1930s Britain was prepared to discuss ways in which India might move towards greater self-government. It recognised that it had to negotiate with the

Indian Congress, inviting Gandhi to take part in *Round-Table conferences in London in 1931 and 1932*. One result of these meetings was a new *Government of India Act* passed in *1935*. This Act gave much more power to both the national and provincial assemblies set up by the 1919 Act (see above). After the election of new provincial assemblies in 1937, most local government was now in Indian hands. Gandhi as a result agreed to call off his campaign of passive resistance.

COLONIALISM AND ITS AFTERMATH: ASIA 15
15.3 Independence and partition

The Second World War had a major impact on India. The Viceroy proclaimed India to be at war without consulting the assemblies or the Congress leaders. This caused widespread resentment, many Indian-controlled provincial governments resigning in protest. After Japan entered the war in December 1941 (p. 97) India was much more directly affected. Having defeated the British in Malaya, Japanese forces invaded Burma and by the spring of 1942 were threatening India's eastern borders. Japanese propaganda also encouraged Indians to join them in driving out the British.

Britain's weakness gave Gandhi an opportunity to launch another campaign of passive resistance designed to force the British to 'Quit India'. The British authorities responded by arresting all the Congress leaders as well as many other nationalists. Most remained in prison for the rest of the war. Britain's action put an end to further campaigns of mass disobedience.

One effect of the arrest of the Congress leaders was to strengthen the position of the *Muslim League*, an organisation that had been set up to defend the interests of India's large Muslim minority. Its leader Mohammed Ali Jinnah demanded that India's Muslims should be allowed to establish a separate state free from Hindu control.

The Second World War made it likely that the British would withdraw from India in the near future. Britain lacked the resources to hold down an increasingly resentful population. Britain's postwar Labour government was also sympathetic to the claims of Indian nationalists. There was disagreement, however, about the form that independence would take, i.e. whether India should be one state or two.

A new Viceroy, Lord Louis Mountbatten, was sent out to India in 1947 to arrange the transfer of power. Mountbatten decided that *partition* was the only solution and managed to persuade the Congress leaders to accept this. After the boundaries between the new states had been settled, *independence was finally achieved in August 1947*. Two new states were formed: India and Pakistan. As you can see on the map on p. 144, Pakistan was divided into two parts separated by a thousand miles.

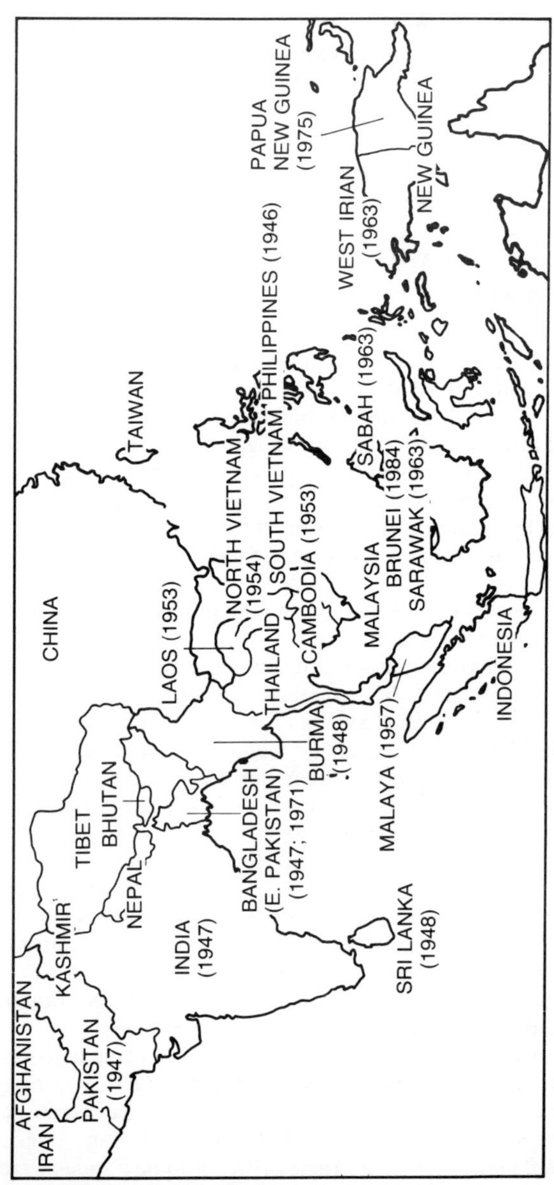

Independence in Asia (showing dates when countries became independent)

Partition was accompanied by a great deal of violence. Hindus and Muslims were intermingled in many parts of the country and partition left many on the 'wrong' side of the frontier. A vast movement of population took place in 1947, in the course of which terrible atrocities were committed on both sides. One of the victims of the violence was Gandhi, assassinated by an extremist Hindu.

COLONIALISM AND ITS AFTERMATH: ASIA 15
15.4 India since independence

Jawaharlal Nehru

India's first Prime Minister was *Jawaharlal Nehru*, the leader of the Congress party in the national assembly. Nehru came from a wealthy Hindu family and had received his education in England. As an opponent of British rule he had spent 14 years in prison. Despite this, he had a great admiration for Britain's system of *parliamentary government* (p. 64) and was keen to establish this form of government in an independent India. At the same time he was also very impressed by the economic achievements of the USSR under Stalin. His aim was to *modernise* and *industrialise* India as Stalin had done in the USSR, but without Stalin's brutal dictatorship (see Chapter 4).

Nehru's main aims were:

(a) The rapid development of heavy industry and power supplies.
(b) The use of the wealth that this produced to tackle India's social problems, e.g. *illiteracy* and poor health care.
(c) The improvement of agriculture in order to feed the country's rapidly growing population.

Nehru's method was the Five-Year Plan, an idea borrowed from the USSR (p. 41). These plans involved close government control of the economy and the nationalisation of many industries. They were therefore to some extent *socialist*. Much industry, however, remained in private hands, as did the lands of the peasants.

The Five-Year Plans achieved a large increase in both agricultural and industrial production during the 1950s and early 1960s. They were hampered, however, by the continuing rise in India's population. Nehru's attempt to tackle this through a programme of birth control met with only limited success.

India after Nehru

Nehru's family has continued to rule India, with only brief interruptions, throughout the period since his death in 1964. Apart from a brief spell out of office in 1977–80, his daughter *Indira Gandhi* ruled the country from 1966 until her death (at the hands of Sikh extremists) in 1984. Indira Gandhi on the whole continued her father's policies, though was sometimes more socialist in her views. Faced with increasing problems in the early 1970s she also resorted for a time to dictatorial powers, something that caused great resentment among the many Indians who were keen not to weaken the system of parliamentary government that the country had inherited from the British. After her death in 1984 power passed to her son *Rajiv Gandhi*.

COLONIALISM AND ITS AFTERMATH: ASIA 15
15.5 India's relations with neighbouring states

Both Nehru and Indira Gandhi adopted a policy of *non-alignment*, that is a refusal to commit India to either side in the Cold War between the USA and the USSR. The Indian government was prepared to receive financial aid from whatever source was willing to provide it, whether this was the USA, the USSR, the United Nations or the British Commonwealth.

India's main conflicts have been with its neighbour *Pakistan*. Border disputes in the Rann of Kutch area led to actual fighting in 1965. There have also been disputes over joint use of the waters of the River Indus. Even more serious was the situation in *Kashmir*, a state situated between the two countries with a Hindu ruler and a largely Muslim population. Fighting in this area in 1947–48 led to the division of Kashmir between the two countries with UN troops trying to hold a cease-fire line between the two.

COLONIALISM AND ITS AFTERMATH: ASIA 15
15.6 Pakistan and Bangladesh

Pakistan was less successful than India in establishing a stable form of government after independence. There were frequent changes of government during the 1950s, followed by a long period of *autocratic* military government between the late 1950s and the early 1970s. Economic policies were similar to those in India, though foreign policies were pro-western.

One of Pakistan's major problems was relations between the two parts of the country. *East Pakistan* had suffered economically from partition, losing its close economic links with neighbouring parts of India. There was also a widespread feeling in the province that the new state was run in the interests of West Pakistan. These resentments led in the late 1960s to growing support for *Sheikh Mujibur Rahman's campaign for a self-governing East*

Pakistan. Civil war broke out in 1971 between the Pakistani army and the Mukti Bahini fighters of Mujibur's Awami League. The Pakistani government was convinced that India was behind all these disturbances and fighting soon broke out between the two armies, both in the east and the west. Indian troops eventually moved into East Pakistan, linking forces with Mujibur to secure the defeat of the Pakistani army. A new state of *Bangladesh* was created, with Mujibur as its first Prime Minister.

The history of Bangladesh since independence has been a troubled one, with enormous problems of poverty and over-population. Democracy proved short-lived when Mujibur assumed dictatorial powers in 1974 only to be overthrown the following year in a military *coup.* After a period of democracy under Bhutto during the 1970s, Pakistan also experienced a long period of military rule.

The differences between the development of India and Pakistan since independence are striking, as indeed are some of the similarities. They are not always easy to explain. It is a useful exercise to think of possible reasons why these countries have developed in such different ways.

COLONIALISM AND ITS AFTERMATH: ASIA 15

15.7 Decolonisation elsewhere in Asia

At the same time as granting independence to India and Pakistan, Britain also withdrew from *Ceylon* (Sri Lanka) and Burma. Ceylon joined the Commonwealth, like India and Pakistan. Burma, however, chose to break its links with Britain altogether. Britain's remaining possessions in *Malaya* and *Borneo* did not receive their independence until much later, partly because of a communist guerrilla revolt that the British wished to suppress before withdrawal. Malaya became independent in 1957 and was joined by Sabah (North Borneo) and Sarawak in 1963 to form the *Federation of Malaysia.* The creation of this federation led to great resentment in neighbouring Indonesia, which launched a war against Malaysia which continued intermittently during the years 1963–66.

France and the Netherlands both found it difficult to resume control of their Asian colonies after 1945. Perhaps because of their humiliation by the Germans in the Second World War, both states were much more reluctant than the British to agree to give up their power. However, the Dutch were unable, with limited resources, to hold down a hostile population, finally granting independence to their colonies in the *East Indies* (now *Indonesia*) in 1949. The French struggled for longer in *Indo-China*, though were finally defeated after the capture of their fortress at Dien Bien Phu in 1954.

15.8 Key historical terms

Nationalists This term has already been defined on p. 56. Its meaning in this chapter, however, is slightly different. It still means being devoted to one's country and believing that its interests come first. Applied to colonial peoples it mainly refers to their strugglee to free themselves from foreign rule. Nationalists in this sense are people opposed to colonialism and in favour of independence.

Other key terms in this chapter include *autocratic* (p. 195), *coup* (p. 195), *dyarchy* (p. 142), *federation* (p. 180), *illiteracy* (p. 196), *industrialisation* (p. 45), *Muslim* (p. 170), *parliamentary government* (p. 64), *partition* (p. 196), *satyagraha* (p. 142), *socialism* (p. 197).

15.9 Questions

Source-based questions

Study the cartoon opposite, first published in the British magazine *Punch* in 1930, and then answer the following questions. The standing figure represents a *genie*, i.e. an imaginary spirit that Gandhi is supposed to have conjured up.

(i) Explain in your own words what is meant by *civil disobedience*. (2)
(ii) Explain what the cartoonist means by describing the standing figure as *A Frankenstein of the East*. (2)
(iii) What does the cartoon suggest about Gandhi's lifestyle? Why did Gandhi try to live in this way? Give reasons for your answer. (3)
(iv) Write a paragraph describing Gandhi's aims and methods during the interwar years. (5)
(v) Write one or two sentences describing the ways in which, during the 1930s, the British government responded to Gandhi's protest movement. (3)

Essay question

During the 1920s and 1930s the Congress movement in India turned into a powerful mass movement that the British government was unable to ignore.

Give reasons (i) why the Congress movement turned into a mass movement and (ii) why the British government was unable to ignore it. (15)

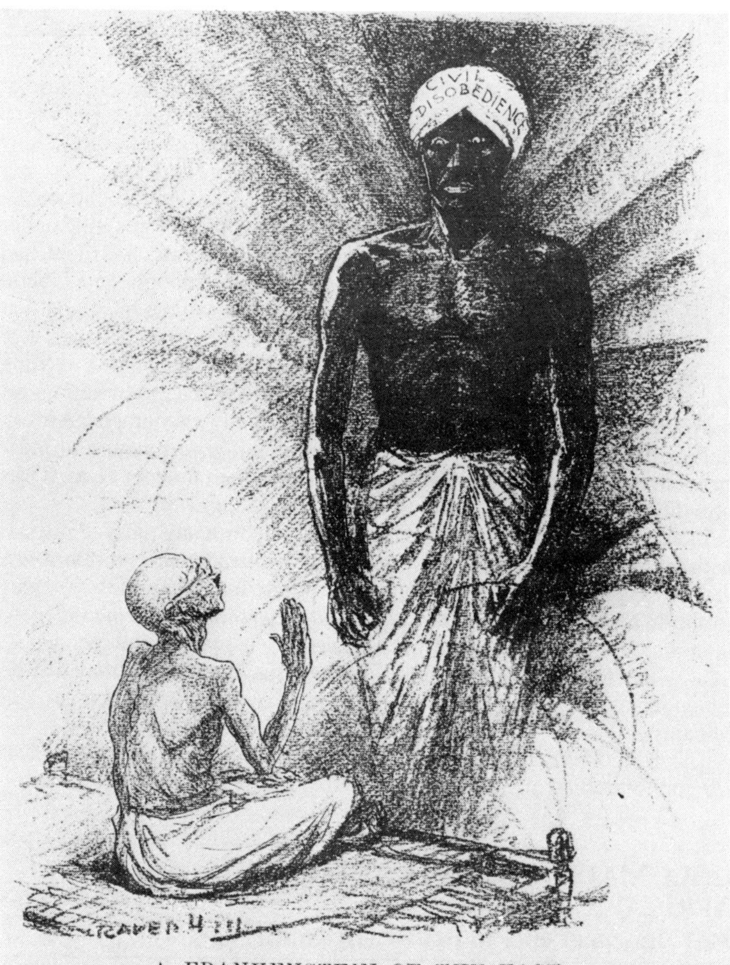
CIVIL DISOBEDIENCE
A FRANKENSTEIN OF THE EAST.
GANDHI. "REMEMBER—NO VIOLENCE; JUST DISOBEDIENCE."
GENIE. "AND WHAT IF I DISOBEY *YOU*?"

COLONIALISM AND ITS AFTERMATH: AFRICA 16

This chapter looks at how *decolonisation* came about in certain parts of Africa. In reading this chapter keep on referring back to Chapter 14 which examines some of the general reasons why decolonisation took place. Many of these apply to the African states you will be reading about.

Decolonisation came later to Africa than to Asia. At the end of the Second World War almost the whole of the continent was still under European rule. The only exceptions were Egypt (to which Britain had granted independence after the First World War), Ethiopia and Liberia (both independent states with African rulers). Few people imagined that Europeans would hand over power in the near future.

Chapter 14 tells you about some of the pressures that helped to bring about decolonisation. A powerful influence was the success of nationalist movements in Asia (see Chapter 15). This greatly encouraged African nationalists to persevere in their struggle for self-government and independence. Once a few African colonies achieved their independence it was also difficult to withhold it from others.

In the end, decolonisation came very rapidly to many parts of Africa, with large numbers of states achieving their independence within a few years of each other (see map opposite). By the mid-1960s most colonies formerly belonging to Britain, France and Belgium had become independent. Portugal's colonies were much slower to achieve their independence, as was the former British colony of Rhodesia, for reasons that will be examined later in this chapter. One part of Africa, South Africa, still remains under white minority rule.

The rest of this chapter concentrates on those parts of Africa most commonly studied in GCSE World History syllabuses.

COLONIALISM AND ITS AFTERMATH: AFRICA 16
16.1 Independence in British Africa: (i) Nigeria

Nigeria was the largest British colony in west Africa, though not the first to obtain independence. A nationalist movement had developed since the Second World War. Many of its leaders were Nigerians who had received a higher education in Britain, but who had been prevented on their return to Nigeria from taking part in the government of their country. Britain's decision in 1957 to grant independence to the Gold Coast (Ghana), another of its west African colonies, made it difficult to justify withholding independence from Nigeria.

By 1960 the British government had come to recognise the strength of

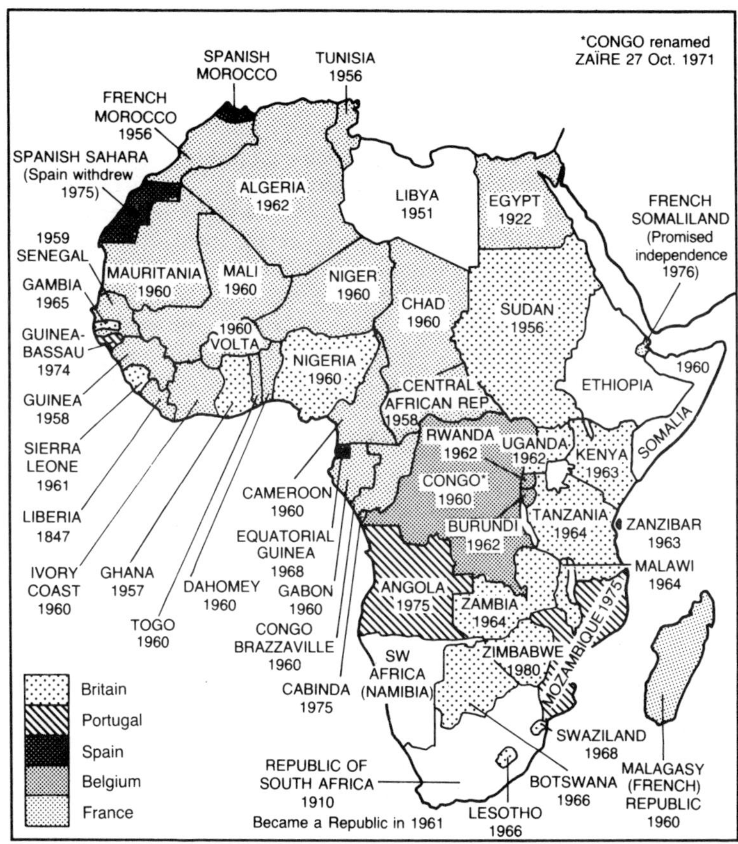

Independence in Africa

nationalist feeling all over Africa. It began to make preparations to hand over power in almost all of its colonies. A very important speech in that year by the British Prime Minister Harold Macmillan, in which he talked about the '*wind of change blowing through the continent*', signalled Britain's decision to withdraw. The British government felt that if they did not withdraw quickly there would be conflict and bloodshed, as in French Algeria (p. 156). By agreeing to leave they hoped that the new states would remain friendly towards Britain and continue as members of the *British Commonwealth* (p. 139).

Nigeria became independent in 1960, becoming a *republic* within the Commonwealth three years later. The *constitution* of the new state, drafted by the British, created a *parliamentary democracy*. It also established a *federal* (p. 180) system of government, with separate governments in each of the three main regions (the North, West and East) under the general authority of a federal Prime Minister based in Lagos, the capital.

Divisions within Nigeria

The 1960s were a very disturbed period in the history of the newly independent state. One of the main reasons for this was the existence of *strong tribal divisions* within the country. Like many former colonies, Nigeria was a very artificial state whose boundaries paid little attention to tribal groupings. The main divisions within Nigeria were (a) between the three main tribal groups, the Hausa (situated in the north), the Yoruba (situated in the south-west), and the Ibo (situated in the south-east), and (b) between members of the country's main religions, *Islam* (largely in the north) and Christianity. There were also growing differences in wealth, e.g. between the poorer northern regions and the more prosperous south-east with its recently discovered oil deposits.

The Nigerian civil war, 1967–70

These many divisions helped to create an increasingly tense political situation which eventually led in 1966 to a military *coup* and in 1967–70 to a full-scale civil war. In 1966 a group of Ibo military officers, headed by General Ironsi, seized power in a bloody *coup* and attempted to create a strong unitary state (i.e. a state with a strong central government) under Ibo control. This led to bitter resentment, especially in the north where people retaliated by massacring large numbers of Ibos. The northern regions threatened to secede (withdraw) altogether from Nigeria and to form a separate state. Ironsi was then overthrown by another military leader *General Gowon*, who in a desperate attempt to keep the country together, proposed a new kind of federal state with twelve rather than four divisions. This was rejected by the Ibos, many of whom were now fearful about their future within Nigeria. The Ibo leader *General Ojukwu* proclaimed the independence of the eastern region in 1967, giving the new state the name of *Biafra*.

Ojukwu's action led to a bitter civil war which lasted until 1970. Gowon was determined to maintain the unity of Nigeria and had far greater resources at his disposal. Ojukwu, however, was an able leader who fought hard, despite increasing losses and appalling starvation among his people. Biafra's eventual defeat proved very costly for all concerned, with terrible suffering among the Ibos, the deaths of many Nigerian soldiers, and heavy financial costs. The civil war also increased the already considerable size and influence of the armed forces.

Gowon after 1970 tried hard to re-unite the country as well as to secure fair treatment for the Ibos. He also presided over rapid economic development during the early 1970s, Nigeria becoming Africa's leading oil-exporting country. He ruled until 1975, when he was overthrown in a military coup.

Nigeria continued to be under military rule until 1979 when power was transferred to a civilian government. At the same time the country was re-organised into a new kind of federal state similar to the USA (see p. 180). Nigeria was divided into 19 states, each with a certain degree of independence to run its own affairs. This, it was hoped, would satisfy the demands of the country's many different tribal and religious groups.

COLONIALISM AND ITS AFTERMATH: AFRICA

16.2 Independence in British Africa: (ii) Rhodesia/Zimbabwe

16

Find Southern Rhodesia (now Zimbabwe) on the map on p. 151. The development of this British colony during the first half of the twentieth century was very different from that of Britain's other African colonies. The main reason for this was the presence in Southern Rhodesia of a substantial minority of white settlers. Since 1923 the colony had been ruled under a *constitution* which gave it a considerable degree of self-government. Power, however, rested entirely in the hands of the white minority.

The Central African Federation, 1953–63

By the early 1950s the British government was beginning to think of ways of reducing the burden of ruling its vast territories in Africa. It was also considering moves towards self-government for some of its colonies. In east Africa, as in the British West Indies, one way of achieving these two aims seemed to be to group a number of neighbouring states into a larger unit or *federation*. In 1953 Britain therefore set up the *Central African Federation*, consisting of Southern Rhodesia, Northern Rhodesia and Nyasaland. Each colony continued to have its own government, but all were now under the overall control of a federal government based in Salisbury, the capital of Southern Rhodesia. The right to vote, both in federal and in local elections, was confined to people with a certain amount of wealth and with certain educational qualifications. This meant that power continued to be held by the whites. The Federation thus strengthened the position of Southern Rhodesian whites who now controlled both their own colony and the federal government.

The Federation may have been popular with most whites. It was certainly, however, very unpopular with many blacks. They feared that rule by white settlers would now be extended into Northern Rhodesia and Nyasaland as well. Able black opposition leaders such as Kenneth Kaunda in Northern Rhodesia and Joshua Nkomo in Southern Rhodesia rose to prominence. They demanded the disbanding of the Federation and the granting of independence to its various parts. Aware of the strength of black feeling, the British government began to make preparations for the transfer of power. As a first step the Federation came to an end in 1963. At the same time Northern Rhodesia and Nyasaland were given self-government. Elections were held under a system of universal suffrage (i.e. each adult to have one vote) and in 1964 both colonies became fully independent under black governments. Northern Rhodesia changed its name to Zambia and Nyasaland changed its name to Malawi.

Rhodesia's Unilateral Declaration of Independence (UDI)

Most whites in Southern Rhodesia were strongly opposed to Britain's decision to withdraw from its colonies. Many felt that they had been betrayed by the British government. More and more gave their support during the early 1960s to the Rhodesia Front, a new party led by *Ian Smith*, that was determined to hold on to white minority rule. They were only prepared to consider independence on condition that the whites retained power. Britain, however, would not grant independence without black majority rule. Seeing that Britain was not going to give way to his demands, Smith in 1965 made a Unilateral (i.e. one-sided) Declaration of Independence. In the eyes of Smith and his supporters Rhodesia (as it was now called) was a fully independent state with no further connection with Britain.

Britain refused to accept Rhodesia's independence, but was unwilling to attempt to recover control by force. It tried instead to undermine Smith's regime by imposing *economic sanctions*. These, however, were largely a failure, mainly because two of Rhodesia's neighbours, South Africa and Portuguese Mozambique (see map on p. 151), were sympathetic to its government and allowed the country to maintain its economic links with the rest of the world. There were a number of meetings between Smith and the British government, in an attempt to settle the dispute, but all failed to reach any agreement because of the fundamental difference of opinion about black majority rule.

Within Rhodesia Smith's government strengthened the position of the white minority. The country was divided into white and black areas, with the blacks receiving the poorest land. All opposition to the regime was firmly dealt with. African political organisations were banned and many of their leaders detained without trial. There was censorship of the press.

Why and how Rhodesia became Zimbabwe

Despite firm government and the failure of sanctions, Smith's regime did not survive into the 1980s. These are some of the reasons:

1 Increasing pressure from black political organisations campaigning for black majority rule. *Groups of black guerrillas*, often based in neighbouring states, carried out more and more attacks on Rhodesian targets. There were two main groups opposed to the government: the Zimbabwe African People's Union (ZAPU) led by Joshua Nkomo and the Zimbabwe African National Union (ZANU) led by Robert Mugabe and Ndabaningi Sithole. In the late 1970s the two groups came together in a Patriotic Front.
2 Black opponents of the regime received *aid and encouragement from some neighbouring black states* such as Zambia and Tanzania.
3 The fall of the Portuguese empire in Africa (p. 157) led in 1975 to the *establishment of a Marxist government in Mozambique.* This deprived Smith of one of his main allies and gave the guerrillas a further useful base from which to attack Rhodesia.
4 The guerrilla war imposed a great strain on Rhodesia's resources. *The small size of the white population* – approximately 250,000 – made it unlikely that Smith would be able to hold off his opponents indefinitely. Fears for the future led more and more whites to leave the country altogether during the 1970s.
5 Even Smith's most important ally, South Africa, began to be less enthusiastic about supporting his regime. The South African government came to feel that a moderate black regime might be an easier neighbour than a country racked by warfare. It was encouraged in this attitude by the USA which feared the establishment of another Marxist state in this part of Africa.

By 1979 Smith therefore had worked out a plan for the transfer to black majority rule. As a result of elections in that year he handed over power to a moderate African leader, Bishop Abel Muzorewa, though continuing himself as a member of Muzorewa's cabinet. The Patriotic Front refused to accept the results of these elections, claiming that they had not been fairly conducted. Further negotiations took place, as a result of which the Rhodesian government finally agreed to hand over power in December 1979. *Britain briefly resumed control* of the country in order to conduct elections for the government of a new state of Zimbabwe. These were held in February 1980 and resulted in a large majority for Robert Mugabe and his ZANU organisation. Two months later the *independent state of Zimbabwe* was proclaimed.

Zimbabwe since independence

Like Nigeria, Zimbabwe has suffered since independence from the effects of tribal divisions. One reason why Mugabe won the 1980 elections was that his party was based to a large extent on the Shona-speaking peoples who form a majority of Zimbabwe's population. The minority Matabele tribe, who supported Nkomo and the rival ZAPU organisation, were unhappy about Mugabe's victory. They were particularly concerned by Mugabe's determination to turn Zimbabwe into a one-party state. Conflicts developed and in the mid-1980s there were many allegations, some of them substantiated, of terrible atrocities against the Matabele people. In other ways Mugabe has shown himself to be a cautious ruler, trying to unite his country and to maintain friendly relations with many different powers.

COLONIALISM AND ITS AFTERMATH: AFRICA 16
16.3 Independence in French Africa

Most of France's large African empire (see map on p. 151) achieved independence in 1960, in which year fifteen independent states were created out of former French Equatorial and French West Africa. France's unsuccessful struggle to hold on to its Asian colonies (p. 147) had shown how difficult it was to deny independence to nationalist groups determined to acquire it.

In Africa the transfer of power in France's colonies was mostly peaceful. The one exception was *Algeria*, which had a well-established white population of approximately one million. These *colons* (white settlers) were strongly opposed to any move towards independence. During the 1950s the French government was engaged in a bitter war against the FLN (the Front for National Liberation), an organisation of Algerian nationalists fighting for their independence. As in Indo-China the French government found it impossible to defeat a determined and organised nationalist movement. The often violent opposition of the colons, who had many supporters in the French army, also made it difficult just to withdraw. Eventually a new French government, headed by General de Gaulle, decided that it had no choice but to transfer power. Despite continuing terrorism from the OAS, the secret army of the colons, Algeria became independent in 1962. Having failed in their attempt to keep an 'Algerie Francaise' (French Algeria), most of the colons now returned to France.

COLONIALISM AND ITS AFTERMATH: AFRICA 16
16.4 Independence in the Congo

The Belgian colony of the Congo received even less preparation for independence than France's colonies in Africa. The decision to transfer power in 1960 was made hastily, with the result that there were virtually no

Congolese with experience of government ready to take charge of the new state. This was particularly disastrous in a country that was so vast and that contained so many different tribes and languages. The result, after independence, was *anarchy* and civil war. You can read on p. 177 how the United Nations intervened to take over the administration of the new state. One of the main problems for the new Congolese government was the *secession* of the province of Katanga, which contained much of the country's mineral wealth. UN forces succeeded in re-uniting the country, withdrawing in 1964 when the country appeared to have begun to settle down. Since 1965 the Congo – renamed *Zaire* – has been under a firm centralised military government headed by *General Mobutu*.

16.5 Independence in Portuguese Africa

Portugal had three colonies in Africa: Angola, Mozambique and Portuguese Guinea (see map on p. 151). It had been the first European power to obtain overseas colonies. It was to be the last to lose them.

Portugal had been ruled since the 1930s by an intensely nationalist right-wing government that was determined not to let go of its colonies. During the 1950s and 1960s, instead of preparing its colonies for self-government (as the British were often doing), the Portuguese government stepped up investment and encouraged emigration. Nationalist feelings, however, spread in all of Portugal's African colonies. Guerrilla movements were formed and Portugal was forced to commit more and more troops and money to try and hold on to its possessions. The strain on a small and poor country eventually proved too great and in 1975, after a change of government in Portugal, all three colonies became independent.

The history of both Angola and Mozambique since independence has been disturbed by internal divisions, both tribal and political. This has been particularly so in Angola where three rival nationalist groups have competed for control. The situation in Angola has been further complicated by the involvement of both Cuba (in support of the Marxist MPLA) and South Africa (in support of UNITA and in pursuit of Namibian guerrillas using southern Angola as a base).

COLONIALISM AND ITS AFTERMATH: AFRICA 16

16.6 South Africa

By the 1980s South Africa was the only part of the African continent still ruled directly by people of European descent. Its history during the twentieth century has been very different from that of any other former European colony. This can be explained by the presence in South Africa of a very large white community. In the early 1980s there were 4.5 million whites in South Africa. Many of these whites can trace their descent from settlers who arrived as long ago as the seventeenth and eighteenth centuries. Unlike whites in some other parts of Africa, South Africa was their only home. They had nowhere else to go. They were thus determined to hold on to *white supremacy* (keeping power in the hands of the whites) at all costs. As you will find out below, their numbers, together with their control of the country's rich mineral resources, have enabled them to do this.

South Africa's peoples

The peoples of South Africa can be divided into the following main groups:

(i) *Afrikaners* (or Boers) These are the descendants of mostly Dutch-speaking settlers who came to South Africa in the seventeenth and eighteenth centuries. They comprise 60% of the total white population. They speak Afrikaans, a language derived from Dutch.
(ii) *English-speaking whites* These are the descendants of British settlers who came to the country after it became a British colony in the early nineteenth century. They comprise 40% of the total white population.
(iii) *People of Asian descent* Most of these are the descendants of Indian labourers brought to the country at the end of the nineteenth century and the beginning of the twentieth century. There are approximately 870,000 of them, most of whom live in the province of Natal.
(iv) *'Coloureds'* These are people of mixed white and black race. Most speak Afrikaans, are Christians and live in Cape Province.
(v) *Blacks* Much the largest group, with a population of 23 million (out of a total South African population of 31 million). They are divided into many different races and languages. Most are Christians.

South Africa 1910–48

During the nineteenth century there had been a great deal of conflict between the British government and the Afrikaners. This had culminated in the Boer War of 1899–1902. After its victory in this war the British government decided to group the various parts of South Africa into a new *Union of South Africa*. This new state became a Dominion of the British Empire in 1910. This meant that in effect it was an independent country, though still recognising the British monarch as head of state.

South Africa's governments after 1910 were entirely white. Despite being led by Afrikaners, relations with Britain were usually good. Given that the two countries had very close economic links, an anti-British policy would have been very damaging to South African interests. Many Afrikaners, however, wished to strengthen even further the position of their own community within South Africa and to sever the remaining links with Britain. After 1933 some of them gave their support to a new right-wing party, the *Afrikaner Nationalist Party* led by *Dr Malan*. When the South African parliament, by a narrow majority, decided in 1939 to join Britain in the Second World War, Malan's Nationalists vigorously opposed this decision. Some even openly sympathised with Nazi Germany.

After the war support for the Nationalists grew. Many South African whites became worried that blacks would begin to rise up and demand their rights, as non-white peoples were doing in Asia and elsewhere. They were therefore attracted by the Nationalist commitment to maintain and strengthen white supremacy. This was the main reason for the Nationalist victory in the general election of 1948. The Nationalists have been in power in South Africa ever since.

Apartheid

Apartheid is an Afrikaans word meaning 'separation of the races'. This was the most important feature of Nationalist policy within South Africa after 1948. The idea was to keep the races apart as much as possible, but in ways laid down by the whites in the interests of white supremacy. South Africa's races were already separated before 1948. The new policy took this separation much further. These were some of the main characteristics of apartheid:

1 The *classification* of everyone according to one of a number of racial types. A person's racial type determined where you could live, what jobs you could do, etc.
2 *Segregation* in all aspects of life, e.g. separate buses, park benches, beaches, and hospitals.
3 *Separate educational systems*, with far more money being spent on schools for whites.
4 Stronger *pass laws*. These were laws requiring non-whites to carry pass books which enabled police to keep a check on their movements.
5 *The removal or limitation of any voting rights* still possessed by blacks and coloureds.
6 *A ban on mixed marriages* and sexual relations between whites and non-whites.
7 *The division of the country into black and white areas*. This led to many blacks being deported from areas reserved for whites. This aspect of apartheid was taken further by the Bantu Self Government Act of 1959,

which provided for the eventual creation of seven *Bantustans*. These areas were to be reserved for blacks of particular racial groups and were to be self-governing. Although some have even been given their independence, they remain heavily dependent on South Africa. They occupy some of the poorest land in the country and offer limited opportunities for employment. Conditions for their inhabitants are often appalling.

Opposition to apartheid

Throughout the twentieth century non-whites have continued to protest about the ways in which they have been treated as second class citizens. They have been supported in their protests by a minority of whites. The authorities have given themselves many new powers to deal with opponents of the regime. These have included the power to ban opposition organisations, prevent the holding of meetings, censor the press and keep people in prison without trial. Some opponents of apartheid have spent long periods in prison. The most famous of these is Nelson Mandela, the leader of the main nationalist organisation the African National Congress (ANC). Others have been beaten up or killed.

Protest has taken many forms. Peaceful protests and *passive resistance* gave way in the mid-1970s to outbreaks of riot and disorder. These were particularly severe in 1976 when black townships all over the country exploded in anger against government policies. Similar outbreaks, on an ever bigger scale, took place in the mid-1980s. The ANC has also resorted to sabotage and to the use of guerrilla tactics.

Government response to protest has usually been very ruthless. A *peaceful demonstration at Sharpeville in 1960* was broken up by force with the loss of 67 lives. The protests of the 1970s and 1980s were also suppressed with considerable loss of life, especially among young blacks. The riots and demonstrations of the mid-1980s were on such a scale that the Prime Minister, Botha, decided to remove some of the worst features of apartheid and to promise greater non-white involvement in government. At the same time even tighter restrictions on the activities of opponents, including stricter press censorship, were introduced.

South Africa's relations with other countries

The policies adopted by South African governments since 1948 have isolated the country from many other parts of the world. In 1960, in a *referendum*, the electorate decided to end its links with the British monarchy and to become a *republic*. In the following year opposition from other states in effect forced it to withdraw from the British Commonwealth. South Africa's policies have often been condemned by the United Nations, which has tried unsuccessfully to impose *economic sanctions*. The United Nations has also had a long-running dispute with South Africa over *Namibia*, a neighbouring state that South Africa has controlled since the end of the First World War and to which it has refused to give independence.

Since the collapse of the Portuguese empire in the mid-1970s and the end of Smith's government in Rhodesia in 1979, South Africa has been surrounded by states hostile to apartheid. South Africa's military forces, however, are far superior to those of all its neighbours put together. *Raids against ANC bases in Mozambique, Botswana, Lesotho and Swaziland in the 1980s* showed the government's determination to strike at its enemies wherever it could find them. South African forces have also raided far into Angola in pursuit of guerrillas belonging to SWAPO, the Namibian independence movement.

COLONIALISM AND ITS AFTERMATH: AFRICA 16.7 Key historical terms 16

Racism This term is often used loosely as a term of abuse for people whose views we don't like. This is a pity, as the word has a precise meaning. A racist is someone who believes that certain groups of people are inferior or superior simply because they happen to belong to a certain 'race'. The Nazis were racists. So too were many of the Afrikaner Nationalists you have read about in this chapter. So too were many (though by no means all) of the Europeans who went out to rule overseas colonies earlier in the twentieth century. So too were some African tribes who regarded members of neighbouring tribes as inferior to themselves.

Most educated people believe that racists are simply wrong. Different groups of people have different attitudes and customs because of the societies in which they happen to be brought up, not because of the 'race' to which they belong. Racism, however, has been a very powerful force in the history of the world in the twentieth century, as this chapter has suggested.

Other key historical terms relevant to this chapter are *anarchy* (p. 195), *apartheid* (p. 159), *British Commonwealth* (p. 139), *constitution* (p. 195), *coup* (p. 195), *decolonisation* (p. 195), *economic sanctions* (p. 172), *federation* (p. 180), *guerrilla warfare* (p. 107), *nationalists* (p. 148), *parliamentary democracy* (p. 64), *secession* (p. 197), and *white supremacy* (p. 158).

COLONIALISM AND ITS AFTERMATH: AFRICA

16

16.8 Questions

Short answer and essay questions

(i) Make three columns headed *Nigeria*, *Congo* and *Zimbabwe*, and then read statements 1–7 below.
Which statements apply to which states? Put the number or numbers of the statements that apply to each state in the appropriate column.
N.B. A statement might apply to all three states, to one or two of the states, or to none of the states. (10)

1 Black majority rule was resisted for many years by white settlers within the colony.
2 Independence was achieved without a long armed struggle.
3 Independence was only granted after many years of self-government by the black majority.
4 Independence was achieved without any involvement by outside powers.
5 Independence was followed by the setting up of a stable parliamentary democracy.
6 Independence was followed by the intervention of outside powers.
7 Independence was followed by considerable internal conflict between different tribal groups.

(ii) Answer the following questions, making use of the tables you have completed for (i) above.
(a) What differences were there in the way in which the Congo and Nigeria obtained their independence in 1960? (5)
(b) Compare the history of the Congo and Nigeria during the first ten years after independence. In what ways, during these years, did these two states develop in (i) similar ways and (ii) different ways? (10)
(c) Why did independence come much later to Zimbabwe than to Nigeria and the Congo? (5)

THE ARAB–ISRAELI CONFLICT

17.1 The Palestine mandate and the origins of the state of Israel

17

As almost all GCSE World History syllabuses concentrate on the Arab–Israeli conflict since 1948 this chapter only looks very briefly at the origins of the state of Israel before 1948.

The history of the Jewish people is an extraordinary one. Driven out of Palestine in Roman times, they had spread all over Europe, North Africa and the Middle East (and indeed beyond). Many Jews, however, continued to hope that one day they might return to their homeland. This hope sustained them during centuries of persecution at the hands of other peoples. At the end of the nineteenth century there grew up among Jews a movement that tried to turn this hope into a reality. This *Zionist* movement encouraged Jews to settle once again in Palestine, an area which at that time was part of the Turkish Empire and inhabited by Arabs. Zionists were active among Jewish communities in many European countries. In Britain some of their supporters had close links with the British government.

The Turkish Empire was one of Britain's enemies in the First World War. During the war the British government made a number of agreements and promises about what would happen to Turkey's Middle Eastern possessions in the event of that country's defeat. These included (a) an agreement to divide them between Britain and France, (b) a promise that the Arabs, in return for help against the Turks, would be given their independence, and (c) a promise that there should be a Jewish national home in Palestine. These promises were difficult to reconcile with each other.

At the end of the First World War Turkey's possessions were given to Britain and France as *mandates*, i.e. territories to be ruled under the supervision of the League of Nations and to be prepared for eventual independence (p. 173). France obtained Syria and the Lebanon. Britain obtained Palestine, Iraq and Transjordan.

Britain's Palestine mandate encouraged more Jews to settle in that area. Jews continued to arrive in substantial numbers throughout the 1920s and 1930s. This caused growing resentment among the Palestinian Arabs. In the 1930s and 1940s there was more and more violence: by Arabs against Jews and by both groups against the British. British restrictions on Jewish immigration, imposed in 1939, seemed heartless at a time of appalling Jewish persecution in Europe (pp. 77–78).

After the end of the Second World War Britain faced the activities of Jewish terrorist groups determined to turn the national home into a national state. These attacks, together with pressure from countries like the USA sympathetic to the Jews, persuaded the British that it was time to withdraw. In 1948 British troops were removed, the mandate came to an end and Palestine was handed over to the United Nations. The UN wished to *partition* the area between Arabs and Jews, a proposal strongly opposed by Arabs who regarded the whole of Palestine as their country. In the midst of mounting violence between the two communities, the Jews took the initiative and in *May 1948 proclaimed the state of Israel.*

THE ARAB–ISRAELI CONFLICT 17
17.2 The First Arab–Israeli War, 1948–49

Causes The establishment of the state of Israel was a moment of great rejoicing for most Jews. For the Palestinian Arabs, who had lost a large part of their homeland, it was a moment of great bitterness. The neighbouring states of Egypt, Syria, Jordan and Lebanon immediately took up arms in defence of the rights of the Palestinian Arabs. From their point of view the state of Israel did not exist and must be destroyed.

Events The war which followed was a victory for the Israelis, who not only held on to their existing territories but also acquired further lands from the Arabs. The Arab armies were poorly equipped and badly coordinated.

Effects The remaining parts of Palestine (i.e. the Gaza strip and the West Bank) were now taken over by Egypt and Jordan respectively. Into these territories flocked three-quarters of a million Palestinians fleeing from the areas now under Israeli control. For these Palestinians and their supporters the struggle to regain their homeland would continue – with the prospect of further wars to come.

THE ARAB–ISRAELI CONFLICT 17
17.3 The Suez Crisis, 1956

Causes Border clashes between Israel and its neighbours continued during the years after 1949. Although Britain, France and the USA agreed in 1950 to guarantee Israel's existing frontiers, none of Israel's neighbours was prepared to recognise the new state. Relations with Egypt were particularly strained after the rise to power of a new Egyptian leader, *General Nasser*, in 1954.

When war broke out between Israel and Egypt in 1956, however, it involved other powers as well. Nasser had come into conflict with Britain and France by *nationalising the company that ran the Suez Canal* (see map opposite), a company in which those countries were the major shareholders. Representatives of the British, French and Israeli governments met at *Sèvres*, near Paris, and agreed on a plan to bring about Nasser's downfall. The plan involved two stages: (a) Israel would attack Egypt across the Sinai desert, and (b) Britain and France would then use this as an excuse to

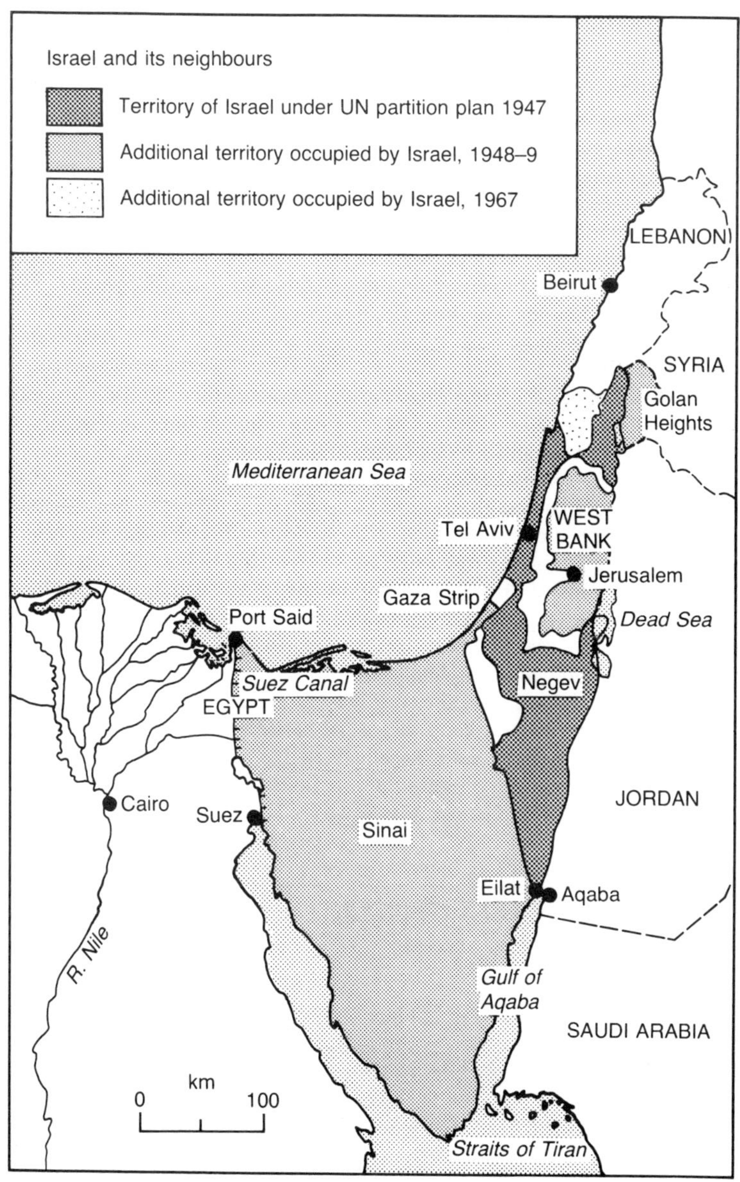

Israel and its neighbours

launch their own invasion of Egypt on the pretext of separating the two sides.

These are some of the reasons why Britain, France and Israel decided to take this action:

(i) *The Israeli government* resented Nasser's refusal to recognise its existence, his support for Palestinian *guerrillas*, and the fact that in 1956 he had closed the Gulf of Aqaba to Israeli shipping. The Israelis suspected him of planning another war against their country.
(ii) *The British government* was concerned about the threat to its trade routes as a result of the nationalisation of the Suez Canal Company. The British Prime Minister, Anthony Eden, also regarded Nasser as a threat to the peace of the Middle East, partly because of Nasser's growing friendship with the USSR.
(iii) *The French government* had close economic and military links with Israel, shared some of Britain's fears about trade routes, and resented Nasser's support for anti-French forces in the French colony of Algeria.

Events Israeli forces attacked successfully across Sinai. Britain and France then demanded that both sides withdraw from the Suez Canal. When Egypt, predictably, refused to do so, Anglo-French forces attacked and destroyed the Egyptian airforce and invaded the Egyptian town of Port Said. The actions of Britain and France met with such strong condemnation, however, (e.g. from the USA) that they were unable to persist with their invasion. A ceasefire was arranged and within a month the Anglo-French forces had been completely withdrawn.

Effects Israel was compelled to withdraw from the Sinai desert and a UN force was sent to try and keep the peace between the two sides. All the other results that Britain and France had tried to prevent now came about, e.g. the canal was closed, oil supplies were interrupted, and Nasser became the hero of the Arab world.

THE ARAB–ISRAELI CONFLICT 17
17.4 The Six Days War, 1967

Causes The basic causes of conflict were the same as they had been in 1948–49 and in 1956, i.e. Israel's determination to survive as an independent state and the refusal of the Arabs to recognise its right to do so. As in 1956, the war in 1967 began with an Israeli attack. As in 1956, however, the Israeli government feared that if it did not attack first it would lose the advantage. During the early months of 1967 Egypt and Syria had increased pressure on Israel in various ways, e.g. Nasser had asked the UN to remove its forces from both Sinai and the Gaza strip, Syria had increased its shelling of Israeli settlements on the Golan Heights, and the Gulf of Aqaba had once again been closed to Israeli shipping.

Events Israel won immediate and spectacular victories, advancing at the same time against Egypt, Jordan and Syria. The Sinai desert was taken from Egypt, the West Bank from Jordan, and the Golan Heights from Syria (see map on p. 165). All three Arab states had agreed to ceasefires within six days of the first Israeli attack.

Effects The Six Days War greatly increased Israel's size. Israel refused to consider handing back its gains until such time as its neighbours recognised its right to exist.

The war, however, heightened the bitterness of the Palestinians, more of whom were now driven into exile. This bitterness found expression in growing support for Palestinian guerrilla organisations such as the *Palestine Liberation Organisation* (PLO). In the late 1960s and 1970s the PLO and other groups tried to harm Israel in whatever ways they could. These included the hi-jacking of aeroplanes, together with atrocities such as the murder of all the Israeli athletes at the 1972 Munich Olympics. The war also increased the number of Palestinians living within Israel, many of whom were bitterly opposed to Israeli rule.

THE ARAB–ISRAELI CONFLICT 17
17.5 The Yom Kippur War, 1973

Causes The basic causes of this fourth Arab–Israeli war were similar to those of previous ones. In this war the Arabs attacked first, imitating Israel's tactics in 1967. They chose as the day for their attack the Jewish religious festival of Yom Kippur (the Day of Atonement), after which the war is named.

Events After some initial Arab successes, the Israelis counter-attacked and once again found themselves penetrating further into both Egyptian and Syrian territory. In Egypt Israeli troops crossed the Suez Canal and advanced to within 65 miles of the Egyptian capital. Fighting ended after a few weeks and once again UN forces attempted to separate the two sides.

Effects The Yom Kippur War demonstrated the extent to which the superpowers had become involved in the Arab–Israeli conflict. Israeli forces were supplied with US weapons, whereas the Arab states mostly received theirs from the USSR. Neither the USA nor the USSR wished to come into conflict with each other in the Middle East. Their search for allies and influence, however, had led them to line up behind different sides.

US aid to Israel angered many Arabs. In retaliation oil supplies to the west were interrupted, causing a world-wide economic crisis.

17.6 The resurgence of the Arab world

'Resurgence' means rising up again or growing in strength. It is a term that is often used to describe what has happened since the 1960s in both the Arab world and the wider world of *Islam*. There are two important aspects of this resurgence: (i) the growth in the power of Arab states as a result of *rising oil prices*; and (ii) *the revival of the Islamic religion*. Both developments have had a major effect on the Arab–Israeli conflict.

Oil

The economic life of many Middle Eastern countries has been dominated by oil for much of the twentieth century. Since the Second World War profits from oil production have transformed the way of life of many Arab states. Profits have risen because of increasing demand for oil and also because oil-producing states have begun to organise themselves better. Since 1969 they have met to fix the price of oil in regular meetings of OPEC (*the Organisation of Petroleum Exporting Countries*). Countries such as the USA were so heavily dependent on Middle Eastern oil that they had little choice but to pay whatever price was demanded. Although OPEC was faced in the 1980s with a drop in world demand for oil, its position remained strong. The oil weapon has undoubtedly strengthened the position of Arab states in negotiations concerning Israel.

The revival of the Islamic religion

In a world where the influence of religion has generally been in decline, the revival of the Islamic religion has shown the continuing importance of religious belief. Islam has over 600 million followers, most of them in Asia, Africa and the Middle East – in countries as widely scattered as Indonesia, China, Bangladesh and the USSR. It is particularly strong in the Middle East, where it began in the seventh century.

The revival of Islam has shown itself in many ways. In particular it has led *Muslims* (followers of Islam) to reject many aspects of western life that seem opposed to Islamic teaching. Muslims who follow a very strict version of their religion have been especially hostile to western influences. These *Islamic fundamentalists*, as they are called, have been particularly active since the 1970s. One of these groups, the *Shia Muslims*, played a major part in the overthrow of the western-style government of the Shah of Iran in 1979. The establishment of an Islamic Republic in Iran, under the Ayatollah Khomeini, encouraged fundamentalists in other Arab countries, for example, in the Lebanon and Egypt (see below).

Islamic fundamentalists have always taken a particularly tough line on the question of Israel. They have totally rejected all proposals to recognise Israel's existence and have often spoken of the need for a *jihad* or holy war against those who they see as the Jewish enemies of their faith.

THE ARAB–ISRAELI CONFLICT
17.7 Peace moves
17

Oil problems prompted the USA to try and bring about some solution to the Arab–Israeli dispute. They were encouraged by the improvement in US–Egyptian relations that took place, as a result of the initiative of Egypt's President Sadat, after the Yom Kippur War. Sadat made the unprecedented move of visiting Israel in 1978, a visit returned by the Israeli Prime Minister Begin. The two sides then met at *Camp David* in the USA where they agreed on the outlines of an Egyptian–Israeli peace treaty. This treaty, which was finally signed in 1979, had two main features:

(a) a gradual Israeli withdrawal from the Sinai desert.
(b) an Egyptian recognition of Israel's existence as a state (the first such recognition by an Arab state).

Sadat and Begin were unable to agree, however, about the future of the Palestinians.

The Camp David agreements marked a major change in Arab–Israeli relations. They were rejected, however, by many Arabs, especially Palestinians, as well as by most Islamic fundamentalists (see above). Sadat probably paid with his life for this bold initiative, being assassinated by Islamic fundamentalists in 1981. His successor, Mubarak, continued the peace initiative. Problems arose, however, as a result of Israel's intervention in the Lebanon.

THE ARAB–ISRAELI CONFLICT
17.8 Israel and the Lebanon
17

The history of the Lebanon in the 1970s and 1980s was one of almost constant violence and civil war. These were the main reasons:

1 For centuries the country has been divided into *Christian and Muslim communities*. The Muslims were further divided into two main groups, the *Sunni Muslims* and the *Shia Muslims*. All three groups were frequently very hostile towards each other. After the Second World War an attempt was made to share power, with the President normally being a Christian, the Prime Minister a Sunni Muslim, and the Speaker of the parliament a Shia Muslim. This arrangement sometimes broke down.
2 The situation was made worse after the Six Days War (pp. 166–67) by the *arrival of large numbers of Palestinian Arab refugees*. After 1970 the PLO made its headquarters in the Lebanon. This further increased tension between the Christian and Muslim communities, leading to full-scale civil war in the mid-1970s.
3 This civil war led to *intervention by neighbouring Syria* in support of the

Lebanese Muslims. Fighting continued between Syrians and Christian Lebanese forces.

4 The use of the Lebanon as a base for PLO attacks on Israel eventually led to *Israeli intervention* as well. A full-scale Israeli invasion took place in 1982. As a result the PLO was forced to leave the country altogether. Israeli forces later withdrew, but within the Lebanon fighting, car bombs and massacres continued as before.

THE ARAB–ISRAELI CONFLICT 17.9 Key historical terms

17

The main terms that you need to understand in this chapter are *Zionism* (p. 167) and *Islamic fundamentalism* (p. 168). Other terms include *partition* (p. 196), *mandate* (p. 173), *guerrillas* (p. 107), *nationalisation* (p. 196) and *resurgence* (p. 168). Further details of the two main religions involved in the Arab–Israeli conflict are given below.

Islam The religion of the Muslims. Followers of Islam believe in one God, whom they call *Allah*. Their holy book is the *Koran*, which they believe was recited by the archangel Gabriel to the prophet Mohammed and is therefore the word of God. The Koran tells Muslims how they should live. There are *five main duties*: to recite the creed (statement of belief); to pray five times a day; to give money to the poor; to fast during the month of Ramadan; to make a pilgrimage to the holy city of Mecca. Muslims accept some of the Christian and Jewish prophets as prophets of Islam. Like the Jews, they regard Jerusalem as a holy city – a fact that has led to much resentment since Israel's occupation of that city.

Most Muslims are *Sunni Muslims*. A smaller number, called *Shia Muslims*, follow the teachings of Mohammed's son-in-law, Ali.

Judaism The religion of the Jewish people. Judaism, like Islam and Christianity, involves a belief in one God. It also involves a belief that God has *chosen* the Jews as the people to whom he has made known his will, e.g. through their sacred books. Judaism lays down very precisely how Jews must behave in many different situations. There are many rules, e.g. about daily prayer and about the keeping of religious festivals. Like Muslims, Jews interpret their religion in different ways. *Orthodox Jews* follow their traditions very strictly. *Progressive Jews* have modified these in various ways. Differences of opinion between various groups of religious Jews have played an important part in Israeli politics.

17.10 Questions

Source-based questions

Study this photograph and its caption and then answer the questions that follow. The photograph was published in the British newspaper *The Independent* on 26 February 1988.

A masked youth waves the banned Palestinian flag during a West Bank demonstration yesterday

(i) Explain where the West Bank is and describe the circumstances in which it was acquired by Israel. (3)

(ii) Give reasons why the youth in the photograph is behaving in the way shown. (5)

(iii) Give reasons why the *Palestinian flag* should have been *banned*. (3)

(iv) What attempts were made during the 1970s and 1980s to bring about a peaceful settlement of the Arab–Israeli dispute? (4)

INTERNATIONAL COOPERATION 18

This chapter looks at some of the ways in which attempts have been made during the twentieth century to bring about greater cooperation between different countries. During this century countries have become more and more dependent on each other: as a result of increased trade and improved communications. Although the world is still divided into a large number of *sovereign states* (i.e. states that are not under the power of any higher body), there has been a growing awareness of the advantages to be gained from greater cooperation. This cooperation has taken various forms. This chapter looks at some of these, firstly at attempts that have been made to set up some kind of the *world authority*, and secondly at the various *regional groupings of states* that have emerged.

18.1 The League of Nations

Origins The League had its origins in the First World War. It was born out of a desire that the sufferings of that war should never happen again. The main influence behind its establishment was President Woodrow Wilson of the USA. It was largely as a result of his efforts that the Paris peace conference in 1919 accepted the *Covenant*, an agreement that laid down the rules of the new organisation. The main purpose of the League was to preserve world peace and to ensure that all countries respected each other's independence.

Organisation Countries signing the Covenant and thus joining the League promised to submit to the League any dispute that they had with another state. If the League were unable to solve the dispute within six months, the states involved could go to war as long as they gave notice that this was what they were going to do. If any member state went to war in any other way, all other members agreed to go to the defence of whichever country was attacked. In these circumstances the League could impose *sanctions* (i.e. measures taken against an offending state). Sanctions might take one of three forms:

(a) *diplomatic sanctions*, i.e. breaking off diplomatic relations.
(b) *economic sanctions*, e.g. breaking off trade links.
(c) *military sanctions*, i.e. taking military action against the aggressor.

In practice the League never established an army and therefore was unable to take military sanctions.

The League consisted of the following bodies:

1 *The Assembly* This met once a year. Each state had one vote. All decisions had to be unanimous. There were 27 original member states, rising to 60 in the 1930s.

2 *The Council* This body dealt with problems as they arose. It had four permanent members (Britain, France, Italy and Japan), rising to five in 1926 when Germany joined. There were also a number of non-permanent members elected by the Assembly. Like the Assembly, this met in Geneva in Switzerland.

3 *The Secretariat* This was the League's civil service.

4 *The Permanent Court of International Justice* Members were not obliged to submit legal disputes to this Court, but if they did so were supposed to accept the Court's ruling.

5 *Specialised agencies* The League set up various bodies dealing with a number of international issues such as refugees, drugs, slavery, etc. These were very important in creating habits of international cooperation. The two best known agencies are described below.

The International Labour Organisation (ILO)

This agency was concerned with protecting the interests of workers all over the world. Its officials worked hard to persuade governments to ensure decent working conditions, to provide insurance against sickness, and to respect trade union rights. Its function, however, was advisory, i.e. it was unable to compel governments to follow its advice.

The Mandates Commission

This body supervised the administration of the colonies that were taken away from the defeated powers at the end of the First World War. These colonies were given to countries such as Britain and France as *mandates*, i.e. to be ruled under the League's supervision and in the interests of the inhabitants. There were three types of mandate:

Type A: to be prepared for independence in the near future. These included all the former Turkish possessions in the Middle East (e.g. Palestine and the Lebanon), which were given to Britain and France.

Type B: where independence was thought to be unlikely for a further 50 years. Most of these were in Africa, e.g. German Tanganyika (now Tanzania) which was given to Britain.

Type C: where, in the eyes of the League, there seemed little prospect of independence ever being possible, e.g. German South-West Africa (now Namibia) which was given to South Africa.

The mandates system was much criticised at the time. To some people it seemed just a device to enable the victorious powers to extend their empires.

Successes of the League

The League succeeded in achieving its aims in a number of important ways. These included:

(i) The work of the *specialised agencies* (see above).
(ii) Its *efficient administration* of areas placed under international control, e.g. Danzig and the Saar (p. 29).
(iii) The *peaceful settlement* of various disputes between member states. These included the Aaland islands dispute between Sweden and Finland, a dispute between Iraq and Turkey over the Mosul area, and one between Germany and Poland over Upper Silesia. The League also succeeded in bringing to an end a war that broke out in 1925 between Greece and Bulgaria. Most of these disputes concerned minor powers.
(iv) Establishing *habits of international cooperation* over a large number of matters.

Failures of the League

During the 1930s the League was much less successful. It failed to prevent or to deal effectively with various acts of aggression by member states. It came to play a smaller and smaller role in world affairs and was eventually ignored almost totally. These are some of the instances when it failed to achieve its aims:

(i) Even during the 1920s the League *failed to take action against a number of states that broke the Covenant*. France ignored the League when it sent troops into the Ruhr in 1923 (p. 59). Italy likewise took direct action in its dispute with Greece in the same year (pp. 53–54). Actions such as these by members of the League Council set a bad example.
(ii) *The Japanese invasion of Manchuria, 1931* (pp. 95–96). Although the League condemned Japanese aggression, sanctions were not even considered.
(iii) *The Italian invasion of Abyssinia, 1935* (p. 54). Economic sanctions were eventually imposed, but with some of the main items (e.g. coal, oil, iron, etc.) excluded. These did not, however, succeed in forcing Italy to hand back its gains.
(iv) A series of *disarmament conferences* during the 1920s and early 1930s failed to dispel the fears of many member states that disarmament would threaten their security. During the 1930s the League was powerless to prevent the rise in arms production that took place in many parts of the world.

Why did the League fail?

The League failed as an instrument for keeping the peace for a number of reasons. These included:

(a) Almost all League members, including members of the Council,

continued to think and act as *sovereign states* (pp. 180–181). They were unwilling to leave decisions that affected themselves to some higher authority.
(b) The League was *associated from the beginning with the victorious powers in the First World War*. As a result it did not always appear to be acting impartially.
(c) *Many major powers did not belong to the League at various times*, e.g. Germany was not admitted until 1926 and the USSR until 1936. The US Senate refused to join the League at the end of the First World War, a decision that greatly weakened the organisation from the start. Members that were in dispute with the League also tended to withdraw from the League altogether, e.g. Japan and Italy.
(d) *The League never had an army* and was thus easy to ignore. Protests, diplomatic sanctions and limited economic sanctions had little effect.

INTERNATIONAL COOPERATION 18
18.2 The United Nations Organisation (UNO)

Origins The possibility of a new and more effective international organisation was being discussed from early on in the Second World War. As in the First World War, there was a desire to prevent similar conflicts from breaking out in the future. A series of conferences among the Allies finalised the arrangements for the new organisation in 1944–45. The UNO came into existence in October 1945.

Organisation The structure of the UNO is as follows:

1 *General Assembly* Meets once a year and all members have one vote. Decisions are by a simple majority or, in major matters, by a two-thirds majority.
2 *Security Council* Can take action at short notice. Can impose sanctions and compel members to apply them. Consists of five permanent members (Britain, France, USA, USSR, and China) and temporary members chosen by the General Assembly. Permanent members have a *veto*, i.e. can prevent action being taken. Since 1950 the power of this veto has been restricted, by a *Uniting for Peace* resolution passed in that year. This allows the General Assembly to by-pass the Security Council in various ways, e.g. by sending observers to a crisis area.
3 *Secretariat* The UN civil service, headed by a Secretary-General.
4 *The Court of International Justice* The successor to the Permanent Court of the League (p. 173). It deals with disputes where both parties have agreed to consult it. It has no power to enforce its decisions.
5 *Trusteeship Council* Supervised former League of Nations mandates (p. 173) as well as territories taken away from the Axis powers at the end of

the Second World War. By the 1980s most of these had gained their independence.

6 *Economic and Social Council* Concerned with promoting 'the economic and social advancement of all people'. It works through various specialised agencies.

7 *Specialised agencies* There are a large number of these. Some were inherited from the League, for example, the ILO (p. 173). Some of the best known are:

Food and Agriculture Organisation (FAO): concerned with agriculture, fishery and forestry. Aims to improve the quantity and quality of foodstuffs. Organises many projects in 'developing' countries.

United Nations Educational, Social and Cultural Organisation (UNESCO): aims to eliminate *illiteracy and to promote cultural contacts between countries.*

United Nations Relief and Works Agency (UNRWA): provides help for refugees who have fled their homes to escape persecution, war, revolution or famine.

World Health Organisation (WHO): tackles a whole range of diseases and other causes of death such as malnutrition.

UNO: successes and failures

In international relations the United Nations has played a bigger part since 1945 than the League did in the interwar years. There are a number of reasons for this:

(a) Unlike the League, UN membership comprises the whole world.
(b) Member states have also tended to stay in the UNO rather than withdraw, even when they have been in dispute with the organisation.
(c) The UN has been prepared to raise an army and to use it in order to keep the peace.

Despite this, the power of the UNO should not be exaggerated. It has failed to prevent numerous small wars that keep on breaking out all over the world. Its decisions have often been ignored. Member states have also frequently taken action without any reference to the organisation of which they are members.

UN involvement

These are some of the areas of the world in which the UNO has been closely involved:

Palestine The UN has often attempted to keep the peace between Israel and its Arab neighbours (Chapter 16). Its presence has often been effective in reducing tension. It has also had many failures, e.g. the expulsion of the UN force in 1967 (p. 166).

Korea You can read about UN involvement in Korea on pp. 125–26. This was the biggest use of force by the UN in the whole of its history. Its intervention protected the independence of South Korea, but failed to bring about a peaceful reunion of the country.

The Congo UN forces intervened in the Congo in 1960 at the invitation of the Prime Minister (pp. 156–57). The Congo had just gained its independence and the country was in a chaotic state. The UN took over the administration of the country and used force to prevent the *secession* p. 197) of the province of Katanga.

Cyprus The UN has been closely involved in the affairs of Cyprus since 1964. It has sometimes succeeded in reducing tension between the Greek and Turkish communities in the island. It failed, however, to stop Turkey's invasion of the island in 1974 or to prevent the partition of the island to which this led.

Rhodesia The refusal of Rhodesia's white minority government to extend voting rights to the black majority led to the imposition of *mandatory sanctions* (i.e. sanctions that all member states were obliged to impose). These were designed to bring about the collapse of the white minority government. In practice they were evaded, a number of states (e.g. Portugal and South Africa) choosing to ignore them. You can read about events in Rhodesia on pp. 154–55.

INTERNATIONAL COOPERATION 18
18.3 Regional cooperation

Since the Second World War there have also been many attempts to strengthen links between states at a regional level. These attempts at regional cooperation have taken three main forms: (a) military, (b) political, and (c) economic.

Military cooperation

Regional military pacts have been a feature of the Cold War that has developed since 1945. They usually involve agreements between states that their military forces will cooperate with each other in certain circumstances. You can read about some of these pacts, e.g. NATO, the Warsaw Pact and SEATO, in Chapter 13.

Political cooperation

Regional groupings of states for political purposes have also developed in certain parts of the world. These have had different aims. For example, the *Organisation of American States* (OAS) was set up in 1948 as a regional branch of the United Nations whereas the *Organisation of African Unity* (OAU), established in 1963, was originally mainly concerned with eradicating *colonialism* from Africa.

There have also been some attempts to bring together a number of small states and to group them into a larger *federation* (p. 180). In each case it was felt that member states would benefit, for example economically, from belonging to a larger organisation. The British government was particularly interested in federations as a way of preparing their colonies for independence. Both the *Central African Federation* (1953–63), discussed on pp. 153–54), and the *West Indies Federation* (1958–62) failed, however, largely as a result of rivalries between different member states. The federation of *Malaysia*, formed in 1963, proved more successful.

Economic cooperation

Since the Second World War many countries have also come to see the advantages of economic cooperation between states. In a world where states are always competing with each other to sell more and more goods, there are obvious advantages, at least for small states, in cooperating with each other. Such cooperation might provide them with a wider market for their exports. It might also help them to compete with more economically successful states such as Japan and the USA.

There have been regional economic groupings in many parts of the world. Examples of such groupings outside Europe include the *Caribbean Free Trade Area* (CARIFTA), established in 1968, and its successor the *Caribbean Community and Common Market* (CARICOM). The rest of this chapter examines the regional economic groupings that have developed in western Europe since the Second World War.

Economic cooperation in western Europe

There were various pressures making for greater unity in western Europe during the years after 1945. These included (a) a desire to avoid another disastrous European war, (b) fear of the USSR, (c) a feeling that economic recovery was most likely to come about through cooperation, and (d) an acceptance that European states would only be able to hold their own in dealings with superpowers such as the USA and the USSR if they combined with each other. At the same time there was a great reluctance on the part of *sovereign states* to hand over power to some higher authority.

These are some of the ways in which western European states have come together since 1945:

1948: *the Organisation for European Economic Cooperation* (OEEC) was set up to administer the US aid that was given to Europe after the war.
1948: *the Benelux Customs Union* (Belgium, the Netherlands and Luxembourg) was formed.

1950: formation of the *European Coal and Steel Community* (ECSC). This was joined by France, Italy, West Germany and the Benelux countries, but not by Britain. It placed coal and steel production under a *supranational authority* (p. 181).

1957: *The European Economic Community* (EEC) was established by the *Treaty of Rome*. This aimed to establish a *common market* among the six member states (the same states as formed ECSC in 1950). This common market involved (a) the removal of trade restrictions between member states, (b) a common external *tariff*, (c) free movement of people, money, etc., within the Community, and (d) common policies on matters such as agriculture. The structure of the EEC consisted of a *European Commission*, staffed by civil servants from the member states, a *European Council*, in which each state had one representative, and a *European Parliament* based at Strasburg.

The EEC proved a great success in terms of most of its aims. During the late 1950s and 1960s trade between members increased enormously. Economic production within the EEC also rose more rapidly than in other parts of the world.

Since its formation membership of the EEC has expanded considerably. Britain at first remained aloof, concentrating instead on its continuing links with the *British Commonwealth*. The British government, however, could

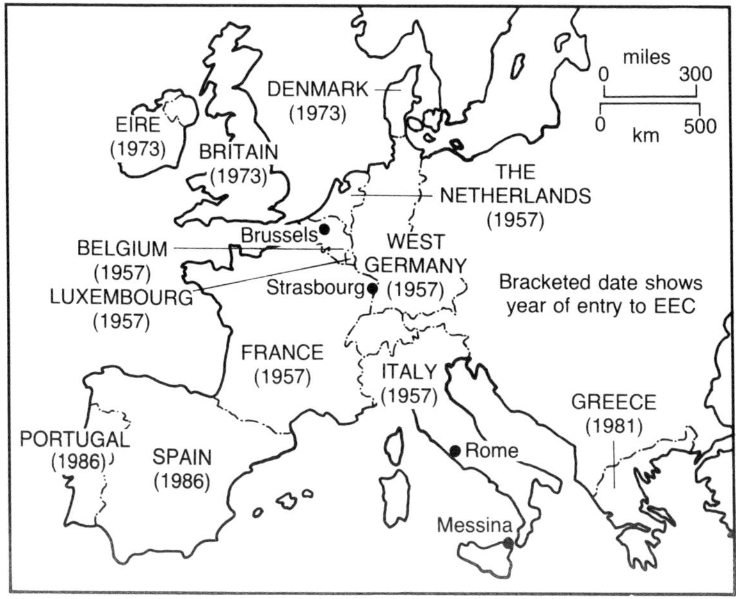

The EEC countries

see the advantages of belonging to a larger economic unit and in 1959 formed its own grouping known as the *European Free Trade Association* (EFTA). Unlike the EEC, EFTA did not involve any *supranational authority*. The greater success of the EEC eventually encouraged Britain to apply for membership. This was vetoed on two occasions by President de Gaulle of France (in 1962 and in 1967), but eventually succeeded in the early 1970s after de Gaulle's fall from power. Britain joined the EEC in 1973, a decision that was approved in Britain's first ever *referendum* in 1974. Denmark and the Republic of Ireland joined the European Community at the same time, to be followed in the 1980s by Greece, Spain and Portugal.

Attempts to create some kind of political union in western Europe have been less successful. Since the late 1970s the European Parliament, however, has been elected directly by the inhabitants of member states. The *Council of Europe*, established in 1949, has also had considerable success through its *European Court of Human Rights* in enforcing the provisions of the European Convention of Human Rights.

INTERNATIONAL COOPERATION 18
18.4 Key historical terms

Common market This is both a general term and a term that is sometimes used to describe the European Economic Community (EEC) established in 1957. As a general term, it refers to a group of states joining together to form a larger economic unit for the purposes of trade. Within a common market trade barriers disappear, i.e. countries can trade with each other without paying import duties. They also usually agree on a common *external tariff*, i.e. will all charge the same import duties on goods coming from countries outside the common market. A common market may also, as in the EEC, involve other measures to bring the economic policies of member states into line with each other.

Federation A group of states joined together in order to form a larger political unit. In a federation there are usually two levels of government: the federal government of the larger state (i.e. of the federation) and the governments of the various parts into which the federation is divided. Some examples of federations are discussed above (p. 178). Many individual states are also of course organised in a federal way, for example, the USA which has both a federal government (in Washington) and governments in each of the various states.

Sovereign state A state is said to be *sovereign* when it recognises no authority above itself. Despite various attempts to create some kind of world authority, the world is still made up of sovereign independent states, few of which recognise any higher power.

Supranational authority *Supranational* means 'above (*supra*) the nation'. A supranational authority has the power to compel national governments, i.e. those that have agreed to accept its authority, to take certain actions. Most states have been very reluctant to transfer some of their powers to such an authority. Despite this, a number of important supranational authorities with substantial powers have been established since the Second World War, for example, the European Community.

Other key terms you need to understand in this chapter include *disarmament* (p. 196), *mandates* (173), *sanctions* (p. 172), and *veto* (p. 197).

INTERNATIONAL COOPERATION 18.5 Questions 18

Evidence question

Study this extract from a conversation between an interviewer and the former British Prime Minister Clement Attlee. The interview was recorded in a book published in 1961. It refers to the San Francisco Conference which met in 1945 to agree on the structure of the UNO. Then answer the questions that follow.

> *Francis Williams:* Were you satisfied with the San Francisco Conference?
> *Attlee:* Yes. There was the veto, of course. One had to have it in the Security Council, but the idea was if one behaved there it wouldn't be used *habitually*, only in the last resort. And at that time on the basis of sovereign independent States one couldn't have got anything through unless the USA and the USSR and we ourselves, I think, had a power of veto in reserve . . . it would have been quite unrealistic to try to make a United Nations in which the vote of the big Powers had no more significance than the small ones. You couldn't have had that. In fact, we went too far in giving a vote to every little Power . . .
> *Williams:* Do you think, looking back, you might have had a better organisation?
> *Attlee:* If we could have got an organisation with a *cession* of sovereignty, then we'd have got somewhere; and power to act. But it would have required a different conception of world government which I suppose we weren't prepared for at that time . . .
>
> (Francis Williams, *A Prime Minister Remembers*, 1961)

habitually: again and again / as a matter of habit
cession: handing over

(i) What questions would you need to ask before accepting this as an accurate record of how Attlee felt about the United Nations in 1945? (3)

(ii) Explain the meaning of (a) *veto*, (b) *sovereign independent states*, and (c) *cession of sovereignty*. (6)

(iii) Describe in your own words Attlee's opinions about the United Nations. (4)

(iv) What do you learn from this extract about British attitudes towards Britain's position in the world at the end of the Second World War? (3)

(v) If you were studying attitudes towards the UNO in 1945 what other types of sources might you wish to use? What might be the advantages and disadvantages of these types of source? (4)

INTERNATIONAL THEMES 19

Most chapters in this book refer to specific regions of the world. One of the most striking features of twentieth-century history, however, is the way in which during this period the world has become increasingly *one world*. Partly because of improved communications, people are now more conscious of the world outside their own countries and of the impact this can have on their own lives. They have also come to appreciate the similarities between their own and other countries, seeing in particular how many of the most important developments in the twentieth century have had similar effects all over the world. The last chapter in this book examines a number of these developments. The ones chosen for study are those included in GCSE world history syllabuses.

INTERNATIONAL THEMES 19
19.1 The population explosion

World population has increased faster during the twentieth century than at any time in the past: from approximately 1,400 million in 1900 to 4,000 million in 1975. The main reason for this dramatic growth has been a drop in the death rate resulting from improved medical knowledge and better medical facilities. The number of child deaths has been greatly reduced, as has the number of deaths from the great killer diseases such as smallpox and typhus. Other reasons include better drainage and water supplies, as well as an improved diet and (in some countries) a higher standard of living.

Population growth since the Second World War has been very much faster in 'developing' than in 'developed' countries, e.g. 3·3% a year in central America during the early 1970s by comparison with 0·4% in north-western Europe. This can be explained by the much higher birth rate in developing countries. Governments in some of these countries, e.g. India and China, have attempted to reduce this high birth rate, and thus to slow down population growth. These attempts have sometimes met with resistance, partly on religious grounds.

The effects of rapid population growth have been of many kinds. These include:

(i) *Overcrowding*, for example, in the slums and shanty towns of some Third World cities, to which people have drifted from the countryside in search of employment.
(ii) *Over-population*, i.e. countries where the resources are insufficient to support a rapidly rising population even at a low standard of living. Some Asian countries such as Bangladesh come into this category.
(iii) *Pressure on food supplies*, which means that in times of droughts and

bad harvests there is sometimes famine and death on a huge scale, as in north-eastern Africa during the mid-1980s.
(iv) Societies where, because of a high birth rate, *a very high proportion of the population is under the age of 20* and needs to be maintained and educated out of limited resources. The opposite problem is to be found in many 'developed' countries where a low birth rate and improved medicine have led to a high proportion of the population being over the age of 60.
(v) *Pollution of the environment* in areas of high population (see p. 187).

INTERNATIONAL THEMES 19
19.2 World poverty

Poverty is what is called a *relative* concept. In other words people are richer or poorer than other people rather than just 'poor' or 'rich'. For example, someone who is considered to be 'poor' in Britain might be thought to be 'rich' in Uganda or Bangladesh. By comparison with conditions earlier in the century many Third World countries might well have experienced an improvement in their standards of living. By comparison with the 'developed' world, however, they are strikingly poorer. Moreover, the gap between 'developed' and 'developing' countries has been getting wider in recent years.

There are many possible explanations for the poverty of the 'developing' world and for the huge gap in wealth that exists between 'developing' and 'developed' countries. A rapidly rising population and a high birth rate (Section 19.1) are often major factors. Some observers argue that under-developed countries are poor because they are part of a world economy in which they are *dependent* on the developing countries. They lack the capital (money), skilled labour or resources to *industrialise* (p. 45) and are therefore dependent on developed countries for expensive essential imports. To pay for these they have to export the only commodities they are able to produce. These are often raw materials of various kinds which they are forced to sell to developed countries at a relatively low price. Others, however, argue that this is not the explanation, pointing out that some Third World countries (e.g. Taiwan and South Korea) have received great benefit from being part of a world economy.

Whatever the reasons for poverty, it remains perhaps the world's worst problem, with millions of people dying every year from famine, malnutrition or preventable diseases. In addition to the many efforts made by developing countries themselves (see, for example, Chapters 11 and 15), the following efforts to tackle this problem have been made:

(i) *Long-term aid programmes* organised by particular countries. Although the amount of aid increased considerably in the 1960s and 1970s,

it still fell far short of 1% of the total annual income of the developed countries.
(ii) Aid programmes of a more ambitious kind organised by a number of states, for example, the *Colombo Plan* of 1950 which committed the more prosperous states of the British Commonwealth to provide aid to less prosperous members such as India and Pakistan.
(iii) The efforts of the various *specialised agencies of the United Nations*, such as the World Health Organisation and the Food and Agriculture Organisation (p. 176).
(iv) *Short-term emergency relief*, to deal with famines and natural disasters, for example, the Ethiopian famine of the mid- and late 1980s.

INTERNATIONAL THEMES 19.3 Communications 19

The twentieth century has been a period of rapid technological change. The Industrial Revolution of the late eighteenth and nineteenth centuries did not come to an end with the twentieth century. Instead it increased in pace, the twentieth century witnessing technological changes that have had a dramatic effect on many aspects of everyday life. These have been particularly noticeable in the field of communications and include some of the following:

1 Land transport It was not until the twentieth century that the impact of the *internal combustion engine*, developed during the late nineteenth century, became fully apparent. Its effects have included:

- revolutionising private transport through the rapid increase in the number of motor cars
- changing the appearance of both cities and the countryside, through the construction of new roads
- creating new patterns of settlement, with people living further away from their place of work
- mechanising agricultural production through the use of tractors, combine harvesters, etc.
- making possible the faster distribution of goods
- using up large quantities of oil resources
- increasing environmental pollution (p. 187)
- creating a major new industry, employing large numbers of workers and increasing demand for a range of other products such as rubber, steel, etc.
- changing the ways in which people spend their leisure time.

2 Air transport The development of aeroplanes during the twentieth century is yet another example of the impact of the internal combustion engine. The growth in civil (i.e. civilian) aviation took place in conjunction with the increasing use of aeroplanes for military purposes. The two world wars in particular stimulated many changes in air transport (e.g. the use of radar in the Second World War).

The growth of air transport has had many consequences: on methods of waging war, for example the blitzkrieg of the Second World War (p. 74); on trade; on tourism and the use of leisure; and on politics, for example by permitting more direct contact between politicians from different countries.

3 Space travel German experiments with rockets in the later stages of the Second World War were followed up and led eventually, during the 1950s, to the launching of the first space satellites. The USSR led the way with its *Sputnik*, launched in 1957. Unmanned satellites were widely used during the 1960s as navigation beacons, for weather forecasting, and for relaying radio and television broadcasts. The first manned satellite was launched in 1961, to be followed at the end of the decade (1969) by the first manned landing on the moon.

Space exploration throughout has been largely the result of initiatives from the USSR and the USA. Its effects on communications have been enormous. Its direct impact on everyday life, however, has perhaps been less than that of the changes in land and air transport mentioned above.

4 Radio, films and television Radio and films began to have a major impact after the end of the First World War. Their importance was more than just the appearance of new ways of spending leisure time. Both were of great importance to governments as means of conveying information and propaganda (e.g. Hitler's use of propaganda film and Roosevelt's use of 'fireside chats' on the radio). Since the 1950s television has become an even more important medium for conveying to an audience a particular view of the world. It has also transformed the way in which ordinary people live their lives.

5 Information technology The increasing complexity and rapid spread of computers since the 1950s have had dramatic effects on the way in which governments, businesses and private individuals organise their affairs. The impact has varied from country to country, the 'developed' countries obviously seeing the greatest changes. There are few areas of life unaffected: industry; banking; shopping; cooking; travelling. This book was written and printed using computers. So too are your GCSE examination papers, the good news (when it comes) about your GCSE results, your actual GCSE certificates, etc. Few would disagree about some of the obviously beneficial effects, for example helping to diagnose and treat illnesses or enabling the severely disabled to acquire basic skills. Other effects, the loss of jobs or the creation of a more impersonal kind of society, are more open to debate.

INTERNATIONAL THEMES
19.4 The environment

19

The rapid growth in population, the development of new methods of agricultural and industrial production, changes in transport, the use of new materials such as plastics, new methods of packaging goods – all these have led during the twentieth century to greater pollution of the natural environment. The last few decades have seen growing concern for *conservation* (i.e. the preservation of those features of the natural environment that seem to be under threat). In some countries political parties mainly concerned with environmental issues have had some success, for example the Green Party in West Germany. There has been a growing awareness that some of the economic and technological changes of the twentieth century are not necessarily a good thing and that the simpler lifestyle of so-called 'under-developed' countries may have many advantages that the 'developed' world lacks.

INTERNATIONAL THEMES
19.5 Key historical terms

19

'Developed' countries This term is usually applied to countries that have an *industrialised* economy (p. 45) and a high standard of living. Such countries tend to have a high proportion of their population living in towns and a low proportion working in agriculture. They also have a high level of literacy (i.e. most people can read and write) and a low birth rate. The 'developed' part of the world includes Europe, North America, Australia and New Zealand, Japan and the USSR.

'Developing' or 'under-developed' countries These are countries which usually have a low standard of living and an economy that is heavily dependent on the production of raw materials (e.g. agricultural products and minerals). Industries are only partially developed and a high proportion of the population is often engaged in agriculture and/or living in the countryside. Levels of literacy are sometimes low and the birth rate is often high. The 'under-developed' part of the world includes large areas of Asia, Africa, Central and South America.

The words 'developed', 'developing' and 'under-developed' are all terms that are often used. They have been put in inverted commas, however, to show that we don't necessarily have to use this set of labels when describing these countries. Some people object to these terms because they imply that being a 'developed' country is superior to being an 'under-developed' country. This is something that not everyone would agree with. For example, you could argue that an 'under-developed' Amazonian tribe, which doesn't possess large quantities of weapons with which to destroy its neighbours, doesn't live in a polluted environment, doesn't have a rising crime rate and doesn't suffer from heart disease or cancer, is in fact superior in many ways to some of the so-called 'developed' societies of the world.

Other terms that are important in this chapter include *conservation* (p. 187), *dependency* (p. 184), *industrialisation* (p. 45), and *over-population* (p. 183).

INTERNATIONAL THEMES 19
19.6 Questions

Source-based questions

Study the map of the world opposite and then answer the following questions.

(i) Referring to the map, identify *three* of the richest countries of the world. (3)

(ii) Referring to the map, identify *three* of the poorest countries of the world. (3)

(iii) Suggest reasons why the countries you have identified in (i) have a very much higher income per head of population than those you have identified in (ii). (6)

(iv) Three of the countries with the highest income per head of population are *not* inhabited by Europeans or people of European descent. Choose *one* of these three countries and give reasons why it has a high income per head of population. (3)

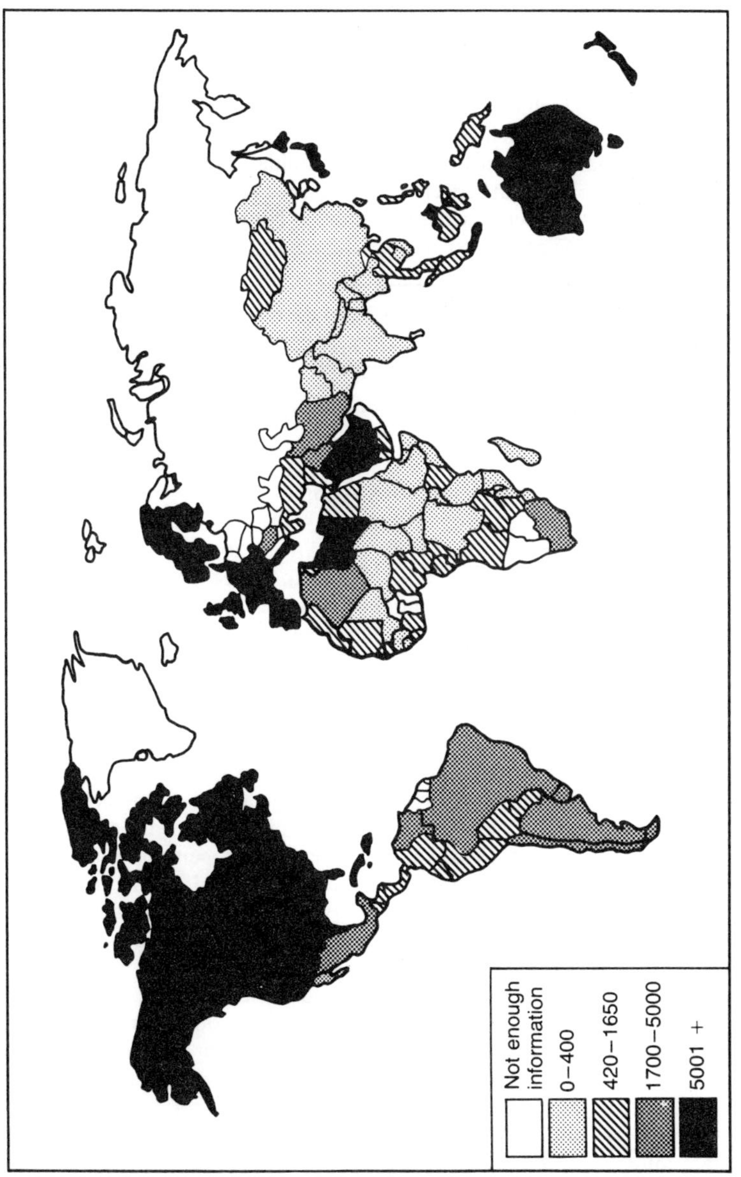

Income (in US dollars) per head of population for the various countries and regions of the world

SPECIMEN ANSWERS 20

This final chapter consists of specimen answers to some of the questions that have been included earlier in the book. These will give you some idea of the standard at which you should be aiming. All answers are the kinds of responses that examiners expect from candidates likely to receive a good Grade A pass. There are specimen answers for each of the three main types of questions discussed in Chapters 1 and 2. Notice how the answers try to follow the advice contained in those chapters.

SPECIMEN ANSWERS 20
20.1 Essay questions

Why were so many Germans deeply resentful about the terms of the Treaty of Versailles? (15)

There are many reasons why German people deeply resented the Treaty of Versailles. One of the most important was that they felt they had not been defeated. Harsh peace terms were very difficult to accept when Germany had not been invaded or occupied by enemy forces. Although Germany probably could not have continued fighting for much longer, many Germans believed that the army had been 'stabbed in the back' by left-wing politicians at home. They believed that Germany need not have accepted such harsh terms. This made them even more difficult to accept.

Many Germans particularly resented the fact that the treaty was a Diktat, i.e. had been imposed on Germany rather than negotiated. The Allies seemed to be treating Germany in a humiliating way. This was made worse by the 'war-guilt' clause which placed all blame for the outbreak of the war on Germany and its allies. The consequence of the war guilt clause was that Germany was forced to pay reparations (or compensation) for having caused the war. These reparation payments were fixed at an incredibly high level. Germany faced the prospect of having to pay them indefinitely – with very harmful effects on the country's economy and on people's standard of living.

The territorial clauses of the treaty also caused much resentment. The Allies were supposed to believe in self-determination, but many Germans were now forced to live under foreign rule without anyone so much as consulting them. This was true of many Germans living in Danzig (given to the League of Nations), the Polish Corridor (given to Poland), and Alsace-Lorraine (returned to France). The Allies also ignored self-determination when they forbade Germany to unite with Austria. In the west, Germany lost control of the Saar, one of its most important industrial districts. This caused further damage to the German economy. Overseas

Germany lost all its colonies, which were mostly added to the empires of the Allies. To many Germans this seemed just another example of the Allies' greed.

For a proud military country like Germany the restrictions on armed forces were also greatly resented. It was to have no airforce or submarines, a tiny navy and an army restricted to 100,000 men. The Rhineland was to be permanently demilitarised and occupied for 15 years by Allied troops. The presence of foreign troops on German soil was another great humiliation – especially when they moved in *after* the end of the war.

All these reasons help to explain why the Treaty of Versailles was so unpopular in Germany. Not all Germans were as obsessed as some of the nationalist parties with getting rid of the treaty. Few Germans, however, can have wanted it to continue.

SPECIMEN ANSWERS 20
20.2 Source-based questions

The questions below refer to the photograph on p. 171.

(i) *Explain where the West Bank is and describe the circumstances in which it was acquired by Israel.* (3)

The West Bank is the West Bank of the River Jordan and before 1967 it belonged to the state of Jordan. In 1967 it was invaded and occupied by Israeli forces during the Six Days' War. In order to forestall an expected attack from its Arab neighbours, Israel had decided to strike first. Israeli forces at the same time occupied the Sinai desert and the Golan Heights.

(ii) *Give reasons why the youth in the photograph is behaving in the way shown.* (5)

The youth is obviously a Palestinian Arab. He is presumably raising the Palestinian flag because he wants his people to get back the homeland that had been taken from them by the Jews. Most Palestinian Arabs have refused to recognise the state of Israel that was created in 1947. This, they claim, is their land and should be returned to them. They resent having to live in what they feel to be an occupied country. Many of them also resent the fact that they have been driven from their homes and are living as refugees in neighbouring countries. If the youth in the photograph is from the West Bank his family may well have fled to Jordan in 1947 only to find their new home in the West Bank taken over by the Israelis when they captured that territory in 1967. He may therefore feel particularly bitter.

The youth in the photograph seems very defiant. Many Palestinians feel very angry and powerless to do much against the Israeli forces. He may also be concealing his face so that the Israeli military cannot identify him.

(iii) *Give reasons why the Palestinian flag should have been banned.* (3)

The Palestinians use this flag as a way of showing that they are a separate nation. They believe that the lands taken from them by the Israelis should be handed back. They want these lands to become an Arab state. The Israeli government is opposed to all this and cannot therefore accept this flag. Israelis believe that Israel is their homeland. They have no intention of allowing the Palestinians to take it from them.

(iv) *What attempts were made during the 1970s and 1980s to bring about a peaceful settlement of the Arab–Israeli dispute?* (4)

Both the United States and the United Nations made various attempts during this period to prevent the Arab–Israeli dispute from getting any worse. For most of the time this was the best they could do, given that relations between the two sides were so bad. In the late 1970s, however, there were more positive steps. President Sadat of Egypt took the initiative in trying to improve relations with Israel. The USA encouraged this and at the Camp David talks in 1978 the two sides agreed on a peace treaty. This treaty provided for Israel's withdrawal from Sinai, which took place in 1982. Many other Arab countries were strongly opposed to Sadat's action and this hostility has made it difficult to carry out some of the other terms of the peace treaty. Relations between Israel and most of the Arab world continue to be very poor indeed.

SPECIMEN ANSWERS 20

20.3 Evidence questions

The examples here have been chosen to illustrate the different kinds of evidence questions you are likely to come across in examinations.

Comprehension questions

Refer to the sources on pp. 82–83. *Describe in your own words what the extract tells you about the film* Desert Victory. (3)

I learn from this extract that the film *Desert Victory* was made during the Second World War and that it was about British victories in the North African campaign. It was made at Pinewood Studios, presumably by the British Army Film Unit. The film obviously included scenes of fighting, though some of these were shot in the studio.

Questions asking you to distinguish between fact and opinion

Refer to the source on p. 108. *Quote one statement of fact and one statement of opinion to be found in these extracts.* (2)

One statement of fact in these extracts is 'I had lunch today with a man named Chun'. One statement of opinion is 'Time and again he has promised to bring in abler men and then appoints the most incompetent he can find'. In the second part of this statement Melby gives his own opinion that these men were 'incompetent'.

Questions asking you to identify the attitudes revealed in a source
Refer to the sources on pp. 134–35. *What do you learn from Source A about the attitudes of its authors? Refer to the source in support of your answer.* (4)

I learn from Source A that its authors were hostile towards the United States. They refer to the United States as 'imperialists', which is a critical term. This suggests that they feel the USA is only concerned with its own interests and therefore has no business being in Vietnam. They also describe US measures against North Vietnam as 'sabotage', another word which suggests that the USA is acting wrongly. They are distrustful of vietnamisation, seeing it as just another means by which the USA is trying to gain a victory. They are also hostile to the USA's allies in Vietnam, calling South Vietnam a 'puppet government'.

Questions asking you about the reliability of particular sources
Refer to the sources on pp. 82–83. *Do you think that this extract is likely to be a reliable source of information about the work of the British Army Film Unit? Explain your answer.* (3)

This extract is likely to be a reliable account of the work of the British Army Film Unit because it is written by someone who served as a member of that Unit. He had taken part in many of the events that he describes. This extract does not suggest that he might have had any reasons for deliberately concealing the truth. On the other hand these are Grant's memoirs and were written nearly 40 years after the events he describes. His memory might not be as good as it seems – though we have no way of telling just on the basis of this extract.

Questions asking you to comment on the value of a source
Refer to the sources on pp. 72–73. *How valuable are these sources to someone studying appeasement during the 1930s? Explain your answer.* (4)

These sources are all valuable in different ways to someone studying appeasement. They all show the attitudes that certain people at the time had towards Hitler and Nazi Germany. These attitudes are likely to have influenced the way politicians behaved. They may well help to explain why a policy of appeasement was adopted. Sources C and D show that some influential people had at least some good things to say about Nazism, though these sources may not tell us what Henderson and Halifax really thought. As it is an unpublished letter, Source A probably tells us what Dawson thought, though he doesn't say much in this extract about *why* he was so keen 'to get going with the Germans'. It is difficult to decide how valuable Source E would be without knowing who Lady Londonderry was. Her views might have been untypical and unimportant. Source A stands out as the only one where the author was opposed to appeasement. This is interesting, but we would need to know how many others shared this view.

Questions asking you to test the evidence against a particular statement
Refer to the source on p. 108. *'US officials after the Second World War were frequently obsessed with the threat from communism.' Was this true of Melby? Explain your answer.* (3)

It is difficult to know what Melby thought about communism just from these brief extracts. If these extracts are typical of the rest of the diary, Melby cannot be described as 'obsessed with the threat from communism'. He quotes a US journalist who reports that the communists were 'behaving very well' and he shows no sign of disagreeing with this or of being very worried about it. He is also very critical of the Kuomintang. Generally he seems to be reporting events in a fairly detached way, without being very involved on one side or the other. But it is difficult to tell just from these extracts.

GLOSSARY

The page references indicate where a term is explained in detail.

anarchy: a situation in which there is no government or where government has broken down
Anschluss: the union of Austria and Germany
anti-imperialist: p. 107
anti-Semitic: hostile to the Jews
appeasement: p. 68
aristocracy: p. 45
authoritarian (government): a government with very strong powers and which is able to use these powers without being answerable to some other body such as a parliament
autocrat: a ruler with strong powers who is able to use these powers in whatever way he/she sees fit
blitzkrieg: p. 74
British Commonwealth: p. 139
capitalist: an economic system in which trade and industry are privately owned (i.e. are not owned or totally controlled by the state)
civil rights: p. 120
civil war: a war within a country, between different groups or different political parties
coalition: an agreement between different groups or different political parties
coexistence: p. 129
Cold War: p. 122
collectivisation: p. 42
colonialism: a system of ruling in which one group of people is ruled by another group of people (from outside the area), largely in the interests of the ruling group. Usually applied to European rule outside Europe.
conscription: compulsory military service
constitution: the way in which a state is governed. Many states (e.g. the USA) have written constitutions
constitutional monarchy: a state headed by a monarch with limited powers
consumer goods: goods that are bought by individuals (e.g. clothes are consumer goods whereas iron and steel are not)
coup: an attempt to seize power, using force or the threat of force
decolonisation: the ending of colonial rule
demilitarisation: removing military forces or installations (e.g. from an area or country)
democracy: p. 64
desegregation: allowing different races to mix (i.e. bringing *segregation* to an end)

detente: p. 29
developed country: p. 187
developing country: p. 187
dictatorship: a government in which the ruler (or dictator) has complete power
disarmament: getting rid of armaments (i.e. reducing the amount of armaments or abolishing them altogether)
Dominion: a self-governing territory within the British Empire
economic depression/recession: a period in which economic production declines (e.g. a fall in profits, a decline in the amount of goods produced, an increase in unemployment)
Fascism: p. 49
federation/federal: p. 180
guerrilla warfare: p. 107
illiteracy: inability to read and write
imperialist: p. 107
Industrial Revolution: p. 45
industrialisation: p. 45
Islamic fundamentalist: p. 168
isolationist: cutting oneself off from the rest of the world. Normally applied to a country's foreign policy
Judaism: p. 170
laissez-faire: leave things alone. Usually applied to government economic or social policies that involve doing very little
liberalism: pp. 55–56
mandates: p. 173
Marxism: pp. 45–46
middle class: p. 46
modernisation: an attempt by a country to make itself more like the 'developed' part of the world (e.g. with a higher standard of living and an economy based on industry rather than on agriculture)
Muslim: p. 170
nationalisation: taking properties (e.g. industries) away from private owners and placing them under state control
nationalism: p. 56 and p. 148
parliamentary democracy: p. 64
partisans: a group of resistance fighters who are not part of a regular army (e.g. resistance fighters in Nazi-occupied Europe)
partition: dividing into different parts
passive resistance: resistance that does not involve the use of force
personality cult: the way in which people in a country are encouraged to think of their government in terms of a particular individual leader, and to regard this leader in a very flattering light
propaganda: attempts to persuade people to adopt a certain point of view

proportional representation: a way of choosing members of parliament in which political parties obtain seats in proportion to the number of votes they have obtained (e.g. a party that obtains 30% of the votes receives 30% of the seats)
public works: projects (e.g. building roads) paid for by the state
putsch: an attempted seizure of power
racism: p. 161
rearmament: building up armaments (after having reduced them)
referendum: a national vote on a specific issue
republic: a form of government that is *not* headed by a monarch
revisionist: a state or individual who wishes to change or revise the existing state of affairs
sanctions: p. 172
secession: splitting away from/withdrawal
self-determination: p. 32
self-sufficiency: p. 98
socialism: the belief that wealth should be owned by the state or community rather than by private individuals. *Socialists* are opposed to *capitalism* and to private enterprise
sovereign state: pp. 180–81
soviet: a council consisting of workers' representatives
tariff: a tax on imports or exports
totalitarian dictatorship: p. 65
total war: p. 74
under-developed: p. 187
veto: the power to prevent something from being done
Viceroy (British India): the leading representative of the British government in India
warlords: military leaders with control over certain parts of a country (as in China during the first quarter of the twentieth century)
welfare state: p. 91
westernisation: p. 98
Zionism: p. 167